Perl
Weekend Crash Course™

Perl
Weekend Crash Course™

Joe Merlino

Hungry Minds™

Best-Selling Books ♦ Digital Downloads ♦ e-Books ♦ Answer Networks
e-Newsletters ♦ Branded Web Sites ♦ e-Learning

New York, NY • Cleveland, OH • Indianapolis, IN

Perl Weekend Crash Course™
Published by
Hungry Minds, Inc.
909 Third Avenue
New York, NY 10022
www.hungryminds.com

Library of Congress Control Number: 2001092894
ISBN: 0-7645-4827-1
Printed in the United States of America
10 9 8 7 6 5 4 3 2 1
1B/QZ/RQ/QR/IN
Distributed in the United States by Hungry Minds, Inc.
Distributed by CDG Books Canada Inc. for Canada; by Transworld Publishers Limited in the United Kingdom; by IDG Norge Books for Norway; by IDG Sweden Books for Sweden; by IDG Books Australia Publishing Corporation Pty. Ltd. for Australia and New Zealand; by TransQuest Publishers Pte Ltd. for Singapore, Malaysia, Thailand, Indonesia, and Hong Kong; by Gotop Information Inc. for Taiwan; by ICG Muse, Inc. for Japan; by Intersoft for South Africa; by Eyrolles for France; by International Thomson Publishing for Germany, Austria, and Switzerland; by Distribuidora Cuspide for Argentina; by LR International for Brazil; by Galileo Libros for Chile; by Ediciones ZETA S.C.R. Ltda. for Peru; by WS Computer Publishing Corporation, Inc., for the Philippines; by Contemporanea de Ediciones for Venezuela; by Express Computer Distributors for the Caribbean and West Indies; by Micronesia Media Distributor, Inc. for Micronesia; by Chips Computadoras S.A. de C.V. for Mexico; by Editorial Norma de Panama S.A. for Panama; by American Bookshops for Finland.

For general information on Hungry Minds' products and services please contact our Customer Care department within the U.S. at 800-762-2974, outside the U.S. at 317-572-3993 or fax 317-572-4002.

For sales inquiries and reseller information, including discounts, premium and bulk quantity sales, and foreign-language translations, please contact our Customer Care department at 800-434-3422, fax 317-572-4002 or write to Hungry Minds, Inc., Attn: Customer Care Department, 10475 Crosspoint Boulevard, Indianapolis, IN 46256.

For information on licensing foreign or domestic rights, please contact our Sub-Rights Customer Care department at 212-884-5000.

For information on using Hungry Minds' products and services in the classroom or for ordering examination copies, please contact our Educational Sales department at 800-434-2086 or fax 317-572-4005.

For press review copies, author interviews, or other publicity information, please contact our Public Relations department at 317-572-3168 or fax 317-572-4168.

For authorization to photocopy items for corporate, personal, or educational use, please contact Copyright Clearance Center, 222 Rosewood Drive, Danvers, MA 01923, or fax 978-750-4470.

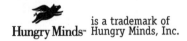

Hungry Minds™ is a trademark of Hungry Minds, Inc.

Credits

Acquisitions Editor
Sharon Cox

Project Editor
Sharon Nash

Technical Editor
Allen Wyatt, Discovery Computing Inc.

Copy Editor
Maarten Reilingh

Editorial Manager
Colleen Totz

Senior Vice President, Technical Publishing
Richard Swadley

Vice President and Publisher
Joseph B. Wikert

Project Coordinator
Dale White

Graphics and Production Specialists
Sean Decker
Jill Piscitelli
Heather Pope
Kendra Span
Erin Zeltner

Quality Control Technicians
Carl Pierce
Marianne Santy

Proofreading
Sossity R. Smith

Indexing
TECHBOOKS Production Services

About the Author

Joe Merlino is a freelance consultant and technical author from Boston, Massachusetts. This is his sixth book.

For Kate

Preface

This book is for people who want to learn to program in Perl. No experience in Perl or in any other programming language is required, although you should have basic familiarity with the PC and whatever operating system you're using, as well as keyboarding skills. The book's focus is Perl as a full-featured programming language used in application development. The book supports any version of Perl greater than 5.0. It provides a CD-ROM with the Perl interpreter software.

Who Should Read This Book

This book is for you if you wish to learn Perl programming. Though the focus is primarily on Unix and Linux systems, Perl interpreters are available for almost every operating system.

Perl Weekend Crash Course™ teaches you the fundamentals of Perl programming in a series of short lessons you can cover in one weekend. The first session starts Friday evening, and the last session ends Sunday afternoon. There are 30 sessions, each requiring approximately one-half hour.

What's in the Book

The book begins by telling you how to get and install Perl. Once you've got the necessary software in place, you can begin writing programs. (The good news is if you're working on a Unix or Linux system, the odds are very good that Perl software is already installed.) With that task out of the way, an overview of the language follows. You'll be introduced to the basic concepts that make up a Perl program, and you'll get a taste of how one is put together.

From here, you shift focus a bit. Before you can start writing programs, you need to know a few things about how programming works in general. You learn to use the Perl interpreter, including the ways in which you can alter its behavior. Then you move to Perl's built-in help system. Any time you get stuck, you can almost always find something in the help system to get you moving again. The final preliminary is getting you comfortable with a text editor. Programs are written as text files; to create and edit a text file, you need to use a text editor. Whether this is the common Windows text editor, Notepad, or one of the many Unix text editors, you need to be comfortable with your editor before you can program effectively.

With these preliminaries taken care of, you begin to address the Perl language. You start by learning about variables and getting to know Perl's three native data types. You see how to use expressions and operators to construct statements and how to put those statements together into sequences that do something. You address input and output and learn to control the flow of your program and to interact with your operating system.

Then you look at some of Perl's most powerful capabilities — text processing, data transformation, and data display. From strictly linear programming, you advance to subroutines, packages, and modules. You learn to use these features to make your programs more efficient, more powerful, and less demanding.

Finally, you look at one of the more popular applications of Perl — programming for the World Wide Web. Perl can be used to create HTML documents *on the fly*; by combining Perl techniques with the common gateway interface (CGI), you can create Web pages that interact with the user and present dynamic content.

Perl is a freeform language, and it's possible — even likely — that some of the Perl code you encounter in the real world will look somewhat, or even quite a bit, different from the code you see in this book. That's okay. One of Perl's many mantras is "There's More Than One Way to Do It."

Organization and Presentation

The book is organized into 30 sessions, each requiring approximately 30 minutes. I divide the sessions as follows:

- Friday evening. Sessions 1 through 4. Reading time: 2 hours.
- Saturday morning. Sessions 5 through 10. Reading time: 3 hours.

- Saturday afternoon. Sessions 11 through 16. Reading time: 3 hours.
- Saturday evening. Sessions 17 through 20. Reading time: 2 hours.
- Sunday morning. Sessions 21 through 26. Reading time: 3 hours.
- Sunday afternoon. Sessions 27 through 30. Reading time: 2 hours.

At the end of each session, I present questions designed to check your progress. The text is sprinkled with icons designed to catch your attention.

**30 Min.
To Go**

The Minutes to go icons mark your progress in the session.

The Tip icons offer suggestions on style and mention shortcuts that can save programming effort.

The Note icons highlight incidental or technical information that clarifies and expands the discussion.

The CD-ROM icon refers to material furnished on the book's CD. Use it to find electronic versions of programs and software elements mentioned in the text.

Contacting the Author

I can't guarantee I can solve all your Perl problems, but I promise to take a look at your questions and see if I can help. If you get stuck, you can contact me at the following e-mail address: joe@nigiri.org.

Acknowledgments

I wish to thank all of those who made this book possible. Getting a beast like this to fly is not an easy task. First, thanks to David "The Wonder Agent" Fugate for all of his usual efforts and to all of the rest of the terrific people at Waterside Productions. Second, thanks to all of the fine folks at Hungry Minds, Inc., especially the Sharons (Cox and Nash). Third, I want to thank my friends at Georgia Tech, to whom I can always turn in a pinch, especially Chris Sidi (for making large chunks of Perl code available to me) and Cameron Perkins (for making those whacks with the clue-by-four almost painless).

Finally, I need to acknowledge the efforts of Jessica Close. Without Jess's assistance, it is very unlikely that this book would have been completed anywhere close to its deadline. Jess's reliability and high standards make her a dream to work with. Jess rules!

Contents at a Glance

Contents

Perl
Weekend Crash Course™

☑ **Friday**

☐ Saturday

☐ Sunday

Part I — Friday Evening

PART

I

Friday
Evening

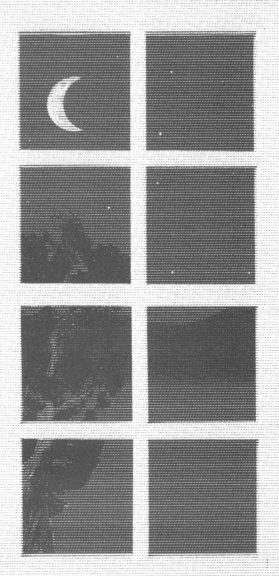

Getting and Installing Perl

Session Checklist

✔ Checking to see if Perl is already installed

✔ Locating Perl packages

✔ Installing Perl

**30 Min.
To Go**

Before you can start writing programs in Perl, you need to have it installed on your computer. Perl programs are written simply as text files, but you need to have a piece of software called an interpreter installed in order to run them. The interpreter converts the programs from text into the binary format that your computer needs in order to execute your program instructions.

Fortunately, the Perl interpreter falls into a category of software often called Open Source or Free Software. The Free Software movement arose in the 80s as a response to the trade secret protection practices of companies like Microsoft and Sun. The "Free" in free software does not necessarily mean that the software is available free of charge (although practically speaking this is often the case); rather Free Software can be freely copied, used, modified, and distributed by anyone. Perl is only one example of Free Software. Other notables include the Linux operating system, and the Apache Web server (both of which will be discussed in brief elsewhere in this book). While you may have little need to involve yourself in Free Software in general, the practical upshot is that anyone with an Internet connection can download the Perl interpreter free of charge.

You May Already Have It

Perl has become very popular over the past few years, primarily owing to its ease of use, and suitability for Internet-related tasks. Because of this popularity, Perl comes as part of the standard suite of packages on many operating systems. (In fact, the Perl Web site suggests that if you don't already have Perl installed as part of your Linux or Unix OS, you may want to rethink your choice of OS. It's become that basic.) If you're running Linux, BSD, or any variant of Unix, the odds are good that you already have Perl installed on your system. You can test this by issuing the command which perl. That command should return the full path name of the Perl interpreter, which should be something like /usr/bin/perl. (If you get a response like this, write it down. You'll need to know the full path later.) If you do not have Perl installed, you should see something like:

```
/usr/bin/which: no perl in (/bin:/usr/bin:/usr/bin/X11:/usr/local/
bin:/usr/bin:/usr/X11R6/bin:/home/joe/bin:/sbin:/usr/sbin:/usr/X11
R6/bin:/home/joe/bin:/sbin:/usr/sbin:/usr/X11R6/bin:/home/joe/bin:
/sbin:/usr/sbin)
```

If you are running another operating system such as Windows or MacOS, your odds of having Perl already installed are a lot slimmer. Unless Perl was installed on your computer by another user, you probably don't have it. Use your file manager or file-finding utility to see if you have it.

Download Sites

If you don't have Perl already installed on your computer, you're going to have to install it yourself. Fortunately, this isn't difficult.

There are two kinds of software packages that you could install: source code and binary packages. Of the two, installing binary packages is far easier, and for something as complex as Perl, is by far the recommended method.

Home base for the Perl distribution is, unsurprisingly, www.perl.com. Here you can find links to Perl packages for just about every Unix variant imaginable, as well as for Windows and Macintosh. Simply click the Downloads link and you should find a link to your operating system.

If you are running a Microsoft Windows system, you may wish to go directly to www.activestate.com. This is the Web site of the ActiveState Corporation, which creates a version of Perl designed to run on Windows systems. While there is a pure Perl distribution for Windows, ActivePerl (the version of Perl created by ActiveState) is much easier to install and maintain. Even the core Perl developers recommend that Windows users use ActivePerl.

Likewise, Macintosh users may wish to proceed directly to www.macperl.com. MacPerl is a Perl distribution designed for the Macintosh. It is easy to install, and comes with lots of helpful applications to get you going.

Read the docs!

You will find that throughout this book I harp pretty consistently on the need to read documentation wherever it appears. While you might get annoyed at the constant admonitions, there's a reason for it. The documentation that comes with programs is written by the programmers themselves, or people working directly with them. The documents that are packaged with software are specific to that version of the software. They are simply the most accurate and specific instructions you can possibly get on any particular piece of software. The downside of the included documents is that they're not always especially user-friendly. That's what books like this are for.

Which Version?

At the time of this writing, the current version of Perl is 5.6.1, however, it is still fairly common to find version 5.005 series installations around. While there have been some changes between the two versions, and you may wish to upgrade, all of the examples in this book should work just fine with either version. However, if you find that you have a version of Perl installed with a version number lower than 5, you should upgrade immediately.

Installing under Linux/Unix

**20 Min.
To Go**

As I mentioned previously, just about any decent Linux or Unix system will probably have Perl already installed. Perl in an integral part of many of these systems, and in addition to the Perl interpreter, you may find Perl programs already on them.

However, on the off chance that you do not have Perl installed on your system, you'll need to install it.

Installing from binary packages

As I said previously, binary packages are by far the easiest way of installing Perl. In most cases, the binary packages come with installation programs that handle all the configuration for you, thus you need only install the package, and you're ready to go.

As an example, here's how you would install Perl under Red Hat Linux:

1. Download the Perl package from the Red Hat Web site (www.redhat.com) or one of its mirrors. (The proper package would be "perl-5.6.0-12. i386.rpm" for the version of Perl that comes with Red Hat Linux 7.1.) Alternatively, if you have the installation CD for your Red Hat system, you should be able to find the Perl package on it.

2. Assume superuser privileges on your computer using the su command.

3. Using the RPM package manager, install the package:

```
[root@fugu joe]#rpm -ivh perl-5.6.0-12.i386.rpm
Preparing...    ############################################# [100%]
1:perl          ############################################# [100%]
```

4. If you are upgrading, substitute U for i in the preceding command.

Once the package is installed, you should be ready to begin writing Perl programs.

If you are using a Debian or Debian-derived version of Linux, you can use the dpkg utility to install the Debian package. Under Solaris, you would use the pkgadd utility, and so on. Some systems will have special installation programs you may have to download and run. Make sure you check the instructions that come with the package you are using.

Installing from source code

Installing from source code is an alternative that you always have even if you can also install from binary packages. The advantages that you have with a source code install are that you can exercise a good deal more control over the installation (for example, where the files will be put, and so on) and that you can install Perl even if you don't have superuser privileges on the machine you're working with. The disadvantages are that it is more complicated, and there are more opportunities for things to go wrong.

If you choose to install from source code, you should at least be familiar with the process in general; ideally, you will have installed a simple software package from source code at least once before. You should also be certain that you have a complete compilation environment: a C compiler, and all the standard C libraries that you would need to build any other software package. Again, if you have a standard Linux or Unix installation, the odds are very good that you have these packages already installed. You should also have the make program installed.

If your compilation environment is complete, and you wish to perform a default install, perform the following steps:

1. Download the source code package, which, if you get the latest version, will be named stable.tar.gz

2. Place the package in a convenient directory, such as /tmp, or /usr/src. (For general housekeeping reasons, I suggest that you do not use your home directory.)

3. Extract the package using the tar utility:

    ```
    [root@fugu src]# tar cvfz stable.tar.gz
    ```

    A lot of filenames should scroll up the screen.

4. IMPORTANT: Before you do anything else, read the documentation that comes with the package. Most especially, read anything with the title README or INSTALL or anything with the name of your operating system in the title. If anything has changed in the particular distribution you're using, or if there are any special instructions regarding compiling on your particular operating system, they will be spelled out in these documents. In case of any discrepancies between this book, and the package documentation, follow the directions in the package documentation.

5. Assume superuser privileges using the su command.

6. Extracting the package will create a new directory that should have the name perl-*x.x.x* (where *x.x.x* is the version number, for example, perl-5.6.1). Change the working directory to that directory.

7. Issue the following commands, in order:

    ```
    rm -f config.sh Policy.sh
    sh Configure -de
    make
    make test
    make install
    ```

Pay attention to the messages that each command produces. If there are problems with the compilation process, they will show here.

When running the Configure program (as shown on line 2), answer any questions the program asks you. To accept the default response, just press the Enter key. The default is almost always okay. The Configure program will also make it possible to customize your Perl installation if you need to. You can find out the details of the configure script by reading the INSTALL document.

Once you have completed all of these steps with no errors, your Perl installation should be ready for action.

Installing under Windows

**10 Min.
To Go**

If you're using any variant of Microsoft's Windows operating system, you will almost certainly want to install a binary package. While source code packages are available for Windows, there's just no reason to put yourself through the hassle of compiling it when the binary distributions work quite well.

As I said previously, I recommend using ActivePerl, ActiveState's distribution of Perl for Windows.

> **If you absolutely MUST install Perl from source code on your Windows system, download the source code ZIP package from the Perl Web site, and extract it. Read all the documentation carefully, especially the file called README.win32. This file contains crucial information about what you need to do to perform the source code installation. In particular, it tells you which compilers can be used, as well as other utilities that you will need to have installed in order for the procedure to work. It is probably best if you have some familiarity with building C packages in a Windows environment. Compiling software is not something most Windows users do, so if you're not familiar with the process, avoid it if you possibly can.**

Before you can install ActivePerl, you'll need to make sure that you have all the prerequisite programs for it to work on your system. If you are using WindowsME, or Windows2000, you need do nothing — you already have everything you need.

If you are using WindowsNT 4, you'll need the following:

- Service pack 5+

- Microsoft Windows Installer, version 1.1 or later (available from `http://download.microsoft.com/download/platformsdk/wininst/1.1/NT4/EN-US/InstMsi.exe`)

- Internet Explorer, version 5 or later (available from `http://windowsupdate.microsoft.com`)

If you are using Windows 98, you'll need:

- Microsoft Windows Installer, version 1.1 or later (available from `http://download.microsoft.com/download/platformsdk/wininst/1.1/W9X/EN-US/InstMsi.exe`)

- Internet Explorer, version 5 or later (available from `http://windowsupdate.microsoft.com`)

- DCOM for Windows 98 (available from `http://www.microsoft.com/com/resources/downloads.asp`)

If you are using Windows 95, you'll need:

- Microsoft Windows Installer, version 1.1 or later (available from `http://download.microsoft.com/download/platformsdk/wininst/1.1/W9X/EN-US/InstMsi.exe`)

- Internet Explorer, version 5 or later (available from `http://windowsupdate.microsoft.com`)

- DCOM for Windows 98 (available from `http://www.microsoft.com/com/resources/downloads.asp`)

- MSVCRT (available from `ftp://ftp.microsoft.com/softlib/mslfiles/msvcrt.exe`)

Once you've installed the necessary prerequisites, you can go ahead and install ActivePerl:

1. Download the package from `www.activestate.com`.
2. Run the program ActivePerl-5.6.0.6xx.msi. This program will take over the installation from this point on. Be aware that the installation program will change your environment and registry settings. This shouldn't be a problem unless you need to modify these settings for some other purpose of your own.

The installation program will put the Perl interpreter in the C:\Perl directory. You will need to reboot your machine in order for the new settings and path directives to take effect.

Done!

REVIEW

This session started by showing you how to find out if you have Perl already installed on your computer system. Then you learned how to find the appropriate Perl packages for your operating system. Finally, you learned how to install Perl on your computer system.

QUIZ YOURSELF
---

1. On a Unix system, how would you go about finding out if you already had Perl installed? (See "You May Already Have It.")

2. Why is it likely that you will already have Perl installed on a Linux or Unix system? (See "You May Already Have It.")

3. As a general rule, is it better to install Perl from binary packages, or source code? Why? (See "Installing from Binary Packages.")

An Overview of the Language

Session Checklist

✔ Learning about the elements of the Perl language

✔ Using statements

✔ Using variables

✔ Using operators

✔ Using functions

✔ Using handles

✔ Using conditional constructs

✔ Using iterative constructs

✔ Using regular expressions

✔ Using packages and modules

**30 Min.
To Go**

This session introduces Perl programs and the way they work. The material in this session will be reiterated and expanded upon in subsequent sessions. The idea is to give you some basic knowledge of how Perl programs work, so that when I refer to certain types of constructs later in the book, you will have at least some familiarity with them, even if they have not been explained in detail.

You should not feel as though you need to learn the entire language in this one session. (You have the rest of the book for that.) In general, you should focus on the terminology, and the basics of program construction.

"Parts of Speech"

Computer languages are a lot like human languages. They're not exactly the same, of course, but they're similar enough that we can make some meaningful comparisons between the two. Like human languages, computer languages have a grammar. They have "nouns" (variables), "verbs" (commands), and "objects" (operands and arguments). In this section, you'll get a look at how some of these ideas are realized in Perl.

Statements

A Perl program (or any program, for that matter) is a series of statements that gives instructions to the computer. In general, these statements can either direct the computer to perform an action, such as printing something on the terminal screen or solving a math problem, or they can tell the computer something about the program itself.

Statements that tell the computer something about the program are often used to change the way the program behaves in response to certain conditions. The components of a statement are functions and expressions. If you compare programming language to human language, functions would be the verbs, and expressions would be complex clauses. You also have nouns in the form of variables. In Perl, every statement ends with a semicolon or with a closing curly brace.

Data

A program isn't very useful without a way of handling information — data. Programs hold data in the form of variables. Variables represent things. These things can be numbers, bits of text, words, expressions, or even other variables.

In Perl, there are three types of variables:

Scalars

Scalar variables hold single values. That is, any scalar value is a single number, a single bit of text, or something similar. Any value held in a scalar variable is considered a single, discreet, indivisible unit. Scalar variables are identified by a dollar sign in front of the variable name, for example, $variable.

Lists

Lists, as their name implies, hold multiple values. A list is also sometimes called an *array*, and I use both terms in this book. Each single item in a list is called a *list element*. Lists are identified by the at sign (@) in front of the variable's name, as in @list.

Lists and scalars are related, in that each element of a list can be considered a scalar. You can have access to an individual list element by identifying it as a scalar, and giving it an index number that corresponds to its position in the list. Thus, the third element of the variable @list can be identified as $list[2]. (Use the number 2 to identify the third element because you start counting from 0. The first element is number 0, the second is number 1, the third is number 2, and so on.) Note that the variable $list — with no index number — is not necessarily related to the variable @list.

Hashes

The third variable type is the hash. The hash is a special type of list wherein the elements are related to each other in a particular way. Elements in a hash are grouped by pairs, and each pair comprises a *key* and a *value*. Values can be accessed by referring to them in terms of their associated key. Hashes are identified by a percent sign in front of the variable's name, as in %hash. The general form of a hash looks like this:

```
%hash = {key1, value1, key2, value2, key3, value3};
```

Each key is generally some kind of identifier, and you can extract any value from the hash by referring to it by its key. In other words, the value of

```
$hash{key2}
```

would be value2. If this seems a little abstruse, consider this hash:

```
%address = (
          "number" => "2135",
          "street" => "Elm St.",
          "City"   => "Hamden",
          "State"  => "CT"
       )
```

(The arrow symbol, =>, is a synonym for the comma. You use it sometimes in writing hashes just to make the key/value pairs very easy to see.)

Now, if you want to extract only the street name from the hash, you can refer to it as

```
$hash{"street"}
```

and that will represent the value Elm St.. Note that as with a list, each element of a hash is a scalar, and so is referred to with the dollar sign.

Operators

Operators describe a relationship between two things. The simplest type of operator to grasp is the mathematical variety. Consider the expression

```
2+2
```

Here the operator is the plus sign, and it tells us that the two numbers have an additive relationship. In addition to mathematical operators, there are comparison operators, such as == ("is equal to"), > (is greater than), < (is less than), and the like. There are logical operators such as and and or, assignment operators such as = and +=, and increment and decrement operators such as ++ and --.

Functions

Functions are the heart of programming. Functions take data and work some kind of operation on it. Consider the statement:

```
print "hello";
```

Here, the data is hello, and the print function takes that data and displays it on the terminal screen.

Each function has its own purpose and its own way of dealing with data. If you want to learn to program effectively, there is no way around the fact that you're simply going to have to put some effort into learning what the functions are, and how they work. Some of Perl's more essential functions are described in Session 13.

Handles

Handles are special keywords that help to identify an entity as a target for certain functions. The most common type of handle is one that is linked to a file. These filehandles can then be used to direct the action of certain commands. For example, a filehandle used in conjunction with the `print` function will cause the output of the `print` statement to be directed to the file that is represented by the handle. Handles can also be created for directories as well as for things like databases and network connections.

**20 Min.
To Go**

"Grammar"

At the risk of pushing the language analogy past the breaking point, it is worth noting that the "parts of speech" are only part of the story. You need to put them together in ways that make sense. In this section, I discuss the logical organization of programs, in particular, the ways in which you can get your programs to make decisions about how to execute themselves.

Conditional constructs

Sometimes you want to segregate certain statements to be executed only under certain circumstances. This is called a *conditional construct* and is denoted by the `if` statement.

An `if` statement takes the general form

```
if (some condition) {

    statement 1;
    statement 2;
    statement 3;
}
```

If the condition inside the parentheses is true, the statements inside the braces will be executed. If the condition is false, the statements will be skipped.

In addition to the `if` statement, you can define an alternative case by using an `else` statement. An `else` statement takes the general form

```
if (some condition) {
    statement 1;
    statement 2;
    statement 3;
}
else {
    statement A;
    statement B;
```

```
    statement C;
}
```

If the condition in parentheses is true, statements 1, 2, and 3 will execute, but statements A, B, and C will not. If the condition is false, statements A, B, and C, will execute, but statements 1, 2, and 3 will be skipped.

Finally, you can specify alternate conditions using the elsif statement. An elsif statement takes the general form

```
if (some condition) {
    statement 1;
    statement 2;
    statement 3;
}
elsif (some other condition) {
    statement A;
    statement B;
    statement C;
}
else {
    statement X;
    statement Y;
    statement Z;
}
```

Now statements A, B, and C will execute only if the first condition is not met, but the second condition is. The preceding statement is exactly equal to

```
if (some condition) {
    statement 1;
    statement 2;
    statement 3;
}
else {
    if (some other condition) {
        statement A;
        statement B;
        statement C;
    }
    else {
        statement X;
        statement Y;
```

```
        statement Z;
    }
}
```

The opposite of the `if` construct is the `unless` construct. `unless` causes a section of code to execute only if the condition is false, in other words,

```
unless (some condition) {
    statement 1;
    statement 2;
    statement 3;
}
```

Iterative constructs

Sometimes you want to have a section of code execute repeatedly under certain conditions. For this, there are several constructs:

while

The `while` construct causes a section of code to repeat as long as a certain condition holds true:

```
while (some condition) {
    statement 1;
    statement 2;
    statement 3;
}
```

If, at some point the condition ceases to hold true, the execution of the program will skip to the line immediately following the closing brace.

until

`until` is the opposite of `while`. `until` causes a section of code to repeat as long as a certain condition does not hold true:

```
until (some condition) {
    statement 1;
    statement 2;
    statement 3;
}
```

foreach

foreach is a special construct that executes the enclosed statements once for each element in a list. The general format of a foreach statement is

```
foreach $scalar (@list) {
    statement 1;
    statement 2;
    statement 3;
}
```

Note that in this construct, it is usual for the enclosed statements to use the variable $scalar in some way. Each time through the loop, the variable $scalar takes on the next value in @list. That is, if you have the code

```
@list = (1, 2, 3, 4);
foreach $scalar (@list) {
    print 2 + $scalar;
}
```

the output will be 3, 4, 5, 6. The first time through the loop, $scalar takes the first value of @list, which is 1. 1 is added to 2, and printed, yielding 3. The second time through the loop, $scalar takes the second value of @list, which is 2, and so on. The construct stops looping when there are no more values in the list.

**10 Min.
To Go**

Regular expressions

Although Perl is a full-featured programming language, one of the areas in which it particularly excels is text processing. Indeed, Perl is so well known for its facility in this area that some people (mistakenly) think that that's all it's good for. Perl's facility with text is related to its powerful handling of *regular expressions*. Regular expressions are sort of a template against which we can test a chunk of text, and it fits the template, we have a match. We create this template by means of *metacharacters*. Metacharacters are symbols that can match a variety of characters under certain conditions. The most basic metacharacter is the dot (.). The dot character matches any other character. Thus the regular expression

```
/b.t/
```

(regular expressions are denoted by being enclosed between slashes) would match bat, but, bit, bet, blt, or nonsense strings like bht, bjt, and so on. An asterisk is a metacharacter that means "zero or more of the previous character." Thus

```
/b.*t/
```

matches all of the preceding words, plus words like `built`, `beat`, and basically anything that starts with a b and ends with a t.

Subroutines

Subroutines are a way that you can create your own functions. Any piece of code can be made into a subroutine by declaring it to be one and giving it a name. Any time that name is invoked, the code denoted by the name is executed. Thus you can define a subroutine:

```
sub mysub = {
    statement 1;
    statement 2;
    statement 3;
}
```

Then, any time you wish to execute `statements` 1, 2, and 3, you can simply call the subroutine by using its name:

```
mysub();
```

Subroutines can appear anywhere in a program, and can be called anywhere in a program. It is typical to group them all at the beginning or the end of a program.

Packages and modules

If you think that your subroutines might be useful in more than one program, you can group them together into a package or module. Such modules make subroutines available to be imported into programs. Once you've imported these subroutines using a `use` or `require` statement, you can use them just as if they were subroutines that you had put in that program itself.

In addition, there are a huge number of packages and modules available from the worldwide Perl archive, CPAN. CPAN is a repository of modules written by Perl programmers from all over the world. CPAN contains modules that provide subroutines to deal with almost any kind of common programming task imaginable.

Done!

REVIEW

In this session, you had a brief tour of almost the entire Perl language. You started by learning about Perl's most basic elements such as statements, operators, data types, and handles. You went on to visit the concepts of conditional and iterative control structures. Finally, you were introduced to regular expressions, subroutines, and packages and modules.

QUIZ YOURSELF

1. What is an operator? Identify the operator(s) in this expression: a+b=c. (See "Operators.")

2. What is a function? How can you create functions beyond those that are native to Perl? (See "Functions.")

3. Give five examples of words that are matched by the regular expression /r.*d/. (See "Regular Expressions.")

Session Checklist

✔ Getting to know the Perl interpreter

✔ Using command line flags with the Perl interpreter

✔ Using Perl on the command line

**30 Min.
To Go**

Before we go full speed into programming in Perl, it's useful to learn a little bit about how the Perl interpreter works. The interpreter is the main engine that allows Perl programs to function, and, when you installed Perl in the previous session, it was primarily the Perl interpreter that you installed. (You installed a few other things as well, but the interpreter is the most important thing.) The interpreter is a piece of software like any other. Its function is to translate the instructions that you write in your programs into binary instructions that your computer's processor can understand.

It may surprise you to learn that the Perl interpreter is not written in Perl. It is written in C. The reason for this is that C is a very good language for dealing with information at the binary level. Unlike Perl, C is a *compiled* language, which means that the raw programming instructions are converted to binary information, and then left in that form. The advantage of this is that binary information can be processed directly by the computer, and thus these types of programs run faster than others. Perl, by contrast is an *interpreted* language, which means that the programming instructions must be converted to binary each time the program is run. This yields a slower program, but on the other hand, it is much easier to modify such a program, because it need not be recompiled each time it's changed.

Which is better? That depends on whom you ask. I know people who think that compiled languages are the only serious programming languages that exist, whereas others shudder whenever they have to use a compiler. In reality, there's no pat answer to that question. As the very construction of Perl itself shows, there are times when compiled languages are better for a certain job, and there are times when interpreted languages best fill the bill.

Invoking the Perl Interpreter

At this point, the question may occur to you, "If the Perl interpreter is just a piece of software, can I simply run it?" The answer to this, perhaps surprisingly, is yes. At a shell prompt, type the following:

```
[joe@ika joe]$ perl
```

What happened? Nothing. But you'll notice that your shell prompt didn't come back. The interpreter is running, but it has nothing to do. Now stop the interpreter by hitting the Control key, and the C key at the same time (Ctrl+C). At this point, your prompt should come back. So now you know how to run the interpreter, but you don't know how to get it to do anything other than sit there idle.

Now try this: at your prompt, type

```
[joe@ika joe]$ perl -v
```

Now you should get some output. It should look something like this:

```
This is perl, version 5.005_03 built for i386-linux

Copyright 1987-1999, Larry Wall

Perl may be copied only under the terms of either the Artistic
License or the GNU General Public License, which may be found in
the Perl 5.0 source kit.

Complete documentation for Perl, including FAQ lists, should be
found on this system using 'man perl' or 'perldoc perl'.  If you
```

have access to the Internet, point your browser at http://
www.perl.com/, the Perl Home Page.

The -v that you added to the perl command is a *command line flag*. We will
discuss flags in more detail in the next section, but for now, just know that a flag
is an addition to the basic command that changes the behavior of that command.
In this case, the -v flag causes the interpreter to output the message that you saw
previously, and then exit.

Now try this:

```
[joe@ika joe]$ perl -e 'print "hi \n";'
```

The output should be:

```
hi
```

Congratulations, you have just written your first Perl program. The -e flag is an
instruction to the interpreter that means "execute the Perl command enclosed in
single quotes that follows." Get comfortable with the -e flag, because it is a very
useful little thing. Any time you think of a simple task that could be done with a
very short Perl program, the -e flag will allow you to run it quickly at the command line, without having to go through the formalities of real programming.

The -e flag is not limited to one-liners. You could just as easily do

```
[joe@ika joe]$ perl -e 'print "hi \n";
> print "howya doin? \n";'
```

to get the following friendly greeting:

```
hi
howya doin?
```

Notice that by omitting the single quote on the first line, you've extended your
program to a second line. The shell prompts for this line with the > character. At
the end of this second line, you close the single quote, which signals the interpreter that our program has ended.

**20 Min.
To Go**

Command Line Flags

So far, you've seen two command line flags, the -v flag, and the -e flag. There are
many others, some of which are commonly used, and others which are quite
obscure.

Command line flags are sometimes referred to as switches or options. In fact, the Perl documentation mostly refers to them as switches.

Selected flags are listed in Table 3-1. Don't worry if some of the descriptions don't make sense to you now. They'll be more accessible when you've learned some of the language.

Table 3-1
Selected Perl Command Line Flags

--	Turns off command line flag processing. If the interpreter sees this flag, any flags that come after (to the right of) it will be ignored.
-c	Causes the interpreter to check the syntax of the program and then exit without running the program. This is very useful for debugging purposes.
-d	Runs the program under the Perl debugger.
-e	Executes the command that follows it from the command line.
-h	Prints a summary of Perl's command line flags. (Think "h for help.")
-I	Lets you add a directory to the list of directories that Perl searches for modules (additional prewritten Perl functions). If you have a module that you keep in a special place, you can specify it using this flag.
-m or M	Allows you to include a module in your program. This is more commonly done from within the program.
-U	Allows you to use unsafe operations in your Perl program. At this point, the only thing that qualifies as an unsafe operation is the unlinking (deletion) of directories when running with root privileges.
-v	Prints the version and patch level of your Perl interpreter.
-V	Prints a summary of your interpreter's configuration.
-w	This is a VERY important flag! This flag will print warnings about various aspects of your program's syntax. If you're writing a program of any complexity, you need to use this flag.

-x	This is an odd flag that you can use to execute a Perl script that might, for example, be part of a text file, or an e-maile-mail message. This flag causes the interpreter to look for a line beginning with the characters #! and containing the word perl (as you shall see, this is how you begin most Perl programs). In order for this to work properly, the Perl program must either be the last thing in the e-mail (or file, or whatever it is that contains the program), or the program must end with the line __END__.

Assuming there are no arguments to any of the flags you're using, you can group them together. For example, if you wanted to use the -U and -w flags at the same time, you could group them together as -Uw.

Arguments are bits of data added to a command line or to a line of a program that give it further information to work with. Thus, the -I flag expects to be given (that is, takes as an argument) the name of a directory, for example, perl -I/home/joe/perl/ mymodules <whatever>**. Some flags take arguments, and some don't. Still others can use arguments if they are provided, but do not require them.**

Using Perl on the Command Line

**10 Min.
To Go**

If you're used to using Unix-style command-line constructs, such as those found in the bash or other shells, it probably won't surprise you to find out that you can use the Perl interpreter in much the same way as you'd use any other Unix command. That means you can use input and output redirection, and especially pipes, to assist you in command-line processing. For example, suppose you have a bash shell script that produces some particular sort of output, and you want to make a change in that output before capturing it to a file, you might use a command line looking like this:

```
[joe@ika joe]$ bashprog | perl -e 's/foo/bar/g;' > outputfile
```

This command line will take the output of the program bashprog, and filter it through Perl's pattern-matching operator, which will change every occurrence of the word foo to the word bar, and then capture the output of that operation in the file called outputfile. In this way, Perl is acting as a stream editor similar to sed.

You can also use the -e flag to embed Perl commands within a shell script:

```
#!/bin/bash

<some bash commands>

perl -e '
        print "hi \n";
        print "howya doin? \n";
        '

<more bash commands>
```

By using the -e flag, you make the `perl` command just the same as any other command under the shell.

While some of these examples may seem silly, Perl and the shell combine to make a very powerful set of tools. Frequently many complex tasks can be performed as Perl or Perl+shell "one-liners;" and having the freedom to embed Perl commands in shell scripts greatly improves the already impressive power of shell programming. (It is also possible to embed shell commands in Perl programs, but that's another topic.)

Done!

REVIEW

This session started with an overview of the Perl interpreter. You learned how to start the interpreter, and how to use it to execute Perl commands from the Unix shell. You then learned about command-line flags, and learned what a number of them do. Finally, you learned how Perl command-line processing can be combined with other Unix tools.

QUIZ YOURSELF

1. Explain the difference between a compiled language and an interpreted language. Which is Perl? (See introduction.)

2. Explain what the -h flag does. Does it take an argument? (See "Command Line Flags.")

3. Discuss at least two reasons why you might want to use the Perl interpreter with the -e flag to enable command-line processing. (See "Using Perl on the Command Line.")

Getting Help

Session Checklist

✔ Using Unix manual pages

✔ Using perldoc

✔ Getting help online

**30 Min.
To Go**

There comes a time in every novice programmer's life — often sooner than we'd like — when we hit a wall. At such times, we need to seek out sources of help. Fortunately, Perl is one of the most helpful languages out there in this regard. Between built-in documentation, an online manual, and an active Internet community, finding help with your particular Perl problem should not be terribly difficult.

Built-in Documentation

In the last session, I mentioned that, in addition to the interpreter, there were a few other things that got installed when you installed the Perl package. One of these things is a whole raft of helpful documents. Taken together, these documents form a complete manual for the language.

Manual pages

If you're a Unix user, you are probably already familiar with the use of *man pages*. You can access Perl documentation via the man program, just as you would for any other Unix program. But, because there is such a huge volume of information, the manual pages are broken down into specific subject areas. If you type man perl at a shell prompt, you will get a very broad overview of the language, including a list of other topics that you can look up. Typing man plus any of the terms in the left-hand column of Table 4-1 will yield a manual page devoted to that topic.

Table 4-1
Available Perl Manual Pages

Title	Subject
perl	Perl overview
perldelta	Perl changes since previous version
perl5004delta	Perl changes in version 5.004
perlfaq	Perl frequently asked questions
perltoc	Perl documentation table of contents
perldata	Perl data structures
perlsyn	Perl syntax
perlop	Perl operators and precedence
perlre	Perl regular expressions
perlrun	Perl execution and options
perlfunc	Perl built-in functions
perlopentut	Perl
open()	tutorial
perlvar	Perl predefined variables
perlsub	Perl subroutines
perlmod	Perl modules: how they work
perlmodlib	Perl modules: how to write and use
perlmodinstall	Perl modules: how to install from CPAN

Title	Subject
perlform	Perl formats
perllocale	Perl locale support
perlref	Perl references
perlreftut	Perl references short introduction
perldsc	Perl data structures intro
perllol	Perl data structures: lists of lists
perltoot	Perl OO tutorial
perlobj	Perl objects
perltie	Perl objects hidden behind simple variables
perlbot	Perl OO tricks and examples
perlipc	Perl interprocess communication
perlthrtut	Perl threads tutorial
perldebug	Perl debugging
perldiag	Perl diagnostic messages
perlsec	Perl security
perltrap	Perl traps for the unwary
perlport	Perl portability guide
perlstyle	Perl style guide
perlpod	Perl plain old documentation
perlbook	Perl book information
perlembed	Perl ways to embed Perl in your C or C++ application
perlapio	Perl internal IO abstraction interface
perlxs	Perl XS application programming interface
perlxstut	Perl XS tutorial
perlguts	Perl internal functions for those doing extensions
perlcall	Perl calling conventions from C
perlhist	Perl history records

While I will cover some of these topics in this book, many of these are advanced topics that you may want to learn about later. Also, the Perl online documentation lists all the options for every aspect of Perl, whereas in this book, I have omitted some options that are not relevant to the topic at hand or that could be confusing to the novice programmer. In other words, whenever you run across something you haven't seen before, or if you're wondering whether a particular function can be used in a particular way, check the online documents.

**20 Min.
To Go**

perldoc

An alternative and supplement to the manual pages is the built-in Perl function, perldoc. perldoc provides access to documentation in a way similar to manual pages, but does not require access to the man program.

In many cases, the perldoc pages and the man pages are identical. Giving the command perldoc perl will display a document that is exactly the same as what you'd get if you'd typed man perl. All of the topics in Table 4-1 exist as perldoc topics as well as man topics. In this way, you have access to the Perl documentation, even if, for example, you're using Perl on a non-Unix system, and don't have the man program.

This is not to say, however, that the perldoc story ends there. Even if you do have the man program, you will still find perldoc useful. This is because perldoc contains documentation about the nuts and bolts of the Perl language itself. Using perldoc you can look up information about any Perl built-in function, simply by using the -f flag, and the name of the function. For example, you have already seen the Perl built-in function called print. Let's see what perldoc has to say about print:

```
[joe@ika joe]$ perldoc -f print

item print FILEHANDLE LIST

=item print LIST

=item print

Prints a string or a comma-separated list of strings.  Returns
TRUE if successful.  FILEHANDLE may be a scalar variable name, in
which case the variable contains the name of or a reference to the
```

filehandle, thus introducing one level of indirection. (NOTE: If
FILEHANDLE is a variable and the next token is a term, it may be
misinterpreted as an operator unless you interpose a C<+> or put
parentheses around the arguments.) If FILEHANDLE is omitted,
prints by default to standard output (or to the last selected
output channel—see L</select>). If LIST is also omitted, prints
C<$_> to the currently selected output channel. To set the
default output channel to something other than STDOUT use the
select operation. Note that, because print takes a LIST, anything
in the LIST is evaluated in list context, and any subroutine that
you call will have one or more of its expressions evaluated in
list context. Also be careful not to follow the print keyword
with a left parenthesis unless you want the corresponding right
parenthesis to terminate the arguments to the print—interpose a
C<+> or put parentheses around all the arguments.

Much of this is beyond our ken at this point, but the important thing is that
the information is all here. If you were to need advanced information on how to
use the print function, you can use perldoc to get it.

perldoc can also search all of the Perl FAQ (Frequently Asked Questions) documents by keyword, using the -q. Suppose you wanted to find out about the concept of objects in Perl:

[joe@ika joe]$ perldoc -q object

=head1 Found in /usr/lib/perl5/5.00503/pod/perlfaq3.pod

=head2 Where can I learn about object-oriented Perl programming?

L<perltoot> is a good place to start, and you can use L<perlobj>
and L<perlbot> for reference. Perltoot didn't come out until the
5.004 release, but you can get a copy (in pod, html, or
postscript) from http://www.perl.com/CPAN/doc/FMTEYEWTK/ .
=head1 Found in /usr/lib/perl5/5.00503/pod/perlfaq4.pod

=head2 How do I define methods for every class/object?

Use the UNIVERSAL class (see L<UNIVERSAL>).

Now you know that if you want to learn about object-oriented programming in Perl, you should check out the Perl tutorial, which you can read by giving the commands man `perltoot` or `perldoc perltoot`.

Admittedly, the manual and perldoc pages are not the best resources for beginners. They tend to assume a good deal of prior knowledge, and the writing in them is not always as clear as it could be, but they are the authoritative source for detailed information about any given topic.

**10 Min.
To Go**

Other Sources of Help

In addition to the built-in documentation, there is quite a wealth of information to be found elsewhere as well. The Perl community is large, diverse, and thriving, and it generates a veritable ton of written material.

The camel book

There are, of course, many books about Perl. (You have demonstrated your superior taste and judgement by selecting this one.) One book stands out, however, and must come in for specific mention. That book is called *Programming Perl*, and is published by O'Reilly and Associates. What is it about this book that would be so compelling as to plug a rival publisher? Simply that this book was written by Larry Wall, who is the creator of Perl, along with Tom Christiansen and Randal Schwartz, who are probably the most well-known Perl experts.

Programming Perl is so authoritative that it is considered official Perl documentation. It is so well known that it is referred to simply as "the camel book," because of the picture of the camel on the cover. (Indeed, the camel has even become the Perl mascot.) It is common, when asking a question about Perl, to receive an answer like, "That's covered on page 252 of the camel book."

The World Wide Web

Like just about anything computer-oriented these days, Perl has a thriving community on the Internet. Web pages devoted to Perl abound, and some of them are quite good.

Ground zero for the online Perl community is www.perl.com. This is the official Perl Web site; here you can find links to Perl software, as well as the latest news, and links to yet more software. There is also a link to the Perl documentation, which is the same documentation you have accessible by the man program. Finally, there is a Resources link that takes you to a page of links to various topics of interest.

- www.perl.org: Home of the Perl Mongers. The Perl Mongers are a group dedicated to Perl advocacy, and one of their areas of focus is helping beginners get started. They host a Perl beginners e-mail list where you can ask questions and get help with specific problems.
- www.tpj.com: Web site for the *Perl Journal*, which is a magazine devoted to Perl. While somewhat advanced, the magazine contains articles on topics of interest to Perl programmers. [NOTE: at the time of this writing, the *Perl Journal* was in a state of management transition, and the Web site was down. They promise to be back up soon, however.]
- www.perlmonks.org: A site maintained by the Perl Monks. The Monks are dedicated to making "learning Perl as nonintimidating and easy to use as possible," as well as to helping Perl programmers hone their skills. The site is a bit dense and tough to navigate, but the amount of information here is huge.

Usenet

In addition to Web resources, there are several Usenet newsgroups devoted to Perl. The primary one is comp.lang.perl.misc. This is a newsgroup devoted to general discussion about Perl. A word of warning on this group, however: its habitues can be a bit prickly, especially if they sense you haven't done your homework. A question that has an obvious answer in the available documentation is likely to be ignored or flamed.

Other newsgroups include comp.lang.perl.announce, where Perl news is announced; comp.lang.perl.modules, where you can discuss various Perl modules (such as are introduced later in this book); and comp.lang.perl.tk, a group devoted to graphical programming in Perl using the Tk toolkit.

Mailing lists

In addition to the Perl Monks' beginners mailing list, there are numerous other Perl-oriented mailing lists. Many of these are devoted to relatively narrow topic areas, and so should be approached with that in mind. A full listing of these lists is available at http://www.perl.com/pub/language/info/mailing-lists.html.

As you can see, there's no excuse for being ill informed on the subject of Perl. Between built-in documentation, the Web, and the various books on the subject, the amount of information at your disposal is enormous, and I encourage you to make liberal use of it.

Done!

REVIEW

In this session, you learned how to get help with Perl. First, you learned how to use the Unix manual pages that pertain to Perl, and then you learned to use Perl's native documentation format, perldoc. Finally, you learned about other sources of help, such as books, the World Wide Web, Internet mailing lists, and Usenet newsgroups.

QUIZ YOURSELF

1. What is the Unix man program? How would you use it to find information about Perl? (See "Manual pages.")

2. Which help topic(s) would you use to get help with object-oriented programming in Perl? (See "perldoc.")

3. How would you go about getting help with the Perl built-in open function? (See "perldoc.")

4. What would you do if you wanted to keep informed about the latest developments in Perl? (See "Other Sources of Help.")

PART

I

Friday Evening

1. On a Unix system, generally, how can you find out if a particular piece of software is installed and available?

2. On what sorts of systems would you expect to find Perl already installed?

3. How can you obtain Perl if you don't already have it installed?

4. What are the advantages of installing Perl from source code, over installing a binary distribution? The disadvantages?

5. How many different types of variables are there in Perl? Name them.

6. Lists and hashes are both plural data types. What differentiates them?

7. What is a function?

8. What is the difference between a compiled and an interpreted language? Which is Perl?

9. What is a command line flag? Give three examples of command line flags that can be used when invoking the Perl interpreter.

10. Which Unix manual page would you look at if you were interested in finding out about Perl's module system?

11. What is the primary difference between man and perldoc?

12. What can you do if you're looking for information on something that is not covered in the perldoc pages?

☑ Friday

☑ **Saturday**

☐ Sunday

PART

II

Saturday
Morning

Using Text Editors

Session Checklist

✔ Using Pico

✔ Using Nedit

✔ Using WordPad

**30 Min.
To Go**

This is the last session we will have before we get down to the business of writing actual Perl programs. We saw in Session 2 that you can use the -e flag with the perl command to execute Perl commands that you enter from the shell's command line. While this is a satisfactory method for executing one-liners or brief one-time scripts, it does not address the need for saving programs in case you want to run them again, or develop them further.

Programs Are Text Files

In order to save your work on a program, you must have some way of creating and saving a file. While most computer users are familiar with creating files by using a word processor, spreadsheet, or other application, programs need to be created in something a little more generic. Office applications tend to use file formats involving a great deal of layout instructions, which make the document look nice but are alien to the Perl interpreter.

The Perl interpreter deals with ASCII text characters. ASCII text is a very simple text format that assigns a number to each character you might type, as well as to a few invisible characters such as the carriage return (or newline) and the tab character. This scheme produces files that may not look very fancy, but that can be read by almost any program — including the Perl interpreter.

Once these ASCII text files are created, they can be saved to your computer's hard drive just like any other file. But how do you create them in the first place? In order to do that, you need to use a program known as a text editor. You can think of text editors as being stripped-down word processors. That is, you can manipulate text, but you can't control the font or other visual attributes of the document beyond what you can accomplish by using spaces, tabs, newlines, and the like. (Some of us prefer to think of word processors as gussied-up text editors, but we're probably hopelessly behind the times.)

While it is theoretically possible to create plain text files with a word processor such as Microsoft's Word, I don't recommend it. Word processors always seem to have their own agendas, and I've found my own attempts at ASCII file creation to have been something of a battle. Text editors make the job much simpler.

I have chosen in this section to discuss three text editors: two of them, Pico and NEdit are Unix or Linux programs, and the third, WordPad is native to Microsoft's Windows family. The reason that I have chosen two Unix editors is because one of them is a character mode editor (that is, it can be used without any kind of graphical software running) and the other is a graphical editor with many nice features. On the Windows side of things, WordPad is pretty much the only game in town. While there are other text editors for Windows, WordPad is probably the nicest of them, and it comes with the standard Windows package, so unless you prefer something else, there's really no reason not to use it.

Linux/Unix Editors

Choosing a Unix text editor is not a task to be undertaken lightly. The decision is fraught with social, political, and dare I say, religious overtones. The choice of an editor is one of many Unix "holy wars." While these jihads are usually good natured, they do sometimes break out into real acrimony. Your author finds the whole thing a bit silly, but raises the subject for a reason. There are those who will almost certainly criticize my choices for this book. They will point out that this or that editor is actually a better choice for Perl programming, and that I am omitting a crucial part of the puzzle by not including their favorite.

In fact, I have chosen the two editors in this section for straightforward reasons. They are both widely available, and they are both extremely easy to learn. While other editors might handle heavyweight tasks better, they are often unfriendly to the novice. With Pico and NEdit, you will easily be up and running by the end of this section. However, if you're an old hand at Unix, and you are already comfortable with another editor, then by all means, use it.

Pico

**20 Min.
To Go**

The odds are good that you already have Pico installed on your system. It's a relatively common editor. To check if you have it, give the following command at a shell prompt:

```
[joe@ika joe]$ pico -h
```

You should get output that looks like this:

```
Possible Starting Arguments for Pico editor:
Argument          Meaning
     -e           Complete - allow file name completion
     -k           Cut - let ^K cut from cursor position to end of
                  line
     -j           Goto - allow 'Goto' command in file browser
     -g           Show - show cursor in file browser
     -m            Mouse - turn on mouse support
     -x           NoKeyhelp - suppress keyhelp
     -q           TermdefWins - termcap or terminfo takes
                  precedence over defaults
     -d           Rebind - let delete key delete current
character
     -f           Keys - force use of function keys
     -b           Replace - allow search and replace
     -h           Help - give this list of options
     -r[#cols]        Fill - set fill column to #cols columns,
                      default=72
     -n[#s]          Mail - notify about new mail every #s
seconds,    default=180
       -s <speller>  Speller - specify alternative speller
```

```
-t              Shutdown - enable special shutdown mode
-o <dir>        Operation - specify the operating directory
-z              Suspend - allow use of ^Z suspension
-w              NoWrap - turn off word wrap
+[line#]        Line - start on line# line, default=1
-v              View - view file
All arguments may be followed by a file name to display.
```

If Pico is not on your system, you should get something that looks like this:

```
bash: pico: command not found
```

If you do not have Pico on your system, you need to get and install the Pine e-mail package. You should be able to find it at whatever WWW or FTP site you normally use to find software for your operating system. Pico is a key component of Pine, and will be installed along with the Pine package.

Once you have it installed, you can start Pico by simply typing pico at the shell prompt. You should see a screen like that in Figure 5-1.

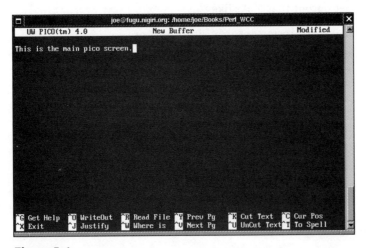

Figure 5-1
The main Pico screen

As you can see, the screen is divided into three parts. At the top is an information line that tells you the version of Pico you're using, plus the name of the file you're working on. If the file you're working on does not yet have a name, you will see the New Buffer legend.

A buffer is an area in your computer's memory that a program reserves for its own use. When you start Pico, it reserves a buffer for the file you're working on. When you save the file, the contents of the buffer will be written to the hard drive.

Below the information line is the text area. This is the area where you actually do your work. Finally, at the bottom, there are two lines that serve as reminders of some of Pico's most commonly used functions. These functions allow you to do such things as save the file, exit Pico, move from page to page, find a particular string of text, and so on.

All functions in Pico are invoked by using the Control key (Ctrl) in combination with letter keys. Thus the combination meaning Exit is ^X.

In Unixese, the carat character, ^, is used to denote the Control key.

You should see a cursor in the text area. To enter text in Pico, simply begin typing. Your text will appear at the cursor. As you might expect, you can use your keyboard's arrow keys to move around in the text. You can also use the sequence ^A to go to the beginning of the current line, and the sequence ^E to go to the end of the current line. If you make a mistake, you can use the Backspace key to delete the text immediately to the left of the cursor. Other control sequences are shown in Table 5-1.

Table 5-1
Pico Control Sequences

Sequence	Action
^G	Display help text.
^F	Move forward a character.
^B	Move backward a character.
^P	Move to the previous line.
^N	Move to the next line.
^A	Move to the beginning of the current line.
^E	Move to the end of the current line.

Continued

Table 5-1   *Continued*

Sequence	Action
^V	Move forward a page of text.
^Y	Move backward a page of text.
^W	Search for text. (Search is case-insensitive.)
^L	Refresh the display.
^D	Delete the character at the cursor position.
^^	Mark cursor position as beginning of selected text. Note: Setting mark when already set unselects text.
^K	Cut selected text (displayed in inverse characters). Note: The selected text's boundary on the cursor side ends at the left edge of the cursor. So, with selected text to the left of the cursor, the character under the cursor is not selected.
^U	Uncut (paste) last cut text inserting it at the current cursor position.
^I	Insert a tab at the current cursor position.
^J	Format (justify) the current paragraph. Note: Paragraphs are delimited by blank lines or indentation.
^T	Invoke the spelling checker.
^C	Report current cursor position.
^R	Insert an external file at the current cursor position.
^O	Output the current buffer to a file, saving it.
^X	Exit Pico, saving buffer.

Two particular control sequences should be highlighted here. Anyone who uses computers much knows the agony of losing a file, and the importance of saving their work frequently. The sequence ^O allows you to save your buffer to your hard drive without exiting Pico. This is useful since you can save your file while still working on it, and doubly useful because, when programming, we often like to make changes to a program, and then run it to see how our change has affected the program's behavior. Since the interpreter will see only that version of the program that has been saved to the hard disk, you will need to save your file using the ^O sequence before your changes will take effect. When you use the ^O sequence, you will be prompted for a filename if you have not saved this file before. Any filename is fine, however, it is traditional to use the suffix .pl to denote Perl programs.

The ^X sequence is used to exit Pico. This sequence will also save your file to disk, prompting you for a filename if the current file doesn't already have one.

It should also be pointed out that the control sequences in Pico are somewhat context-sensitive, which is to say that a sequence may take on a slightly different meaning, depending on what mode Pico is in at the time. For example, if you have used the ^G sequence to pull up Pico's built in help text, the ^X sequence will mean "Exit the help text" rather than "Exit Pico." When in doubt, you should always look to the bottom two lines of the screen to see the options that are available at any given time.

NEdit

NEdit is a very good and largely overlooked graphical text editor. As a graphical editor, it is capable of using your mouse for such functions as moving the cursor around, and highlighting text for cutting-and-pasting. It also has the ability to control the look of the text in the editor. For example, you can set the font and point size of the text in the text area. Note that this only affects the look of the text when it is displayed in NEdit, and will not affect the text in the file itself.

Another very useful function of NEdit is the ability to highlight certain portions of text based on the syntax of various programming languages, including Perl. This makes it a good deal easier to catch typographical mistakes such as failing to close parentheses.

Assuming NEdit is installed on your machine, start it by typing nedit at a shell prompt (or, if you are using a graphical environment that supports it, you may wish to place a launcher icon on your desktop). You will see a basic text window (empty at this point), above which are several drop-down menus. To create a new file, simply start typing. To open an already existing file, click on the File menu and select Open from the list that appears. You will then see a dialog that will allow you to select the file you wish to open.

Once NEdit is up and ready to go, simply click in the text area and begin typing. You can use the arrow keys to navigate around, and you can use your mouse to move the cursor. To cut text, click and drag over the text you wish to cut, and then select Cut under the Edit menu. To paste the text, place the cursor where you want the text inserted, and select Paste under the Edit menu.

If you wish to use syntax highlighting, click on Preferences, and select Language Mode. You will see a submenu. Click on Perl.

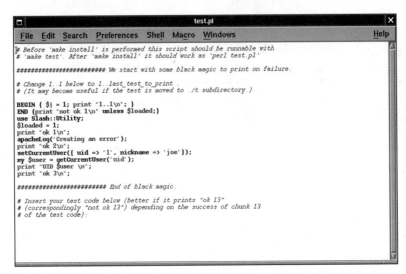

```
# Before 'make install' is performed this script should be runnable with
# 'make test'. After 'make install' it should work as 'perl test.pl'

######################### We start with some black magic to print on failure.

# Change 1..1 below to 1..last_test_to_print .
# (It may become useful if the test is moved to ./t subdirectory.)

BEGIN { $| = 1; print "1..1\n"; }
END {print "not ok 1\n" unless $loaded;}
use Slash::Utility;
$loaded = 1;
print "ok 1\n";
apacheLog('Creating an error');
print "ok 2\n";
setCurrentUser({ uid => '1', nickname => 'joe'});
my $user = getCurrentUser('uid');
print "UID $user \n";
print "ok 3\n";

######################### End of black magic.

# Insert your test code below (better if it prints "ok 13"
# (correspondingly "not ok 13") depending on the success of chunk 13
# of the test code):
```

Figure 5-2
NEdit with a syntax-highlighted Perl program

When you wish to save your work, click on File, and select Save from the menu. This will bring up a dialog box that will allow you to name the file. If the file already has a name, it will simply save the new version of that file under the old name.

When you're done working on your file, click on File and select Exit from the menu. If the file has been modified since the last time it was saved, you will be given the opportunity to save it. Be advised that if you are working on more than one file, and you select Exit, all files will be closed. If you wish to close only one file, use the Close option instead.

NEdit auto-saves your work periodically. If something should happen that results in NEdit exiting before you have saved your work (if, for example, you were to log out without saving your work), you may not have lost everything. Look for a file with the same name as the file you're working on, but with a tilde (~) character prepended to it. Thus if the file were named foo, the backup file will be named ~foo. It may not have all of your latest work, but the odds are good it will have at least some of it. (These backup files have saved this author countless hours of work.)

WordPad for Windows

Lest we forget the Windows users out there, we'll now look at the default Windows text editor, WordPad. WordPad is not terribly different from NEdit described previously, although it lacks syntax highlighting, and has rather more options for text formatting. However, like NEdit, it is a graphical editor, and allows you to use your mouse to cut and paste text, and to position the cursor.

Open WordPad by going to your Windows Start menu, and selecting the Programs submenu. Under Programs select Accessories, and there you will find WordPad. Click on WordPad, and you should see the main WordPad screen.

Click in the text area, and begin typing. You can move your cursor around using the arrow keys, or you can use your mouse to position the cursor in an exact location. By clicking and dragging, you can highlight text, which can then be copied, cut, or pasted by using the corresponding entries in the Edit drop-down menu.

When you wish to save your work, click on File, and then Save. A dialog will appear, prompting you to give your file a name. Enter the name, and make sure to select Text Document in the field labeled Save as type.

Do not save your file as Rich text or Unicode text. The Perl interpreter will not be able to understand these formats.

REVIEW

In this session we started by learning that Perl programs are stored in the form of ASCII text. Then we learned how ASCII text files differ from the kinds of files produced by word processors. Subsequently, we learned how to use three different text editors. We started in the Unix world, learning to use the character mode editor, Pico, and the graphical editor NEdit. We then moved on to the Windows platform, and learned to use WordPad.

Quiz Yourself

1. Why is it advantageous to use a text editor rather than a word processor to create Perl programs? (See "Programs Are Text Files.")

2. How does the -w flag modify Pico's behavior? (See "Pico.")

3. What does the ^K sequence do in Pico? (See "Pico.")

4. Describe the method for turning on syntax highlighting in Nedit. (See "NEdit.")

5. What format should you save your files in when using WordPad? (See "WordPad for Windows.")

6

Basics of Programming Style

Session Checklist

✔ Understanding programming style

✔ Using comments

✔ Using indentation

✔ Code blocks

**30 Min.
To Go**

This morning we will be getting into actual Perl programming. Before we start programming, however, we need to talk a little bit about programming style. To a beginning programmer, the notion of style might seem a little out of place when talking about programming. After all, style is for artists, isn't it?

Programming Style

So what do I mean by programming style? In a nutshell, style means two things: First, it means the way your program looks to a reader. This may seem like a trivial consideration, but I assure you, it is quite important. A clear and readable program is not only a thing of beauty, it is also something that will pay dividends in the future. But why should you care? After all, you are only writing this program for yourself, and only for a small problem that exists only temporarily, right? This may be true, but you'd be amazed at how easy it is to forget what you were thinking when you wrote a bit of code. It is quite easy to write a piece of a program one day, and come back the next to finish it, only to find that you have no idea what you were thinking the day before. A well-styled piece of programming should make the thought process clear.

Second, programming style refers to the elegance and efficiency with which a programmer solves a particular problem. Ideally, the problem should be solved with as few steps as possible. Programs that solve a problem in a roundabout way are usually disdained as kludgy or "spaghetti code." These programs are not only inelegant from an intellectual point of view, the also operate inefficiently, using more time and computing power than necessary, thus wasting system resources.

This session focuses on the first definition of style. The second definition is something that mainly relates to a programmer's understanding of general programming technique and the particular language in use, as well as to her own ingenuity in problem solving. As such, it is not particularly suited to a short session. That kind of style is acquired through much study and practice. So, here I focus on clear structuring and presentation of your programs.

Why Programs Look the Way They Do

Consider this typical piece of Perl code:

```perl
# This subroutine acts like a Server Side Include. It takes the
# name of a file as an argument, and includes that file in the web
# page.

sub SSI {

        open(CONTENT, "$_[0]");
        while (<CONTENT>) {
                print "$_\n";

                if (/^\n/) {
                        print "<P>";
                }

        }

close (CONTENT);
```

```
print "<BR>";

}
```

Don't try to figure out what this code does — you have the rest of the book to learn that. Rather, look simply at the visual aspect of it. You can see a couple of unique features. First, the lines preceded by hashmarks (#) don't look like programming code at all. Second, several programming instructions are enclosed in various parentheses and braces, and indented to various degrees. Finally, a number of braces are on lines by themselves. Although it may not be obvious at this point, this is all organized in a very specific way.

Comments

The lines preceded by hashmarks (#) are comments.

```
# This subroutine acts like a Server Side Include. It takes the
# name of a file as an argument, and includes that file in the web
#page.
```

These are notes that are ignored by the Perl interpreter; they exist merely as a way for the programmer to leave notes, either to himself or to other programmers. Many novice programmers think comments are trivial or unnecessary. Nothing could be further from the truth. Comments make the work of deciphering someone else's work, or your own old work, much, much easier.

In this example, the comment tells what the piece of code is designed to do. Comments can also be used to remind yourself of how you were going about attacking a problem, of another idea you had for a similar piece of code, to keep notes about what you changed in the program and when, or for any other purpose whatsoever.

You may think, "Oh, this program is only a one-off, I don't need to comment it," but you may be surprised at how often you find yourself revisiting old one-off programs because you've run across another task that can be accomplished more quickly by adapting an old program, rather than by writing a new one from scratch. Reusing old code is one of the most reliable ways of increasing your efficiency as a programmer, but it only works if you don't have to spend a lot of time figuring out what you did the first time you wrote the program.

It is a far, far better thing to overcomment than to undercomment. A comment costs you nothing except the time it takes to type it. Since comments are completely ignored by the Perl interpreter, they have no effect on the running of your program. While some may chide you for your prolix commenting style, you can retort by chiding them for the amount of time they spend relearning old code.

In many, if not most Perl programs, you will see a special kind of comment. It is usually the first line of any program, and it looks either exactly like, or very similar to this:

```
#!/usr/bin/perl
```

This is, in fact, not really a comment at all, even though it begins with the hashmark. By following up that character with the exclamation point character, you've alerted the computer that this is a program, and the /usr/bin/perl part tells it that the rest of the file should be handled by the Perl interpreter, which is named perl and is in the /usr/bin directory. (If your Perl interpreter lives in a different directory, use the path name of that directory instead.)

*20 Min.
To Go*

Indentation

Look again at this section of the previous listing:

```
sub SSI {

        open(CONTENT, "$_[0]");
        while (<CONTENT>) {
                print "$_\n";

                if (/^\n/) {
                        print "<P>";
                }

        }

close (CONTENT);
```

Notice that certain lines are indented, double-indented, or triple-indented. Why is that? Believe it or not, this is done for readability. Any indented section is actually a part of the section inside of which it sits. For example, in the section:

```
if (/^\n/) {
        print "<P>";
}
```

The print statement exists *inside* of the if statement. This inside-ness is denoted further by the use of curly braces ({ and }). In fact, that entire statement could be rewritten to look like this:

```
if (/^\n/) { print "<P>"; }
```

While this may seem straightforward enough, imagine if there were many other lines of code besides the print statement. Putting them all on a single line would make the code very confusing. Not only that, it is possible to enclose such a statement inside another similar statement. Thus, the statement

```
if (something) { if (/^\n/) { print "<P>"; } }
```

is possible. Likewise the statement

```
if (something else) { if (something) { if (/^\n/) { print "<P>"; }
} }
```

and so on is possible. The level of complexity here is practically unlimited. You can see that beyond a certain level of enclosure, it becomes difficult to discern exactly which statements are enclosed inside which. By placing each statement on its own line, and indenting lines that are enclosed in other lines, the chain of dependency becomes obvious:

```
if (something else) {
    if (something) {
        if (/^\n/) {
            print "<P>";
        }
    }
}
```

This also explains the brackets on the lines by themselves. By closing off each block with a bracket on its own line, we create a visual enclosure for the block inside. To find the beginning of a particular block one need only scan up from the bracket until a line that begins at the same indent level is found. All statements to the right of that indent level will be inside. This makes it much easier to isolate a section of for editing purposes.

Code blocks

You will notice as you look at more Perl programs that there are blank lines scattered liberally throughout most of them. From a functional point of view, these lines are not necessary at all, however it is a convention of style that blank lines are inserted between sections of code that perform different functions.

Look at this fragment:

```
sub portalbox {
    my($width, $title, $contents, $bid, $url) = @_;
    return unless $title && $contents;
    my $constants = getCurrentStatic();
    my $user = getCurrentUser();

    $title = slashDisplay('portalboxtitle', {
        title    => $title,
        url      => $url,
    }, { Return => 1, Nocomm => 1 });

    if ($user->{exboxes}) {
        $title = slashDisplay('portalmap', {
            title       => $title,
            bid => $bid,
        }, { Return => 1, Nocomm => 1 });
    }

    fancybox($width, $title, $contents, 0, 1);
}
```

Obfuscated Perl

If you find that you have a sufficiently sadomasochistic personality, you may want to try your hand at *obfuscated Perl*. Obfuscated Perl is just one example of the zany and fun-loving nature of the Perl community. It is code that has been deliberately designed to frustrate the reader. Such frustration can take the form of deliberately breaking all the rules of programming style, and cramming as many characters on a line as possible, or it may involve attempting to perform a simple function in as many steps as possible, or some other offense against good and clear programming practice. The idea is to make it as difficult as possible for a reader of the program to figure out what the program actually does.

I should stress here, that obfuscated Perl is something that is done for *recreational purposes only*. Obfuscation is not considered a good way to save space or to keep your programming techniques secret. When programming with serious intent, always follow good programming style.

Note the blank lines. These lines serve to break this bit of code into four sections. While all of these sections are related to a single function, each section performs a discreet and distinct piece of the puzzle.

Such sections of code are often referred to informally as *blocks*. This is a term that should be used with some care, however, as an accurate definition of "block" usually refers to a section of code enclosed within braces.

The Perl interpreter ignores whitespace. This means that it doesn't matter what line a statement is on or where on the line it appears. The interpreter will simply ignore any space, tab, or newline characters that appear in the file. Thus, this code:

```
if ($user->{exboxes}) {
    $title = slashDisplay('portalmap', {
        title       => $title,
        bid=> $bid,
    }, { Return => 1, Nocomm => 1 });

}
```

Could be rewritten to look like this:

```
if($user-
>{exboxes}){$title=slashDisplay('portalmap',{title=>$title,bid
=> $bid,},{Return=>1,Nocomm=>1});}
```

This code would run just as well, but any more than a line or two of this kind of thing quickly becomes unreadable.

The moral of the story here is that you should use whitespace liberally. Anywhere you think you could make the program more readable by inserting a space, tab, or blank line, go ahead. Yes, it will make it take a little bit longer to scroll through the file, but it's easier to do that than it is to disentangle needlessly compressed code.

Formal Perl Style

10 Min. To Go

What I have described in this session is a rather informal definition of programming style. There are, however, accepted ways of doing things, which, while not ironclad rules, have become a sort of de facto standard among Perl programmers. It is up to you exactly how closely you want to follow these conventions, however, if

you plan on releasing any of your code to the world at large, you probably ought
to follow the guidelines reasonably closely.

- Do not indent to more than four columns. If you need to use more than
  four levels of dependency in your code, there's probably a better way to
  do it.
- Closing braces should be placed at the same level of indentation as the
  keyword that began the construct. In other words,

```
if (something) {
    something else;
    some other thing;
}
```

is correct, whereas

```
if (something) {
    something else;
    some other thing;
    }
```

and

```
if (something) {
    something else;
    some other thing;
    }
```

are wrong.

- If your conditional block is only one statement, you can put it all on one
  line, like so:

```
if (something) { something else;
```

- If the conditional part of your statement wraps over more than one line,
  put the opening brace on a line by itself:

```
if (something very, very, very, very, very
    very, very long)
{
    something else;
}
```

- In all other situations, err on the side of readability. Put spaces around operators (for example, x = y rather than x=y), line up corresponding elements vertically, and so on.

Done!

REVIEW

In this session, you learned to understand and use the various aspects of programming style. You learned that programming style includes the use of visual layout attributes that make your code more understandable to those reading it. You learned to use comments to explain your code, and to use indentation and whitespace to make the structure of your code apparent. Finally, you learned the common conventions of Perl style.

QUIZ YOURSELF

1. Explain why it is important to use good programming style, even your program works, and you know that you are the only person who will ever see it. (See "Programming Style.")

2. What is a comment? How is a comment signaled? (See "Comments.")

3. Explain the purpose of #!/usr/bin/perl. How does it differ from #/usr/local/bin/perl? (See "Comments.")

4. Is the following correct or incorrect? Why?

```
If ( $x = 125 )
{
  print $x;
}
```

(See "Code Blocks.")

Variables 1: Scalar Data

Session Checklist

✔ Understanding variables

✔ Scalar data vs. list and hash data

✔ Manipulating scalar data with operators

30 Min.
To Go

Enough with the metaissues, already. It's time to get down to actual programming. In this session, I introduce the first and most important programming concept: the variable. Why is the variable the most important programming concept? Because the variable turns a program from a rote list of static instructions into a dynamic processing machine capable of making decisions about how to run itself.

What's a Variable?

Anyone who's ever taken algebra in high school has at least some idea of what a variable is, but we need to review the concept for several reasons: 1) not everybody was in school that day, 2) some of us have been out of school long enough that we've forgotten, and 3) the concept is slightly different when we talk about it in a computing context.

Briefly put, a variable is a name that we can associate with one or more values. For example, consider the algebraic equation:

X=100

Here, the X is the name, and 100 is the value. We can also be less direct about it:

X=50+50

and we can even define it in terms of another variable:

X=10Y (where Y=10)

Even though the right side (the value side) takes different forms, the value of X remains the same in all three examples.

However — and this is the key part — there's no particular reason why the value of X has to be 100. It just so happens to be in all of these examples, but that's purely a contrivance on the part of the author. X could also be 1, 512, or, stepping out of a mathematical context, the word "fish."

In programming, we also add another dimension to picture; the value of any particular variable can change — so we have to think about not only *what* the value of a variable is, but *at what point in the program's execution* it holds that value.

One way to think about variables is to think of any variable's name as a container — say, a can. At one point, the can may be empty, at another point, it may be filled with water. At still another, it may be filled with sand. This is useful because the name of the can is always the same. At any point, you are able to say, "Let's see what's in 'can X' right now," or you can decide to dump out the contents of "can X" and fill it with something else.

Why would you want to do this? For one thing, you can make decisions based on the contents of your can. We have already seen the if construct in previous sessions. Although we haven't treated it formally, its function is fairly obvious — it executes code based on a certain condition. In other words, you can say the programming equivalent of:

```
if ("can X" is filled with coffee) {
     fry an egg;
}
```

If there is water in the can, and not coffee, the egg will not be fried. Likewise, if there is sand in the can. The egg will only be fried if the can is filled with coffee. You can see that in this way, you can make decisions about what your program is to do by manipulating the values of your variables.

You can also use variables to describe actions to be taken even when you don't actually know the variable's value. For example, you can take input from a person using the program. You can say, in effect, "Here — *you* fill the can, and depending on what you put in it, I'll figure out what to do."

It should be dawning on you about now exactly how much possibility there is in the idea of variables. But Perl actually adds another layer of complexity. Perl variables come in three flavors: scalar, list, and hash. To stretch the can metaphor to the breaking point, scalar variables allow you to put one thing in the can, while list and hash variables allow you to put groups of things in the can. I'll discuss list and hash variables in the next session, and for the remainder of this one I'll focus on scalar variables only.

What Do We Mean by Scalar Data?

**20 Min.
To Go**

Scalar data is a special kind of data in that it consists of only one element. That is, you're only allowed to put one thing in the can. Here are some examples of scalar data:

- 4
- "dog"
- 2+2

Here is an example of nonscalar data:

- 4,2,6,44,34,64,23,75,23,2,664

So, it should be clear at this point that a scalar variable has only one value at any given time.

As a rule, variables are created either by declaration or by assignment. However, declaration happens only in programming languages where you have to specify the type of data you're going to store in your variable. Perl does most of the work of creating the variable for you, so you need only assign a value to a name to be off and running:

```
$name = "joe";
```

There are a couple of interesting features of the preceding line. Let's take them in reverse order from right to left. Note first that the line ends with a semicolon. This is one of only two ways to let the Perl interpreter know that you've ended a line. Every statement in Perl must end with a semicolon, unless it is a construct that uses curly braces to enclose a block (like the previous if statement). If it doesn't end in a semicolon or a curly brace, the interpreter has no way of knowing where the end of the line is.

Second, notice the quotes around the word joe. This lets the interpreter know that the data is in the form of text. (Actually this isn't really necessary. Perl is pretty relaxed about the use of quotes. I could have left them out.)

Third, there is the equals sign (=). In this context, it acts as an assignment operator, letting the interpreter know that there is a value coming up (we'll talk more about operators in Session 10).

Finally, there is the dollar sign ($) preceding the name of the variable. This dollar sign is how we tell the interpreter that we are creating a scalar variable. Other characters are used to signal list and hash variables. It is very important that you always put a dollar sign in front of any scalar variable name for two reasons: 1) if you leave it off, the interpreter won't know it's supposed to be a variable name, and will think it's a command word that it doesn't know, and 2) if you use the wrong character, the interpreter may think it is a list instead of a scalar. This can cause problems because some Perl functions work differently depending on whether they're being used in a scalar or list context.

Variable Substitution

One of the more important things you can do with variables is to use their names as a sort of placeholder for where you want their values to go. That way, you can use the value for various purposes without having to know in advance what that value actually is.

Here's an example. We've already seen the print function. It simply prints out whatever is given to it. So if you give the command

```
print "joe";
```

it will print the word "joe" on a line, and exit.

Now consider

```
$name = "joe";
print $name;
```

This will give the exact same result.

Kinds of Scalar Data

The types of data that can be stored in scalar variables are not unique to scalars. Numerical and textual data can just as easily be stored in list or hash variables.

Numbers

Probably the easiest type of scalar data to grasp is numerical data, and scalar numerical data is the simplest type.

Making the statement

```
$number = 1;
```

is certainly straightforward enough, and has a direct correlation with X=1 of our high school algebra. And like algebra, it is possible to give an expression on the right hand side of the statement that evaluates to a number. Thus, the statement

```
$number = 5 - 4;
```

gives us the same result as assigning 1 directly. This may seem somewhat trivial, but remember that we can use variable substitution here. Thus,

```
$first_number = 5;
$second_number = $first_number - 4;
```

will achieve the same thing.

Text data

Another kind of data we can store in scalar variables is text data.

We have already seen an example of this previously:

```
$name = "joe";
print $name;
```

Using variable substitution, we get the slightly more complex

```
$name = "joe";
print "My name is $name";
```

Special characters

No discussion of textual values in Perl is complete without a mention of the special characters that are available. These are characters that are invisible on the screen, but that have meaning in the context of text formatting or other invisible text functions.

Let's bring back the last example:

```
$name = "joe";
print "My name is $name";
```

There is a minor problem with this program. When we run it, it will return our system prompt without a carriage return, so that the session would look like this:

```
[joe@ika joe]$ perl -e '
> $name = joe;
> print "My name is $name";
> '
```

Perl then returns,
```
My name is joe[joe@ika joe]$
```

Notice how the new prompt is stuck on the end of the output line. To fix this, we need to insert a newline character onto the end of our print statement. We do that like so:

```
$name = "joe";
print "My name is $name \n";
```

Now when we run the program, the output looks a lot better:

```
[joe@ika joe]$ perl -e '
> $name = joe;
> print "My name is $name \n";
> '
My name is joe
[joe@ika joe]$
```

The newline is indicated by the character sequence \n. In Perlese, this is called an escape sequence, because the backslash is used to escape the normal function of the n character.

This works in reverse, too. In order to type a literal backslash character, you would use \\.

Tip

Table 7-1 is a list of common escape sequences:

Table 7-1
Common Text Escape Sequences

Sequence	Meaning
\n	newline
\r	return
\t	tab
\b	backspace
\a	bell (probably more like a beep on your computer)
\0	octal ASCII character (For example, the expression print "\077"; will give "?" because the output the octal number 077 represents the question mark character.)
\x	hexadecimal ASCII character (For example, \x2E is equivalent to a dot [.] character.)
\c	control character (For example, \cX = <ctrl>+x.)
\\	literal backslash
\"	literal quotation mark

Scalar Operators

Operators are special characters that can manipulate data. So far, we have seen the assignment operator, = (the equals sign), but there are others, as you can see in Tables 7-2 and 7-3.

Table 7-2
Operators for Numerical (Mathematical) Functions

Operator	Function
+	addition (6 + 6 = 12)
-	subtraction (6 - 6 = 0)
*	multiplication (6 * 6 = 36)
/	division (6 / 6 = 1)
**	exponentiation (6 ** 6 = 46656)
%	modulus (remainder after division: 10 % 3 = 1)

Table 7-3
String (Text) Operators

Operator	Function
.	concatenation ("hello" . "hello" = "hellohello")
x	repetition ("hello" x 3 = "hellohellohello")

Be sure that you don't mistake the x for a mathematical multiplication character. The expression 5 x 2, does NOT evaluate to 10. Rather it evaluates to 55. That is, in this context, the 5 is interpreted not as a numerical value, but as a textual value, thus it is actually 5 x 2 (that is, 5 letter-x 2), and not the 5 * 2 you were probably expecting.

10 Min. To Go

<STDIN> — A Special Case

There is one special way of assigning a value to a variable, and that is taking it from the person using the program. This person will most likely be typing it at the computer's keyboard, and in most cases, the keyboard is designated as the program's standard input. Data coming from the standard input is represented by the operator <STDIN>. So let's modify our name program a bit, so that the name is taken from the keyboard:

```
# we'll now go ahead and make this a formal program instead of
# a one-off command line job.
#!/usr/bin/perl
print "What is your name? \n";
$name = <STDIN>;
print "Your name is $name. \n";
```

Save this under the name "names," make it executable, and run it from the command line:

```
joe[joe@ika joe]$ ./names
What is your name?
joe
Your name is joe

.
[joe@ika joe]$
```

Why is the period on a line by itself? When I entered my name, I hit the enter key. This added a newline character to the end of my name. When the interpreter saw the newline character, it moved the cursor to the beginning of the next line, thus, the period. When using <STDIN> in this way, this kind of thing is a persistent problem, so the Perl developers added a function to strip off the trailing newline character. This function is (somewhat colorfully) called chomp. Let's add a chomp to your program:

```
#!/usr/bin/perl
print "What is your name? \n";
$name = <STDIN>;
chomp($name);
print "Your name is $name. \n";
```

Now when you try it,

```
 [joe@ika joe]$ ./names
What is your name?
joe
Your name is joe.
[joe@ika joe]$
```

Much better.

You can combine the assignment and the chomp like so:

```
chomp($name = <STDIN>);
```

Done!

REVIEW

In this session, you learned about scalar data. You started by learning that a variable is a name to which one or more values can be assigned. You learned that scalar variables can only hold one value at any given time, but that the value can be any textual or numerical expression. You learned about some of the operators that can be used to manipulate scalar data. Finally, you learned to use the <STDIN> token to accept scalar data from keyboard input.

QUIZ YOURSELF

1. Explain how the concept of a variable in programming differs from the standard mathematical idea of variables. How are they the same? (See "What's a Variable.")

2. How does scalar data differ from list data? (See "What Do We Mean by Scalar Data?")

3. How do we signal the Perl interpreter that we are creating a scalar variable? (See "What Do We Mean by Scalar Data?")

4. How would you go about adding together two numerical scalar variables? (See "Numbers.")

5. Explain the purpose <STDIN>? (See "<STDIN> - A Special Case.")

6. What does the chomp() function do? (See "<STDIN> - A Special Case.")

Variables 2: List and Hash Data

Session Checklist

✔ Creating list variables

✔ Manipulating list data

✔ Creating hash variables

✔ Manipulating key/value pairs

✔ Using <STDIN> in a list context

**30 Min.
To Go**

I n the last session, we saw how to use variables to store a particular kind of data. Scalar data is the simplest form of data in that each scalar variable holds only one value at any particular time. This session shows how to use Perl's two other built in variable types — the list and the hash — to store a group of values all at once.

In some other programming languages you may see the word array used to describe variables that hold multiple values. This is essentially the same idea as the list. In fact, there was a time when lists were called arrays in Perl, and hashes were called associative arrays. The names were changed, ostensibly to provide shorter and more easily remembered terms for them.

What's a List?

A list is just what it sounds like it might be. That is, a list is a simple group of items, organized under a single name. List variables are signified with the @ character, and the elements are grouped inside parentheses, and separated by commas. For example, you could create a list this way:

```
@dogs = ( "husky", "shepherd", "collie", "dane", "greyhound" );
```

As you can see here, we have the variable name, introduced by the @, and we have a group of elements, which together comprise the variable's value.

Look again at our example list:

```
@dogs = ( "husky", "shepherd", "collie", "dane", "greyhound" );
```

The value part of this, that is the part in parentheses, is called the list literal. The way this list literal is shown — each value with its own set of quotation marks and comma separation — is probably the most explicit way of assigning the variable, but it's also fairly clunky and a pain to type.

I mentioned in an earlier session that Perl has a fairly relaxed approach to quoting. While certain types of quotation marks can mean very specific things, if the situation you're in is a common one, there is usually a shortcut. In this case, we can use the quote word function, qw():

```
@dogs = qw( husky shepherd collie dane greyhound );
```

The qw() function in a list context (remember, context is important with some Perl functions) interprets any whitespace as a separator, and builds the list from any character strings separated by it. It is not necessary that this whitespace be simple spaces, either. For example, you might find it preferable to render your list like so:

```
@dogs = qw( husky
            shepherd
            collie
            dane
            greyhound
);
```

However you choose to handle the quoting, you need to be aware of where you have constant textual values, and where you might have variable values, or numerical data.

For example, you might have a variable with mixed data types:

```
@stuff = ( "car", 4, $wagon );
```

You can even include other lists inside your list:

```
@my_lists = ( @dogs, @stuff);.
```

Note that the value of @my_lists now includes all the values of both lists it contains, in other words, the command

```
print(@my_lists);
```

would return the output

```
huskysheperdcolliedanegreyhoundcar4
```

There are a couple of things to notice here. The first and most obvious is that there is no intervening whitespace printed between the list elements. This has to do with the way the print() function works. (I'll show you ways to deal with this in a later session.) The second is that there is no output relating to the scalar variable, $wagon. This is because you have not defined it. Instead of giving an error, as would happen in some other languages, the interpreter creates the variable, but leaves it unassigned. Had it been assigned, we would have seen the value in the output of our print() statement.

How List Variables Work

So, we've seen that lists are plural variables, and that they can contain any sort of data we choose to put in them. The question now arises, how do we use them?

Accessing values

First of all, it would probably be a good idea to know how to access any particular element of the list. Let us return to our earlier example:

```
@dogs = qw( husky shepherd collie dane greyhound );
```

Here are five elements. Here's the good part: for each element of the list, there is a related scalar that represents it. These scalars are indexed by a number that represents each element's position in the list, beginning, as all good programming languages do, with the number 0. Thus, the first element of the list @dogs, is $dogs[0], the second is $dogs[1], and so on. So, if, after assigning the previous list, you were to give the command:

```
print $dogs[0];
```

You would get the output husky. The output for $dogs[1] would be shepherd, and so on.

There are a couple of things to note here. The first it that we must always bear in mind that any single element of a list is a scalar, and is therefore identified with the $ character. While it may seem logical to identify a list element as @list[0], this is not correct, and will cause the program to fail. Second, it is important to distinguish between any scalar $dogs[n], and the scalar variable $dogs. The first is an element of list @dogs, whereas the second is a separate variable, with no intrinsic relationship to the list.

Manipulating list data

We may find that in addition to accessing values in a list, that we wish to change the values. We may, for example, wish to add a new element to the array. There are several ways to do this.

20 Min. To Go

By assignment

If we want to add a value to the beginning of the list,

```
@dogs = ("weimaraner", @dogs);
```

If we want to add it to the end of the list,

```
@dogs = (@dogs, "weimaraner");
```

If we want to add the new element at a particular position,

```
$dogs[2] = "weimaraner";
```

In addition, we can put list literals on the left-hand side of the assignment, so long as they only contain variable references (that is, variable names):

```
($dog, $cat, $horse) = ("Lassie", "Morris", "Trigger");
```

This is the same as

```
$dog = "Lassie";
$cat = "Morris";
$horse = "Trigger";
```

and is a good way to assign a lot of variables at once. Another variation on this idea is

```
($singer, @actors) = (“Donovan”, “Brando”, “DeNiro”, “Nicholson”);
```

This will assign Donovan to the variable $singer, and the other three to the list @actors. (If you do this, however, the list reference must be the last element in the left-hand list literal, and there can be only one. This is because the list reference will claim all the remaining values on the right-hand side, so if there is anything to the right of the list reference, it will not receive any of the values.)

By functions

In addition to manipulating list data through assignment, there are several Perl functions that are specifically for the purpose of working with lists.

push() and pop() If you've ever done any programming with stacks, the concept of pushing and popping should be familiar to you. If not, it can be a tricky thing to understand. A stack is a bunch of data elements that are lined up to be used in order. Think of the stack as a Dixie Cup dispenser, and the cups as the data elements. As we use data elements, we pull cups off the bottom of the stack. This is popping. If we want to add a new element to the stack, we must push the cup up into the dispenser. Once we've pushed a cup, it will be the first one off the next time we pop.

To translate that into more immediate terms, we can think of the right-hand side of a list literal as the bottom of the stack. Using the push() function adds an element to right-hand side of the list, while the pop() function removes one. For example, if we have

```
@dogs = qw( husky shepherd collie dane greyhound );
```

and then we do

```
push(@dogs, “pug”);
```

the new value of @dogs will be

```
qw( husky shepherd collie dane greyhound pug)
```

Likewise, we can add more than one new element at a time:

```
push(@dogs, “pug”, “weimaraner”, “chihuahua”);
```

will yield

```
qw( husky shepherd collie dane greyhound pug weimaraner chihuahua)
```

Using the pop() function, we can grab that last value off the list:

```
$lastdog = pop(@dogs);
```

This gives us

```
$lastdog = "chihuahua"
```

and @dogs is now

```
qw( husky shepherd collie dane greyhound pug weimaraner )
```

shift() and unshift() What push() and pop() do to the right-hand side of a list, shift() and unshift() do to the left. That is, shift() adds a value to the left side, and unshift() removes one. In other words,

```
@dogs = qw( husky shepherd collie dane greyhound );
shift(@dogs, "pomeranian");
```

gives us a value for @dogs of

```
qw( pomeranian husky shepherd collie dane greyhound )
```

Likewise,

```
@dogs = qw( husky shepherd collie dane greyhound pug weimaraner );
$firstdog = pop(@dogs);
```

gives us husky for the value of $firstdog, and

```
qw( shepherd collie dane greyhound pug weimaraner )
```

for the value of @dogs.

sort() and reverse() The sort() and reverse() functions affect the order of elements in a list. sort() arranges the elements in ascending order of their ASCII values (that is, in ascending numerical or alphabetical order). If we have a list

```
@num = (2,4,3,7,5,6,1);
```

and then we do

```
@num = sort(@num);
```

we will now have a value for @num of

```
(1,2,3,4,5,6,7)
```

reverse(), as you might expect, simply reverses the order of a list's elements, so if we now do

```
@num = reverse(@num);
```

we will get

```
(7,6,5,4,3,2,1)
```

as our value for @num.

> **If you wanted to sort a list in reverse order, you could do**
>
> ```
> @num = reverse(sort(@num));
> ```

**10 Min.
To Go**

What's a Hash?

If you're anything like me, the first thing that comes to mind when you hear the word hash is a tasty concoction of meat and potatoes. In Perl, however, the hash is our third and final data type. A hash is similar to list in that it contains multiple elements, but it is distinct from a list in that the elements have a particular relationship to one another. Specifically, the elements of a hash come in pairs.

You can create a hash as you would any other variable, except that the leading character is the percent character, % (for example, %my_hash).

> **You might be wondering at this point what would happen if you created the variables $var, @var, and %var all at the same time. The answer, perhaps somewhat surprisingly, is nothing. Perl maintains separate *namespaces* for each type of variable. If you create a scalar and, say, a hash with the same name, these are considered to be two separate, distinct, and wholly unrelated variables by the Perl interpreter — unless the variables were somehow thematically related. However, this would be considered a bad programming practice, as it would tend to be confusing.**

Each pair of elements in a hash has a key (the first element) and a value (the second element). Each of these is associated such that for any key, we can retrieve the corresponding value, and vice versa. The idea is a little clearer if you think about an example.

Imagine that you are a teacher, and you want to record the grades that your students got on your most recent test in a Perl program for easy processing later.

The obvious way to do it would be with a hash, using each student's name as the key, and his or her score as the value:

```
%grades = ("betsy", 84, "jim", 76, "alex", 92, "melissa", 88);
```

Because of the built-in association between key and value, you can extract the value associated with any particular key with a little variable-type sleight of hand:

```
print $grades{jim};
```

will output the number 76.

What you have done here is to access the value of a special scalar that is created implicitly when we created the hash. If you have a hash called %hashname, then for any scalar represented by $hashname{key}, you will retrieve the value that corresponds to that key.

Unlike lists, hash variables do not have any particular order. sort(), for example, is meaningless when we're talking about hashes. The reason for this is that the Perl interpreter stores hash data in such a way as to maximize the speed with which key/value pairs can be associated. While it is possible, using certain Perl modules, to mess with this order, doing so results in a serious loss of efficiency. If you need hash-type data in a particular order, odds are there's probably a better way to accomplish your task using lists.

How hash variables work

We have already seen how to use a key to extract its corresponding value. We can do the same by using the reverse() function, which, in a hash context, swaps the order of keys and values. Let's bring back your teacher's gradebook example to see how this would work.

```
%grades = ("betsy", 84, "jim", 76, "alex", 92, "melissa", 88);
```

Say you know that the highest grade in the class was a 92, but you can't remember who got it. You can reverse your hash:

```
%rev_grades = reverse(%grades);
```

and then print out the information we need:

```
print $rev_grades{92};
```

and you discover that alex was your high-scorer.

Hash-specific functions

There are a couple of aspects that are unique to working with hashes, and these require some special functions.

keys() and values()

The keys() function is used to extract only the keys from the hash. For example, you extract the names of your students like so:

```
%grades = ("betsy", 84, "jim", 76, "alex", 92, "melissa", 88);
@names = keys(%grades);
```

The list @names now contains the names of your students.

Likewise, you can extract just the scores by using the values() function:

```
%grades = ("betsy", 84, "jim", 76, "alex", 92, "melissa", 88);
@scores = values(%grades);
```

Now the @scores list will contain just the values from the hash.

delete()

The final hash function makes it possible for you to remove a key/value pair from a hash. Suppose that Melissa has moved out of town, and you need to remove her data from your record book. You simply use the delete() function, like so:

```
delete $grades{melissa};
```

and her key/value pair will be expunged from the hash.

Hash slices

Despite being another Perl term that sounds like food, hash slices are actually a way of streamlining the process of assigning key/value pairs to a hash. Suppose that you've just had a bunch of new students assigned to your class. You give them all a test, and now you need to insert their scores into the %grades hash.

The obvious (but slow and clunky) way to do this would be to simply assign them each individually:

```
$grades{"jane"}=79;
$grades{"dean"}=71;
$grades{"susan"}=83;
```

A slightly more streamlined way to do it would be:

```
($grades{"jane"}, $grades{"dean"}, $grades{"susan"}) = (79,71,83);
```

But despite combining all three assignments into a single line, this really hasn't saved you much in the way of clunkiness. Using a hash slice, you can do the whole thing much more elegantly:

```
@grades{"jane", "dean", "susan"} = (79,71,83);
```

By using the @ character to denote a list, along with the curly braces that denote hash keys, you are able to tell the interpreter that you're creating a list of hash keys that can all be processed at once.

<STDIN> in a List Context

In the last session, you saw that the <STDIN> construct could be used to accept input from the keyboard. You saw that, in the scalar context, a newline character terminates the input, and that the entire line is treated as a single value.

But what do you do if you need input that's going to span more that one line. Suppose you want the program's user to be able to input huge piles of data in a single session? What do you do then?

List processing to the rescue. If you define <STDIN> in terms of a list variable, rather than as a scalar variable, it behaves slightly differently.

```
@var = <STDIN>;
```

will accept multiline input. Each line of text, terminated with a newline character, will be treated as an element of the list @var. <STDIN> will continue to accept input until the user sends the End of Record character, which, on most keyboards is generated by the Ctrl+D sequence.

Conveniently, the behavior of the chomp() function is also modified in the list context, so that the trailing newline character is stripped off each element.

Here's how this might work in our gradebook example. Say you want to be able to input the student's grades interactively. You might write code such as this:

```
#!/usr/bin/perl

%grades=(); # We'll start with an empty gradebook.

print "Enter students names (press <CTRL>+D when done): ";
```

```
@names = <STDIN> ;
chomp @names;
print "\n\n";
print "Enter corresponding grades (press <CTRL+D when done): ";
@scores = <STDIN>;

@grades{@names} = @scores # use hash slice to assign scores to
names
```

The hash %grades will now be populated with the names and scores of all of your students. Naturally, this isn't a complete program. This is only a routine for getting data into the hash. What you do with the hash is a subject for other sessions.

REVIEW

Done!

You started by learning what a list variable is and how to create one. Then you learned how to manipulate list data using assignment and functions. You then went on to learn how to create and use hash variables, learning their functions, and how to use hash slices. Finally, you learned how to use <STDIN> in a list context to deal with multiline input.

QUIZ YOURSELF

---

1. What is the main substantive difference between a list variable and a scalar variable? (See "What's a List?")

2. What is wrong with the following statement?

   ```
   (@dogs, $cat) = ("fido", "spot", "bowser", "kittykins")
   ```

   (See "Manipulating list data.")

3. Both lists and hashes contain multiple data elements. How are the elements handled differently between the two data types? (See "What's a hash?")

4. What will be the output of the following statement?

   ```
   %ID = ("Smith", 00001, "Jones", 00002);
   print (keys(%ID));
   ```

   (See "Hash-specific functions.")

9

Statements and Expressions

Session Checklist

✔ Learning the properties of expressions

✔ Simple vs. compound expressions

✔ Evaluating expressions

✔ Learning the properties of statements

✔ Simple vs. compound statements

✔ Learning how statements execute

✔ Learning the properties of blocks

***30 Min.
To Go***

Expressions and statements are the respective atomic and molecular units of programming. These concepts are so basic to programming that it can actually be very difficult to describe exactly what they are because by the time you've learned a programming language or two, the concepts have become so ingrained that you almost never think about them. Nevertheless, a good understanding of expressions and statements is crucial to being able to construct viable programs.

What's an Expression?

Expressions are the work engines of a program. You use expressions to assign the values of variables, perform computations, evaluate conditions, and so on. It is through expressions that the logical action of the program is articulated.

In formal terms, an *expression* is a series of variables, constants, operators, functions, and/or methods that evaluates to a single value. That last part is important. In order to be a valid expression, the result of combining all the elements you've put together must be a single unary value.

This may sound a little esoteric, but in practice, it's very simple. Here's an example of an expression:

```
1+2
```

It doesn't get much simpler than that, but if you look at it, you'll see that we've satisfied the requirements: we have an operator, the plus sign, and two constants. When you combine these through the action of the operator, you get a single resulting value: 3.

It is not necessary for an expression to be a mathematical one. The comparison of text strings is also an expression. Consider

```
"tiger" eq "lion"
```

In this expression, the eq operator tests two text strings to see if their values are the same. In this case, they are not the same, so the value of the expression is false. In the eyes of the Perl interpreter, the condition of falsehood is represented by the number 0, which, of course, is a single unified value.

Expressions can become more complicated as well. For example,

```
2x+3y(2xy)
```

can be a valid (non-Perl) expression, provided that you know the values of x and y. Likewise logical expressions can be complex. For example,

```
("tiger" eq "lion") or ("horse" eq "horse")
```

is a complex expression that evaluates as true (or 1) since the right side is true, and the logical or operator returns a value of true if either side of the expression is true.

Some operations return a value depending on the success or failure of some other task. For example,

```
$a=1;
```

assigns the value 1 to the variable $a, but in the context of being an expression, it is true if the assignment was carried out successfully. (I can't think of any reason that such an assignment wouldn't be successful, but there are other functions that might, for example, access a certain file on your computer. If the file did not exist, the attempt to open it would be unsuccessful, and the expression would evaluate as false.)

Simple vs. compound expressions

Most of the examples in the previous section are examples of simple expressions. Simple expressions are expressions that cannot be reduced to other expressions. The expression

```
1+2
```

is a simple expression, because there is no way to reduce it further without just evaluating the whole thing. By contrast, the expression

```
1+2+3
```

is a compound expression, because it can be seen in terms of two separate expressions.

To evaluate the expression, we first reduce it to another expression,

```
3+3
```

and then finally, to its unified value, 6.

In programming, it is quite common to see an expression such as

```
$a = $b + 1;
```

Here we have a compound expression in that we have an assignment, but the value that is being assigned is the result of another expression (the addition).

Previously, we saw a compound logical expression:

```
("lion" eq "tiger") or ("horse" eq "horse")
```

This is fairly obvious as a compound expression, but look at it formally. There are actually three expressions here:

1. ("lion" eq "tiger")
2. ("horse" eq "horse")
3. (value of left side) or (value of right side)

Evaluating expressions 1 and 2 first, we come up with the final expression
(false) or (true)

Since the logical or operator evaluates as true if the argument on either side of it is true, in this case, the value of the entire compound expression is true.

**20 Min.
To Go**

How expressions evaluate

Usually, it's relatively clear how expressions evaluate. Most operators work from left to right, just as you would read them. Expressions inside parentheses evaluate before expressions outside. Mathematical operators work generally according to algebraic order of operations (thus, 3*2+6 is equal to 12, not 24).

Some expressions, however, evaluate to the right. An example of this is the unary increment operator ++. This operator is called *unary* because it only takes one argument. Given the code

```
$i = 0;
$i++
```

after the increment operation, the value of $i is 1.

Beyond that, operators evaluate in order of their precedence, which, from highest to lowest are

1. Terms and list operators

- ->
- ++, --
- **
- !, ~, \
- =~, !~
- *.*, /, %, x
- +, -, .
- <<, >>

2. Named unary operators

- <, >, <=, >=, lt, gt, le, ge
- ==, !=, <=>, eq, ne, cmp
- &

- |, ^
- &&
- ||
- ..
- ? :
- =, +=, -=, *=, etc.
- ,, =>

3. Rightward list operators

- not
- and
- or, xor

Don't worry if you don't know what all of these are. Many of these are explained in Session 10, and most of the rest are explained throughout the rest of the book.

Statements

If expressions are the atoms of programming, statements are the molecules. Statements are the commands that tell the Perl interpreter what to do. Statements are also the means by which expressions are put into action. If expressions are the engine of programming, statements are the controls. To make an analogy with natural language, statements are roughly analogous to sentences, whereas expressions are more like phrases and clauses.

A statement is not the same thing as a line of code. It is possible for a line of code to contain more than one statement. Indeed, like expressions, you can have compound statements (more on this in a bit). It is also the case that a line of code is not the same thing as a line of text in the program file. (Remember that a line of Perl code must be terminated with a semicolon or rightward-facing curly brace. It is entirely possible, and indeed common, for a single line of Perl code to span several textual lines in a file.)

In reality, it is probably best to define a *statement* as the minimum unit of execution in a program. That is, a statement is the smallest instruction required to actually get the Perl interpreter to do something.

It is possible for a piece of code to be both a statement and an expression. Take for example the line

```
$a = 1;
```

This is an expression, in that it evaluates to a single value, but it is also a statement, in that it directs the interpreter to perform an assignment operation.

More often, we see expressions as a *part* of a statement, as in

```
print(1+1);
```

(Even in cases where `print` might have no argument, there is still an expression, since `print` will operate on the implicit variable $_.)

Simple vs. compound statements

Like expressions, statements can be of either a simple or a compound nature. Take for example, the common statement

```
chomp ($x = <STDIN>);
```

This statement consists of two other statements:

```
$x = <STDIN>;
```

and

```
chomp $x;
```

In a case such as this, the statements execute from the inside out — the assignment happens first, and then the `chomp`. If for any reason the inner statement fails, the outer statement will also fail.

Now, let us add another layer of complexity by extending the statement:

```
chomp($x = <STDIN>) or die "couldn't chomp";
```

In this case, we've added a third statement (the `die`), and a comparison operator. If the `chomp` operation is successful, the `or` operator knows that one side of the expression is true. Therefore, the entire expression is true, and it doesn't bother to test (that is, in this case, execute) the code on the right. Packed into this short line are three statements and four expressions. (Remember, many functions can operate as expressions because their output is a single value.)

Another way of creating compound statements is by use of flow control structures. We met these briefly in Session 2, and will discuss them further in Session 12. If you have a structure that looks like

```
if (expression) {
    statement 1;
    statement 2;
    etc.
}
```

the statements inside the curly braces are stand-alone statements in and of themselves, but are also considered to be part of the if statement.

**In Perl, an expression is an expression is an expression. It doesn't
matter, for example, if the expression given as a condition in an
if statement is a simple test of equality, as in**

```
if ($x == 1){}
```

or a statement that functions as an expression, as in

```
if (print($x)) {}
```

**As long as the expression or statement (or whatever) reduces to
a single value, it's an expression, and can function in the same
way any other expression can.**

**10 Min.
To Go**

Statement blocks

We met blocks back in Session 6, as a way of keeping code visually organized. But
blocks of statements serve more than just an aesthetic purpose. Blocks of code
enclosed inside curly braces comprise a type of compound statement. When we
talk about flow control structures, we will see that a block of statements that follows a conditional statement is the code that will be executed if the condition is
true. Likewise, when creating a subroutine, the block of code that follows a subroutine assignment is the code that comprises the subroutine.

If you have a piece of code that needs to be considered as a single unit, you can
simply enclose it in braces:

```
{
    statement 1;
    statement 2;
    statement 3;
}
```

Code that is enclosed this way can take on special properties. It can be named,
and certain control constructs can be called on it. For example, the control command LAST can be called like this:

```
{
    statement 1;
    LAST if (something);
    statement 2;
    statement 3;
}
```

The LAST command will stop execution of the block if the condition expressed as (something) is met. (In this respect, you can think of blocks as loops that only execute once.)

Irrespective of these special properties, however, you can think of a brace-enclosed block as a single big compound statement.

Done!

REVIEW

In this session, you learned how to conceptualize expressions and statements. First, you learned that expressions are the simplest unit of programming, and that they must always evaluate to a single indivisible value. You learned that expressions can be combined to yield compound expressions. You learned how expressions evaluate, and saw the order of precedence for the operators in Perl. You then went on to learn the properties of statements. You learned that statements are the commands that are given to the Perl interpreter in order to get it to perform your desired tasks. You learned that statements, like expressions, can be of a simple or compound nature. You learned that compound statements evaluate from the inside out. Finally, you learned that blocks of statements, whether part of a control structure or freestanding, can be considered compound statements.

QUIZ YOURSELF

1. Is

   ```
   print ($x=1)
   ```

   a simple statement, a compound statement, a simple expression, a compound expression, or some combination? Explain your answer. (See "Simple vs. compound expressions.")

2. Identify all expressions (if any) or statements (again, if any) in the line given in question 1. (See "Simple vs. compound expressions.")

3. Explain what a block is. How are blocks used? (See "Statement blocks.")

Session Checklist

✔ Using arithmetic operators

✔ Using string operators

✔ Using assignment operators

✔ Using file test operators

**30 Min.
To Go**

You have already seen operators at work in this book. Indeed, it is almost impossible to program without them. The operators we have seen so far have been the assignment operator, =, a few arithmetic operators (+, -, *, **, and %), and a couple of text string operators (. and x). There are many more operators than these, however, and it's well worth devoting some time to looking at them in detail.

What's an Operator?

An operator is a way of modifying or combining terms in an expression. For example, we have seen the assignment operator functioning like so:

```
$x = 1;
```

Here, the operator is combining the terms $x and 1 in such a way as to establish an equivalence between them. Likewise, the expression

```
$x+1
```

uses the addition operator to combine two terms so as to produce their sum. Note that the preceding expression is not a complete statement, because nothing actually happens with the sum. In order to make a statement out of it, you need to add another operator, like so:

```
$y = $x+1;
```

Both = and + are *binary* operators. That is, they require two terms (one on each side) in order to function. (Obviously, the expression =$x makes no sense.)

But there are also *unary* operators. These are operators that modify a single term. An example of a unary operator is the ! character. The ! operator negates any term that follows it. For example the statement

```
if ( $x ) {
    something;
}
```

will execute the something if $x represents a true expression.

You can reverse the effect of this by changing the statement to

```
if ( !$x ) {
    something;
}
```

Now the something will only execute if $x represents a false condition.

Types of Operators

So far, we have limited ourselves to just a couple of types of operators. We have had assignment, mathematical, and a couple of string operators. But there are also other kinds:

- **Binding:** Ties an expression to another expression. (We'll talk more about this one when we get to Session 17, "Regular Expressions.")

- **Relational:** Used to compare one value to another. Use them to see if a given expression is less than, greater than, or equal to another expression. Relational operators come in both numerical and textual flavors.
- **Logical:** Used to evaluate one expression in terms of another. In other words, the overall truth of an expression using a logical operator is dependent on the truth of both expressions being evaluated, as well as on the particular operator being used.

Numeric Operators

As the name would indicate, numeric operators are operators that are designed to manipulate mathematical data.

We have already seen the arithmetic operators, which are displayed in Table 10-1:

Table 10-1
Arithmetic Operators

Operator	Function
+	Addition
-	Subtraction
*	Multiplication
/	Division
**	Exponentiation
%	Modulus

Table 10-2 shows the comparison operators:

Table 10-2
Numeric Comparison Operators

Operator	Meaning	Example
>	Greater than	10>2
>=	Greater than or equal to	10>=2, 10>=10

Continued

Table 10-2 *Continued*

Operator	Meaning	Example
<	Less than	2<10
<=	Less than or equal to	2<=10, 2<=2
==	Equal to	10==10
!=	Not equal to	10!=9, 10!=11
<=>	Comparison with signed result	Given $x<=>$y, if $x is greater than $y, $x is less than $y, operator returns +1. If $x is equal to $y, operator returns 0.

A couple of things deserve mention here. Note that the comparison operator that denotes equivalence is a *doubled* equal sign (==). This is to distinguish it from the assignment operator, the single equal sign. One of the most common sources of errors for beginning Perl programmers is forgetting to double the equal sign.

The comparison with signed result operator (<=>) only makes sense in terms of return value. A *return value* is the value that is returned as the result of the working of an operator or a function. These return values are used in some cases to represent the truth or falseness of a condition. For example, the == operator returns a value of 1 if the condition is true, and "" (undefined), if the condition is false. Other functions, such as the if statement, can use these return values as inputs to their own operations.

20 Min. To Go

String Operators

String operators exist for the purpose of working with text. For the sake of clarity, Perl makes an effort to make string operators look different from numeric operators, but many of the string operators behave similarly to their numeric counterparts. For example, the string operator lt stands for less than. It is the textual counterpart for the numeric operator <. The lt operator compares the binary values of two text strings, and returns a value of true (or 1) if the string on the left hand side has a lower value than the one on the right.

Because of the way the ASCII character set is arranged, the practical value of this is that a letter that appears earlier in the alphabet will be considered "less than" a letter that appears later. In other words, the expression

```
"a" lt "b"
```

is true, whereas the expression

```
"b" lt "a"
```

is false.

Note that if you use numbers in a string expression, the expression will be evaluated based on the numeric characters' ASCII values, and not their numerical values. Table 10-3 presents the string operators.

Table 10-3
String Comparison Operators

Operator	Meaning	Example
gt	Greater than	"b" gt "a"
ge	Greater than or equal to	"b" ge "a" or "b" ge "b"
lt	Less than	"a" lt "b"
le	Less than or equal to	"a" lt "b" or "a" lt "a"
eq	Equal to	"a" eq "a"
ne	Not equal to	"b" ne "a"
cmp	Comparison with signed result	"a" cmp "b" returns -1, "b cmp "a" returns +1, "a" cmp "a" returns 0.

For practical purposes, string comparison operators are generally used to test the equivalence of two strings, as in

```
if ($name eq "Joe") {
    something
}
```

Here, you are testing the string value of the data stored in the variable name. If the value is equal to the string value Joe, the conditional block (the something) executes. If not, it doesn't.

The gt, ge, lt, and le operators can be used to establish the alphabetical order of strings. (However, before you go writing complicated sorting routines using them, you might want to check if the sort() function will do the job for you.)

Quoting operators

I have said in previous sessions that Perl is fairly relaxed about how you go about
making quotations. This is true, up to a point. For most practical purposes, you can
use quotes, or not, as you choose. However, when you are trying to construct very
specific sorts of quotes, the rules about how it is done become very important.

Double quotes

The double quote character, ", is the standard quote that we use most of the time.
This operator renders the enclosed string, but also allows for *interpolation*.
Interpolation means that if you include a variable name in your string, the value
of that variable will be substituted for the name. Thus if you were to write:

```
$name = "Joe";
print "My name is $name";
```

the output would be

```
My name is Joe
```

In addition to variable names, the double quote operator allows for the interpolation of escape sequences. You will recall that if you want to insert a newline
character in your output, you use the sequence \n. Thus

```
$name = "Joe";
print "My name is $name. \n";
```

will print

```
My name is Joe.
```

and then move the cursor to the start of the next line before printing the prompt.
     The construction qq() is a synonym for the double quote operator. The
statement

```
print "My name is $name. \n";
```

is exactly the same as

```
print qq(My name is $name. \n);
```

Single quotes

The single quotation mark, ', quotes a string exactly with no interpolation. Thus the statements

```
$name = "Joe";
print 'My name is $name. \n';
```

will return the output

```
My name is $name. \n
```

The construction q( ) is a synonym for the single quote.

Think "Single quote, single q, double quote, double q."

Finally, the qw( ) construction is used as a synonym for putting quotes around all the elements of a list. Thus the construction

```
@stones = ("Mick", "Keith", "Bill", "Charlie");
```

is exactly the same as

```
@stones = qw(Mick, Keith, Bill, Charlie);
```

Instead of using double quotes, qq( ) or qw( ) (in a list context), you can simply omit quotes all together. The statements:

```
@stones = ("Mick", "Keith", "Bill", "Charlie");
```

and

```
@stones = qw(Mick, Keith, Bill, Charlie);
```

are the same as

```
@stones = (Mick, Keith, Bill, Charlie);
```

You need to use some caution if you do this, however, as there are certain words (such as "my") that if used unquoted and in certain contexts can confuse the Perl interpreter and cause an error. When in doubt, use the quotes.

Assignment Operators

You have already seen the basic assignment operator =. This operator takes a variable name on the left side, and an expression on the right. Thus,

```
$a = 2+3;
```

assigns the value of the expression 2+3, or 5, to the name $a. In addition, there are a bunch of ways to work a mathematical operation into the assignment.

Consider the following:

```
$a = 1+1;
$a += 1;
```

The value of $a after these two statements is 2. The += operator simply adds the value on the right-hand side to the current value of the variable. In other words the expression

```
$a += $b;
```

is the same as

```
$a = $a + $b;
```

Likewise, the -= operator performs the same operation, but incorporates subtraction. That is,

```
$a -= $b;
```

is the same as

```
$a = $a - $b;
```

Similarly, *= applies multiplication, /= applies division, and **= applies exponentiation.

Increment and Decrement Operators

The increment and decrement operators work along the same lines as the mathematically active assignment operators described previously. The function of an increment operator is to raise the value of a variable by 1, and the function of a decrement operator is to lower the value of a variable by 1.

Consider the code

```
$a = 1;
$a++;
```

The ++ operator causes the value of $a to increase by 1, thus the value of $a after the operation is 2.

Now the decrement:

```
$a = 1;
$a--;
```

As you may have surmised, the value of $a at this point is 0.

Logical Operators

Logical operators are operators that allow you to combine expressions in such a way that the truth or falseness of the compound expression is dependent on the truth or falseness of either or both of the simple expression. That sounds a lot more high-concept than it actually is.

Consider the sentence:

```
I will buy fruit from Johnny only if he has lemons and limes.
```

This sentence contains the logical operator and. Johnny must have BOTH lemons AND limes in order to get my business. If he has lemons and no limes, or limes and no lemons, I'll do my shopping elsewhere.

Now, contrast that with this sentence:

```
I will buy fruit from Johnny only if he has lemons or limes.
```

In the second sentence, we have changed the logical operator from and to or. Now, if Johnny wants my business, he needs to have lemons OR limes. Either will suffice, with or without the other.

In other words, an and expression requires both conditions to be true, whereas an or expression requires at least one of the conditions to be true.

The and and or operators in Perl are, not surprisingly, and and or. Consider:

```
if ( $a==2 and $b==3 ) {
    something
}
```

In this example, the conditional code will only be executed if both conditions are met. If $a were equal to 2, but $b were equal to 4, the code would not be executed. Shifting gears,

```
if ( $a==2 or $b==3) {
    something
}
```

gives us a situation in which $b being equal to 4 would not necessarily cause the conditional code to be skipped.

Because of the way logical or statements are evaluated (the left-hand expression is evaluated first and then the right-hand one), it is very common to use logical or statements to create a kind of miniconditional. Since most Perl commands return true if they are successful, you can create a statement like the following:

```
print "hello \n" or die "couldn't print";
```

If the print command is successful, the interpreter knows that the entire expression will evaluate to true. Thus, it does not need to evaluate the right-hand side. However, if the left-hand side is unsuccessful, returning false, the interpreter needs to evaluate the right-hand expression. If that expression is a command, the command will be executed. Thus, the die part of the statement (die is a command that causes the program to exit, optionally printing an error message), will only be executed if the print part is unsuccessful.

The Perl synonyms for the and and or operators are && and || respectively. Thus,

```
$a && $b
```

is the same as

```
$a and $b
```

Likewise,

```
$a || $b
```

is the same thing as

```
$a or $b
```

File Test Operators

The final class of operators is those used for testing the attributes of files. In using these operators, you will wander into that area of programming known as system programming, because you will be using Perl to call on functions of the operating system.

Very often when programming, you may want to open a file or a directory for reading or writing purposes. I'll discuss the procedure for doing this in Session 14, but for now, you simply need to be aware that this is a common way of getting data into and out of your programs.

However, sometimes before you attempt to open a file, you may want to determine if a file exists; or perhaps you want to test the type of file, its owner, its permissions, or other attributes. Perl gives you a number of operators, shown here in Table 10-4, to deal with these kinds of situations.

Table 10-4
File Test Operators

Operator	Function
-e	Tests that file exists
-s	Returns file size
-z	Returns true if file has size 0
-f	Returns true if file is a plain file
-d	Returns true if file is a directory
-l	Returns true if file is a symbolic link
-p	Returns true if file is a named pipe
-S	Returns true if file is socket
-T	Returns true if file is a text file
-B	Returns true if file is a binary file
-r	Returns true if file is readable by UID under which program is running

Continued

Table 10-4   *Continued*

Operator	Function
-w	Returns true if file is writable by UID under which program is running
-x	Returns true if file is executable by UID under which program is running
-u	Returns true if file has setuid bit set
-g	Returns true if file has setgid bit set
-k	Returns true if file has sticky bit set

In use, an expression using a file test operator might look something like this:

```
if ( -e /home/joe/myfile) {
    something
}
```

In this case, the conditional code would only be executed if the file /home/joe/myfile existed.

 Some of the file test operators may not work, or may work differently on operating systems other than Unix, or Unix-derived. File systems on those operating systems may not have the attributes that some of the file test operators test for. When in doubt, consult documentation.

Done!

REVIEW

This session started with a general overview of the concept of operators. You learned what operators are, and how they are used in programming. Then you learned the Perl operators that are used for mathematical, textual, assignment, logical, and file-testing purposes.

QUIZ YOURSELF

1. Explain the functions of the following operators:

   =

   ne

   +=

   (See "Assignment Operators", "Increment and Decrement Operators", "String Operators", and "Numeric Operators.")

2. What is the difference between the = and the == operators? (See "Numeric Operators.")

3. Are the following expressions true or false?

   "a" le "b"

   "a" ne "a"

   (5+2) >= (2+2+3)

   (See "String Operators" and "Numeric Operators.")

PART

II

Saturday Morning

1. How do files generated by word processors differ from files generated by text editors?

2. What are the implications for programming of your answer in question 1?

3. What is the primary difference between Pico and NEdit?

4. When using WordPad, what is the proper format in which to save your files?

5. What is meant by the term *programming style*? Why is it important?

6. Why are some lines of program code indented?

7. What is a comment? Why are comments important?

8. Explain the significance of the (apparent) comment `#!/usr/bin/perl`.

9. Why is it common in Perl programs to see rightward-facing curly braces on a line by themselves?

10. What is a scalar variable? How is it identified?

11. Given the code,

    ```
    $name = "jake";
    print "My name is $name \n";
    ```

    what will be the output?

12. Explain the \n in question 11.

13. What is a list variable? How is one identified?

14. Given list @list, how is the second element of that list identified?

15. What is a hash variable? How is one identified?
16. What is the most important characteristic of an expression?
17. What is a statement?
18. What is an operator?
19. Explain the function of the operator eq.

PART

III

Saturday Afternoon

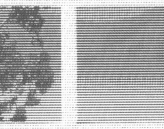

Basic Input and Output

Session Checklist

✔ Passing data on the command line

✔ Reading data from the keyboard

✔ Writing output to the screen

✔ Using the diamond operator

30 Min.
To Go

While it's possible to write programs that don't require anything in the way of input or output, such programs are not likely to be very useful. You need to be able to communicate with your programs in order to make them really work. There are many ways to get data in and out of your programs; command line arguments, the keyboard and monitor screen, files, other processes, and so on. In this session, I'll focus on the most basic — command line arguments, and the keyboard and screen.

Passing Data on the Command Line

Remember how you told the Perl interpreter to execute a command by putting the -e flag and command on the system's command line, like this:

```
perl -e 'some command;'
```

The -e flag and the command are *arguments* to the perl command. They give the interpreter extra information about what it's supposed to do. This is one of the most basic kinds of input there is. We can use the same principle to get data into our Perl programs, by using the special variable @ARGV. The @ARGV variable is a list that contains all of the command line arguments — that is, anything that appears on the command line after the name of the program. Here's an example:

```
#!/usr/bin/perl

print "@ARGV \n";
```

We save this program under the name argtest.pl. Now if we run the program like so,

```
argtest.pl foo bar baz bim
```

the output will be

```
foo bar baz bim
```

We could modify the program slightly:

```
#!/usr/bin/perl

print "$ARGV[0] \n";
print "$ARGV[1] \n";
print "$ARGV[2] \n";
print "$ARGV[3] \n";
and now the output would be
foo
bar
baz
bim
```

The thing to remember here is that the arguments start with the first term after the name of the program, and each successive word (that is, each successive string of alphanumeric characters separated by whitespace), is a subsequent argument. Another thing to bear in mind is that the numbering of arguments starts with 0. In all respects, @ARGV acts like any other list. Any of the operations that can work on an array will work on @ARGV.

The shift function

One very helpful function for processing @ARGV values is `shift`. This function returns the leftmost value from the list, and then chops it off the list, shortening the list by one. Thus, the previous program could be rewritten as

```
#!/usr/bin/perl

shift(@ARGV);
print;              # first value is passed via the $_ variable
shift (@ARGV);
print;
```

and so on.

In fact, since the name @ARGV can be passed implicitly, you could even pare that down to

```
shift;
print;
shift;

print;
```

and so on; or even to

```
print(shift);

print(shift);
```

on so on.

Reading Data From the Keyboard

You have already seen how to accept data from the keyboard, but it's worth reviewing because it's something you'll do quite frequently. As you will recall, you use the construction

```
$var = <STDIN>;
```

to read input from the keyboard in scalar form, and

```
@var = <STDIN>;
```

to read it in list form.

Thus, we can do something like

```
print "input your name: ";
$name = <STDIN>;
print "Your name is $name \n";
```

Or, in the case of list data, we can do something like

```
print "input a paragraph: \n";
@para = <STDIN>;
```

In the latter case, each line in the paragraph is an element in the list, thus:

```
$first_line = $para[0];
$second_line = $para[1];
$third_line = $para[2];
```

and so on.

We use the token STDIN because we are taking our data from the *standard input*, which is usually the keyboard. (I say "usually" here because it is possible to change the thing to which the standard input is attached. For example, on a Unix system, if you have your input piped from another process, or you have the input redirected from a file, STDIN will use that instead. Throughout this book, however, and for the great majority of practical purposes, we are talking about the keyboard.)

Writing Output to the Screen

20 Min. To Go

We have already done a great deal of writing output to the screen. The statement

```
print "Something";
```

does that automatically. There is, however, an assumption that the output of the print function is to be sent to the standard output. The *standard output* is usually the terminal screen. (Although, as with the standard input, this can be changed.) If we wanted to make the assumption in the print statement explicit, we could do it like this:

```
print(STDOUT, "Something");
```

At this point, you might be wondering why, since the print statement assumes that the standard output is the place to go, we need to use a token at all. The answer has to do with the fact that there are certain nonstandard places we may want to send the output (or look to for the input). These places can be files or other processes. We will discuss them in Session 14. Other than the fact that STDIN and STDOUT are the standard and often the default, there is nothing particularly special about them.

STDERR

One place we might want to send output other than the standard output, is the *standard error*. This is the default location for error messages. The Perl token for the standard error is, not surprisingly, STDERR. Very often, the standard error is the same as the standard output, but not always. Under Unix systems, for example, it is possible to redirect the standard error to some place other than the terminal screen. For example, you may want to direct the standard error to a log file like so:

```
unix_prompt> myprog.pl 2>logfile
```

Files and devices

In fact, STDIN and STDOUT actually represent files. As we will see in Session 14, any input or output can be taken from or sent to a file. This points up Perl's Unix heritage. In Unix, everything is represented as a file. Text files, binary files, programs, directories, hardware devices and so on are all files in the eyes of Unix — albeit files with particular types of attributes. Using the tokens STDIN and STDOUT merely tell the program — and by extension, the operating system — which files are being used. Every time you run a program in Unix, three files, or *streams* are opened, standard input, standard output, and standard error (see the next section). Under normal circumstances, the files that are associated with these are device files that correspond to the terminal at which the program was started.

Under Unix it is easy to reassign the files to which standard input, standard output, and standard error correspond, because, special attributes not withstanding, a file is a file.

Other operating systems have their own ways of dealing with input and output, and you should be aware of those, but aside from some particularities regarding naming conventions, the basic methods described in this session should work on any platform.

In this case, any statement in myprog.pl that sends output to STDERR will end up sending it to the logfile (the 2 here is the Unix *file descriptor* that refers to the default location for the standard error. By redirecting the default location elsewhere, you can manipulate this output.) To construct such a statement, you would do something like:

```
print (STDERR, "That's an error");
```

The point to keep in mind here, is that STDIN, STDOUT, and STDERR are defined by the operating system, so if you want to change them, you need to do so there.

The Diamond Operator

You will have noticed that the STDIN token is enclosed in angle brackets when it's used to take input from the keyboard. The angle brackets are actually an operator, and when they are used, they return either a line of input (if used in scalar context), or a list of all the lines input (if used in list context).

Using the angle brackets without anything inside them is a special way of dealing with input, and it has its own name — the *diamond operator*. The diamond operator takes input from files that you name on the command line (and so constitutes an alternate way of using command line arguments). For example, if you did:

```
#!/usr/bin/perl

while (<>) {                    # This is a loop. Loops are
    print $_;         # discussed in Session 12.
}
```

and then saved this program with the name myprog, you could invoke it with the names of one or more files on the command line, as in

```
myprog file1 file2 file3
```

and it would print each line of every file. (We haven't discussed looping yet, so for now just assume the while statement will repeat everything between the curly braces for as long as there is data to process.)

The handling of command-line arguments is implicit in the diamond operator, so you don't need to set up any special handling of @ARGV. The thing to keep in mind is that in this sort of context, the <> represents the next line contained in the file(s). Thus if each file has three lines, the fourth line handled by the <> operator is the first line of the second file. (For this reason, the diamond operator is sometimes referred to as the *readline operator*.)

**10 Min.
To Go**

Mixing Argument Types

What if you have a situation where you want to process some files on the command line using <>, and also use other types of arguments as well? This is possible, provided you are careful to keep things arranged so that you can keep them separate.

The <> operator uses @ARGV, but does so implicitly. For example, consider a program like this:

```
#!/usr/bin/perl

print(shift, "\n");
while (<>){
        print;
}
And invoked it like this:
myprog.pl hello file1 file2
the output would be
hello
first line of file1
second line of file1
first line of file 2
second line of file 2
```

and so on. Because we know that the first argument will not be a file, we can handle it separately — in this case splitting it off with the shift function and printing it. The remainder of the arguments are handled using the <> operator.

This will only work, however, if you know what the format and order of the command-line arguments will be. If you don't, you will need to use @ARGV explicitly, and use other techniques to access the contents of any files named on the command line. We will talk more about this sort of thing in Session 14.

If there are no filenames given as arguments on the command line, the diamond operator takes its input from the standard input. Thus, in a program invoked with no arguments,

```
$input = <>;
```

is the same as

```
$input = <STDIN>
```

Recall our program

```
#!/usr/bin/perl

while (<>) {            # This is a loop. Loops are
     print $_;          # discussed in Session 12.
}
```

If invoked with no arguments, the program will simply pause for input from the keyboard. When input is given, it will simply echo the line back to us. It will continue to do this until the program is killed, or until we give it the end of file (EOF) character (Ctrl+D under Unix, possibly different on other operating systems).

Some Examples of Handling Input

Here are some recipes for common things you might want to do using input and output.

- Reading a file from the command line into an array:

    ```
    @var = <>;
    ```

- Reading several files from the command line into an array:

    ```
    @var = <>;   # Will contain contents of all files named on the
                 # command line
    ```

- Reading the first line of a file into a scalar:

    ```
    $var = <>;
    ```

- Taking a line of input from the keyboard:

    ```
    chomp($var = <STDIN>);
    ```

or:

```
    chomp($var = <>); # if no command line arguments are given
```

- Taking multiple lines of input from the keyboard:

    ```
    chomp(@var = <STDIN>); # continues until EOF is read
    ```

These examples should cover most common situations. We will see more ways to handle input and output in Session 14, but for common situations involving interactive sessions, these techniques should stand you in good stead.

Done!

REVIEW

In this session, you learned some simple ways of getting information into and out of your programs. You learned that data can be passed on the command line in the form of arguments, and used in your program by accessing the value of the special list variable @ARGV. You went on to learn that data can be taken interactively from the keyboard using the readline operator with the standard input token (<STDIN>). Likewise, you learned that you can use the <STDOUT> expression to send data to the terminal screen (although it is assumed that this is what you want to do unless you state otherwise). You learned that the diamond operator, <>, can be used to take information from files used on the command line. Finally, you saw some common examples of passing information.

QUIZ YOURSELF

1. Explain the function of the @ARGV variable. (See "Passing Data on the Command Line.")

2. What are STDIN, STDOUT, and STDERR? How are they used? (See "Files and devices" and "STDERR.")

3. Explain the function of the diamond operator. (See "The Diamond Operator.")

Control Structures

Session Checklist

✔ Using flow control

✔ Using conditional structures

✔ Using iterative structures

**30 Min.
To Go**

C ontrol structures make the difference between a program that is a rote set of instructions that get carried out the same way every time and a program that is a dynamic piece of software that can react to input and varying conditions and make decisions about how to handle particular sets of circumstances. Control structures provide the "thinking" framework of any program.

What Is Flow Control?

When we talk about *control structures*, what we're talking about is the particular constructs that allow the programmer to control the flow of the program. When the Perl interpreter runs a program, it starts at the top and executes each step in sequence. Control structures are used to alter this top-to-bottom flow by telling the interpreter to skip a certain section, or to repeat a certain section depending on certain conditions.

The most common form of a control structure is

```
control-operator ( expression ) {
    code;
}
```

However, it is also possible under certain circumstances to have

```
{
    code;
} control-operator (expression )
```

The difference between the two of these is that in the first, the expression is evaluated before the code is executed, whereas in the second, it is evaluated after. In the second instance, the code will always be executed once, whereas in the first, depending on the expression, it may not be executed at all. (Of course, Perl being Perl, there are ways of bending the rules here.)

Conditional Structures

The easiest control structure to grasp is the conditional type. Conditional structures allow us to write a block of code that will only be executed if a certain condition is true or false.

if

We have already seen many examples of if constructs. if allows us to create a block of code that will only be executed *if* the expression evaluates as *true* (that is, returns a value of 1). Consider the following:

```
$name = "Bill";

if ( $name eq "Bill" ) {
    print "The name is correct! \n";
}
```

In this example, the print statement will only be executed if the variable $name holds a value of Bill. In this case it does, so the print statement is executed. If we were to change the first line to

```
$name = "Sandy";
```

then the condition would evaluate as false, and the code between the braces (that is, the print statement), would simply be skipped. When this happens, the flow of the program will be directed to the line immediately following the closing brace. Since the closing brace is the last line in this example, the program will simply exit.

if/else

Sometimes we may want to specify an either/or type of operation where if a condition is met, one block of code is executed, and another skipped, and if the condition is not met, the first block is skipped and the second executed. For this, we can add an else clause onto our if statement, like so:

```
if ( condition ) {
    something;
}
else {
    something else;
}
```

Here, if the condition evaluates as true, something is executed, and something else is skipped. *In all other cases*, something is skipped, and something else is executed. Here's how that might work in a more concrete context:

```
$name = "Bill";

if ($name eq "Bill") {
    print "The name is correct! \n";
}
else {
    print "Sorry, wrong name. \n";
}
```

Now, you get a response from the program regardless if the name is right or wrong.

if/elsif/else

Sometimes you have more than two alternatives to deal with. In that case, you can use the elsif (think "else, if") statement:

```
if ( condition ) {
    Block 1;
```

```
}
elsif (alternative condition) {
    Block 2;
}
elsif (alternative condition) {
    Block 3;
}
else {
    Block 4;
}
```

Here we have four possibilities. It could just as easily have been three or five, or nine. There is no limit to the number of elsif statements you can use. Here's a concrete example:

```
$name = "Bill";

if ($name eq "Bill") {
    print "The name is correct! \n";
}
elsif ($name eq "Bob") {
    print "Close, but no cigar! \n";
}
else {
    print "The name is incorrect. \n";
}
```

In this case, the message Close, but no cigar! is printed only if the variable $name is equal to Bob.

Note that when using the if construct (with or without elsifs and elses), the expression being evaluated as the condition does not necessarily have to be a comparison expression. It can be any expression that evaluates to a value of true, or, as you've seen, 1. Since most commands return a value of 1 if they are successful, any successful command can be used as the expression. For example, it would be possible (though of dubious usefulness) to say:

```
if ($a = 1) {
    print "Assignment successful."
}
```

(Note that here we are using the assignment operator =, and *not* the comparison operator ==.)

This bit of code will print the message if the assignment of the value 1 to the variable $a is successful. Unless there is a major problem, such an assignment is always successful. Therefore the code within the construct is always executed. Another example displaying some degree of uselessness might be

```
if ( print "hello" ) {
    print "OK";
}
```

This code will print the message OK if the message hello was printed successfully.

unless

The unless construct is sort of the opposite of if. unless executes the enclose block if the condition evaluates to false. In other words,

```
unless ( condition ) {
    something;
}
```

is the same as

```
if ( !condition ) {
    something;
}
```

If you had the following:

```
$name = "Jeff";

unless (name eq "Jeff") {
    print "The name is incorrect. \n"
}
```

The message would not be printed.

Tip

The creators of Perl have gone to some trouble to make it as freeform a language as possible. Both the if and unless constructors can be used after a statement to render it conditional. For example, the statement

```
if (name eq "Jeff") {
```

```
    print "I'm Jeff. \n";

}
```

could also be rendered as

```
print "I'm Jeff. \n" if ($name eq "Jeff");
```

This is seen most commonly with the `unless` **constructor:**

```
print "I'm not Jeff. \n" unless ($name eq "Jeff");
```

**20 Min.
To Go**

Iterative Structures (Loops)

In addition to the strictly conditional `if` and `unless` structures, Perl also provides us with a set of iterative structures. These structures cause the enclosed block of code to execute repeatedly until or unless a certain condition holds true. (Pedants may note that that this is also a form of conditionality, but we don't pay much attention to pedants.) Looping constructs have the same general form as conditional constructs. That is,

```
constructor (condition) {
     code block;
}
```

while

The first iterative constructor to look at is the `while` statement. This causes the enclosed code to repeat as long as the condition evaluates to `true`. Consider the following:

```
$a = 0;

while ($a < 10) {
     print "Still looping...\n";
     $a++;
}

print "Done. \n"
```

The output of this code should be:

```
Still looping...
Still looping...
Still looping...
Still looping...
Still looping...
Still looping...
Still looping...
Still looping...
Still looping...
Still looping...
Done.
```

Let's break this down. The constructor specifies that the enclosed code is to be repeated as long as the value of $a is less than 10. The initial value of $a is 0. At the start, the condition is evaluated. Since 0 is less than 10, the condition is true. The message Still looping... is printed, and the value of $a is increased by one. The program now returns to the top of the loop. The condition is evaluated again. The value of $a is now 1, which is less than 10, so the message is printed, and $a is increased by one again. The program goes back to the top, and so on. At the tenth iteration, the value of $a is 9 (because we started at 0). The conditional block is executed, and the value of $a is increased by one to 10. Back to the top again, the condition is evaluated. This time, the program sees that 10 is not less than 10, so it skips to the line immediately following the closing brace. The message Done. is printed, and the program exits.

until

until is to while what unless is to if. until causes a section of code to repeat *until* a condition is met (or, to put it another way, for as long as the condition is not met). Thus, we could rewrite the previous example to look like this:

```
$a = 0;

until ($a == 10) { # note the double equal sign!
    print "Still looping...\n";
    $a++
}
print "Done.\n";
```

The while and unless constructors can also be placed at the end of the block, if we use a do statement at the top, like so:

```
$a = 0;

do {
    print "Still looping...\n";
    $a++;
} until ($a == 10 );
```

But you should be aware that if you do this, the block will always execute once before the condition is evaluated.

for and foreach

The `for` and `foreach` constructors are synonyms. They are used to iterate over elements in a list. For example, suppose you have a list of names, and you want to process each name in turn. You could do it like this:

```
@names = qw(Scooby, Shaggy, Velma, Daphne, Fred);

foreach $name (@names) {
    print "Look out, here comes $name! \n";
}
```

Because the scalar $names has not been defined prior to the `foreach` statement, the interpreter creates it, and assigns it a value of $names[0]. Each time through the loop, it increases the position, so that the second time through $name is equal to $names[1], and so on until the end of the list is reached.

Perl really does a good chunk of work for you here. Here's how you might have to do that in some other languages (but using Perl syntax):

```
$a = 0;
@names = qw(Scooby, Shaggy, Velma, Daphne, Fred);
if ($names[$a] ) {
  print "Look out, here comes $names[$a] \n";
  $a++;

}
```

See how you would have to create an index variable, and use that to change your position in the array? Perl does that implicitly with the `foreach` construct.

Nested Structures

Consider the following:

```
$b = 0;

until ($b == 10) {
    $a = 0;
    print "$b \n";
    until ($a == 10) {
            print "$a ";
            $a++;
    }
    print "\n"
    $b++
}
```

Before reading on, can you figure out what's going on here?

We have two loops. They are *nested*. That is, one is inside the other one. Both loops are to iterate 10 times, but since the inner loop is inside the outer loop, the inner loop will iterate ten times for each one time that the outer loop iterates. Thus, the inner loop will iterate a total of 100 times.

Our output will look like this:

```
0
0 1 2 3 4 5 6 7 8 9
1
0 1 2 3 4 5 6 7 8 9
2
0 1 2 3 4 5 6 7 8 9
3
0 1 2 3 4 5 6 7 8 9
4
0 1 2 3 4 5 6 7 8 9
5
0 1 2 3 4 5 6 7 8 9
6
0 1 2 3 4 5 6 7 8 9
7
0 1 2 3 4 5 6 7 8 9
8
0 1 2 3 4 5 6 7 8 9
```

9
0 1 2 3 4 5 6 7 8 9

Loop labels

One of the interesting features of loops is that they can be named. It is possible to attach a *label* to a loop, and then use that label to exercise a greater degree of control over the iteration of the loop than might normally be possible. Loops are named by putting a name plus a colon before them, like so:

```
MYLOOP: foreach $sca (@lis) {
   etc...

}
```

Naming the loop allows you to use the control commands `next`, `last`, and `redo`.

For example, say you have the following:

```
@names = qw(Scooby, Shaggy, Velma, Daphne, Fred);
HUNT: foreach $name (@names) {
   if ($name eq "Daphne") {
         print "Got it! \n";
         last HUNT;
   }
   else {
         print "Nope...\n";
   }

}
```

Here, the program is searching through the list for the name Daphne. For each name other than Daphne, we get a `Nope....` BUT, once it's found Daphne, it doesn't need to search any more. So, once Daphne's been found, the `last` command tells the interpreter to stop the loop, and skip to the end.

Likewise, `next` causes the loop to stop executing, and to return to the beginning with the next value (good for cutting short complicated processing if you don't need it), and `redo` causes the loop to restart from the first value.

Interpreting this output, we notice that the single digits on lines by themselves represent the value of $b, whereas the strings of digits represent the value of $a.

Any control structure can be nested inside any other control structure, and we can nest to multiple levels:

```
$b = 0;

until ($b == 10) {
    $a = 0;
    print "$b \n";
    until ($a == 10) {
        $c = 0;
        until ($c == 10) {
            print "$c ";
            $c++
        }
        print "\n";
        print "$a ";
        $a++;
    }
    print "\n"
    $b++
}
```

(though Perl style recommends that you do not nest more than four levels deep).

Also, it is not necessary that your nested structures be of the same type. if statements can live happily inside of while loops, or for loops, and vice versa. Any control structure can be nested inside any other structure.

A Nested Loops Example

10 Min. To Go

Here's a slightly more full-fledged program to give an idea of how these control structures really work in a more complete context.

Returning to the teacher's gradebook example of past sessions, let's imagine that you want to write a program that will allow you to compute each student's test average, given a set of four tests. Your data looks like this:

Test 1.

Jim	86
Sally	92
Chloe	71
Alfred	90
Jane	84

Test 2.

Jim	91
Sally	88
Chloe	68
Alfred	92
Jane	86

Test 3.

Jim	85
Sally	83
Chloe	60
Alfred	90
Jane	88

Test 4.

Jim	94
Sally	100
Chloe	65
Alfred	94
Jane	90

And here's the program:

```perl
#!/usr/bin/perl

print "Enter names of students: \n";
chomp( @names = <STDIN> );

foreach $name (@names) {
        $sum = 0;
```

```
            $avg = 0;
            print "Enter $name\'s scores: \n";
            chomp( @scores = <STDIN> );
            $num = 0;
            foreach $score (@scores) {
                    $sum += $score;
                    $num++
            }
            $avg = $sum / $num;
            print "$name\'s average is $avg. \n\n";
}
```

When you run the program, here's what happens:

```
[joe@ika joe]$ ./scores
Enter names of students:
Jim
Sally
Chloe
Alfred
Jane
Enter Jim's scores:
86
91
85
94
Jim's average is 89.

Enter Sally's scores:
92
88
83
100
Sally's average is 90.75.

Enter Chloe's scores:
71
68
60
65
Chloe's average is 66.
```

```
Enter Alfred's scores:
90
92
90
94
Alfred's average is 91.5.

Enter Jane's scores:
84
86
88
90
Jane's average is 87.

[joe@ika joe]$
```

No doubt there are ways in which this program could be improved, but it does what it set out to do — compute the average of each student's scores.

Done!

REVIEW

You started this session by learning about the concept of flow control. You then learned to use flow control in your program by applying the various control structures, beginning with the simple conditional, and moving to the iterative (looping) constructs. Finally, you learned about nesting structures, and saw how multiple structures might be combined to produce complex behavior.

QUIZ YOURSELF

1. Explain the significance of the curly braces ({}) in flow control structures. (See "What is Flow Control?")

2. Which control structure would you use to prevent code from being executed only under a single condition? (See "unless.")

3. How does placing a condition at the end of a conditional block affect the execution of the block's code, as opposed to placing the condition at the beginning of the block? (See "What is Flow Control?")

Functions I: Perl Native Functions

Session Checklist

✔ Learning about functions

✔ Using functions in your programs

✔ Learning individual functions

**30 Min.
To Go**

Now that you've got the grammar of Perl under your belt, it's time to work on the vocabulary. When I talk about the grammar of Perl, I'm talking about the main structural elements of the language. Data types, variables, operators, statements, flow control constructs, and the like, all provide the structure upon which you build your programs.

But there is another side of the language as well, and that is the function. Functions provide the vocabulary of Perl, in that they allow us to actually do something. A language with grammar but no vocabulary might be formally interesting, but we wouldn't be capable of expressing much with it. Similarly, a programming language with only structures and no functions might be interesting to a student of languages, but it wouldn't allow us to get much work done.

There are two types of functions, native functions and user-defined functions. *User-defined functions* are functions that you create. We will discuss those in more detail in Session 20. In this session we discuss *native functions*, which are functions that are built into the language itself. (Functions are also provided by modules.

These are someone else's user-defined functions that have been packaged and distributed publicly.) Some languages, such as C, have a relatively small number of native functions. These languages provide extended functions through libraries (files full of archived functions). Other languages, such as Perl, have quite a few native functions. (There are Perl libraries, of course, but the point is that the number of native functions in Perl is far greater than that of, say, C.)

What's a Function?

You've already seen several examples of functions throughout in this book. One of the most frequently used has been the `print` function. As we have seen, `print` takes a chunk of text and prints it to the terminal screen. There are also, as we shall see later, ways of making `print` print to other places, such as files. In the most general sense, the `print` function has a *job*, and that job is to take text and put it somewhere. We can use operators and options to modify the way it does this, but the basic essence of the function — the placement of text — remains intact.

In general, all functions share this quality. They have a job, whose essence remains the same, but whose behavior can be modified by means of options and arguments. The basic syntax of a function looks like this:

```
function(arguments);
```

Arguments to a function are the same as arguments given on your operating systems command line. Much in the same way that we used command line switches such as `-e` to modify the behavior of the Perl interpreter, we can use various options to modify the behavior of functions. Arguments can also represent data being given to the function for processing. Perl being Perl, the parentheses around the arguments are often optional. For example with the `print` function, I often don't use parentheses because the quotation marks provide the same type of clarity.

Using Functions in Programming

Functions are used in programming as simple command statements. That is, you use a function as a simple command wherever you want that function's job carried out.

Like control structures, functions can often be nested inside one another. When this happens, the functions are processed from the inside outwards, with the return value of the inner function acting as the data being passed to the outer function. Thus

```
$input = <STDIN>;
chomp $input;
```

is the same as
```
chomp ($input = <STDIN>);
```

You might notice here that the first function in the preceding example does not actually contain a function, but only an operator. In fact, the creators of Perl have gone to some lengths to create ambiguity between what constitutes a function and what constitutes an operator (according to the camel book, 2nd ed., page 141). There is some validity to this. The difference between what constitutes an operation, and what constitutes a function is not always clear.

In any case, you can think of a function as a sort of *black box*. You throw data into the box, and something else comes out. For practical purposes, it doesn't matter how it gets done, as long as it does.

Passing Data to Functions

As mentioned previously, data is passed to functions in the form of arguments. Like command-line arguments, this data is given to the function at the time you want the function to use it. The best way to see how this is done is to look at an example. Take the length function. length takes a scalar value as input, and returns the length of that value:

```
$phrase = "Hello there";
$len = length $phrase;
print $len;
```

The preceding code will output the value 11, as there are eleven characters in Hello there (the space counts).

A much easier way to do the previous code would be

```
print(length "Hello there");
```

Some Perl Native Functions

The remainder of this session is devoted to describing a selected set of Perl native functions. These functions will be used throughout the rest of this book, and, as they are fairly common functions in Perl, it's a good idea to memorize them as fully as you can. You should also feel free to use what follows as a reference for further work. If a function deals with a concept we haven't met yet, I will note it.

**20 Min.
To Go**

abs

Syntax: abs(*expression*)

Description: Returns the absolute value of a particular expression. (If the expression is omitted, it uses $_).

atan2

Syntax: atan2(*x,y*)

Description: Mathematical function which returns the arctangent of *y*/*x* in the range of -[pi] to [pi].

chdir

Syntax: chdir(*expression*)

Description: Changes the working directory to the directory represented by the expression. If the target directory does not exist, the function fails, and returns a value of 0.

chmod

Syntax: chmod(*value, list*)

Description: Changes the permissions on a list of files to the permission represented by the value. The value must be in numerical form, for example:

```
chmod(0666, $file1, $file2);
```

chomp

Syntax: chomp(*scalar or list variable*)

Description: Removes the trailing newline character from a value, or from a list of values. Usually used when receiving input from the keyboard.

chown

Syntax: chown(*UID and/or GID, list of files*)

Description: Changes the ownership of the specified files to the owner and/or group specified by the UID and/or GID. UID and GID must be in numerical format. For example:

```
chown(501, $file1, file2);
```

close

Syntax: close(*filehandle*)

A *filehandle* is a way of allowing your Perl program to have access to a file, either for reading from, or for writing to. I'll discuss filehandles in Session 14.

Description: Closes an open file.

closedir

Syntax: closedir(*directory handle*)

A *directory handle* is a way of allowing your Perl program access to a directory. I'll discuss directory handles in Session 15.

Description: Closes an open directory.

cos

Syntax: cos(*expression*)

Description: Mathematical function that returns the cosine (in radians) of the expression.

defined

Syntax: `defined(expression)`

   Description: This is a Boolean function (meaning that it returns a yes or no answer) that is used to find out if the expression has a real value or not. For example, a variable that has not been declared or defined in a particular program has a value of `undef`. If you wanted to discover whether a variable had been created, you could do something like

```
if (defined $myvar) {
    print "Variable is defined \n";
}
else {
    print "Variable is not defined \n";
}
```

delete

Syntax: `delete(expression)`

   Description: Deletes a specified key, and its associated value from a hash. (See Session 8.)

die

Syntax: `die(list)`

   Description: Causes a program to abort, printing the message(s) specified in the list. This message can be a simple text string:

```
defined $myvar || die "Couldn't find my variable!"
```
or we can pull in specific information by using special tokens:
```
defined $myvar || die "Couldn't find variable in ", __FILE__ , "
at line ",                                   __LINE__;
```

which would print something like:

```
Couldn't find variable in myprog at line 26
```

(Note that I had to stick spaces in the text strings. `die` simply concatenates all the arguments in the list, and if you don't put the spaces in yourself, you won't have any.)

do

Syntax: do {

> *code block;*
> }

Description: do executes a block of code. It is usually used with a trailing flow control structure such that the control structure's conditional statement isn't evaluated until after the block has executed. (See Session 12.)

each

Syntax: each(*hash*)

Description: Returns a list consisting of one set of a key and a value from the specified hash. Using each repeatedly allows you to iterate over all the keys and values of the specified hash, for example,

```
%myhash = (joe, 56, jim, 60, sally, 25);
while (($key, $value) = each %myhash) {
    print "$key, $value".
}
```

would give the output:

```
joe, 56
jim, 60
sally, 25
```

The data extracted from the hash in this way will not necessarily be output in the order in which you put it. Recall that the hash stores the data in the most systemically advantageous way, not in the way that you put it in there.

exists

Syntax: exists(*expression*)

Description: Determines if a specified key exists in a particular hash. For example,

```
if (exists $hash{$key}) {
    print "Key exists. \n";
}
```

exp

Syntax: exp(*expression*)

Description: Mathematical function that returns the value of the constant e raised to the power specified by the expression.

hex

Syntax: hex(*expression*)

Description: Interprets the expression as a hexadecimal (base 16) number, and returns the corresponding decimal number. Here are some examples:

```
print( hex("1") );
```
will output the number 1.

```
print( hex("a") );
```

will output the number 10.

```
print( hex("f") );
will output the number 15
```

lc

Syntax: lc(*expression*)

Description: Forces all characters in a particular string to be lower case. For example,

```
print( lc(HELlo) );
```
would output
```
hello
```

lcfirst

Syntax: lcfirst(*expression*)

Description: Same as lc but only operates on the first character of the expression.

length

Syntax: length(*expression*)

Description: Returns the length in bytes of the expression if the expression is a scalar. Don't try to use length with a list or hash.

log

Syntax: log(*expression*)

Description: Mathematical function that returns the value of the natural (base e) logarithm of the expression.

mkdir

Syntax: mkdir(*directory name, mode*)

Description: Creates a directory with the specified name and permission mode.

my

Syntax: my(*expression*)

Description: Creates a *private* variable. That is, the variables created by the my function exist only within the subroutine, loop, or block of code in which they are created. In other words, given the code

```
while (something) {
    my $var = something;
    (block of code)
}
```

the variable $var exists only inside the enclosing while loop. By doing this, you are able to have variables existing in different places in your program, but having the same name and not conflicting with one another.

The use of private variables is strongly recommended wherever possible.

**10 Min.
To Go**

oct

Syntax: oct(*expression*)

Description: This function is similar to the hex function, except that it interprets the expression as an octal (base 8) number. For example, the statement

```
print( oct(256) );
```

produces the number 174 as output.

open

Syntax: open(*filehandle, expression*)
   Description: Creates a specified filehandle and associates it with the file given by the expression. (Filehandles and the open function are covered in depth in Session 14.)

opendir

Syntax: opendir(*directory handle, directory*)
   Description: Similar to open, but creates a directory handle instead of a file-handle. (Directory handles and the opendir function are covered in depth in Session 15.)

ord

Syntax: ord(*expression*)
   Description: Returns the ASCII value of the first character in the expression. For example,

```
print( ord(a) );
```

produces the output 97.

pop

Syntax: pop(*array*)
   Description: Treats the specified array as a stack and takes the last value from the list, shortening it by one value. (See Session 8.)

print

Syntax: print (*expression*)
   Description: Prints a string, or a list of strings.

push

Syntax: push(*array,* *list*)
Description: The opposite of pop. Treats the array as a stack, and appends the list of values to its end. (See Session 8.)

rand

Syntax: rand(*expression*)
Description: Returns a random number between zero and the value of the expression. Return value can be fractional. If no expression is given, the number returned is between zero and one.

reset

Syntax: reset(*expression*)
Description: Used at the top of a loop to clear the values of any variables that are altered in the course of the loop's execution, so that the loop will work again.

return

Syntax: return(*expression*)
Description: This function is used primarily when creating user-created functions. When your function exits, you can use the return function to make sure a particular value is returned. (This function will be covered in more detail in Session 20.)

reverse

Syntax: reverse(*list*)
Description: Reverses the order of the elements in a list.

scalar

Syntax: scalar(*expression*)
Description: Forces a list-aware function to evaluate a list in a scalar context. For example, you saw previously that the length function operates only on scalars. If you want to find the length of a list, you can do

```
$len = length( scalar(@list) );
```

shift

Syntax: shift(*array*)
 Description: Returns the first value of an array, shortening the array by one value. (Same as pop, but operates from the left instead of the right.)

sin

Syntax: sin(*expression*)
 Description: Mathematical operator. Returns the sine of the expression.

sort

Syntax: sort(*list*)
 Description: Sorts a list in ascending alphabetical or numerical order.

sqrt

Syntax: sqrt(*expression*)
 Description: Mathematical operator. Returns the square root of the expression.

sub

Syntax: sub name {

        block of code;
        }

 Description: Used to identify a subroutine. (Subroutines are less formal versions of user-created functions. They will be described in more detail in Session 20.)

substr

Syntax: substr (*expression, offset, length*)
 Description: Extracts a portion of the given expression, starting after the number of characters given by the offset, and comprising the number of characters given by the length. For example,

```
$phrase = "Jackdaws love my big sphinx of quartz.";
print( substr($phrase, 4, 3) );
```

would produce the output:

```
daw
```

If the offset number is negative, the substring will begin that many characters from the end of the string.

system

Syntax: system (*expression*)
   Description: The system function is used to run external programs. The expression is the command line that you would give at a system prompt.

undef

Syntax: undef(*expression*)
   Description: Sets the value of the variable given by the expression to undef.

unlink

Syntax: unlink(*list*)
   Description: Deletes a file or list of files. Use carefully.

unshift

Syntax: unshift(*array, list*)
   Description: The opposite of shift. Adds values in the list to the front of the array.

values

Syntax: values(*hash*)
   Description: Returns a list of all values in the specified hash.

Done!

REVIEW

In this session, you began by learning what a function is, and how to use functions in programming. You then learned a group of selected Perl native functions.

QUIZ YOURSELF

1. What do we mean when we refer to a function as *native*? (See "Introduction.")

2. What function would you use to get the fourth and fifth characters from a string? (See "Some Perl Native Functions.")

3. What would be the output of the following statement? hex(b); (See "Some Perl Native Functions.")

Advanced Input and Output: File Manipulation

Session Checklist

✔ Using files for input and output

✔ Understanding filehandles

✔ Creating and destroying files

**30 Min.
To Go**

You have already seen that the `<STDIN>` token enables you to take input from the keyboard, and the `print` function enables you to send output to the terminal screen. You've also seen how to pass arguments on the command line. These are fine for dealing with interactive situations involving fairly small amounts of data, but what about those times when you might want to use other sources of input, and other output destinations?

In this session, you'll learn how to use files for input and output. Although I will be discussing only text files, the techniques developed in this session can be used for binary data as well. However, dealing with binary data is an advanced topic, and outside the scope of this book.

Using Files

As you recall from Session 4, text files are nothing more than groupings of ASCII data identified by a name and a location on your computer's hard drive. Files are a great way of dealing with fairly large amounts of text, which is something for which Perl is well suited. Moreover, if you're doing something like maintaining a Web site, you are probably dealing with text files already. (While it is true that a Web site uses HTML files, HTML is just text with formatting tags.) Perl makes it easy to read, parse, and modify files fairly quickly. Or perhaps you intend for your program to run automatically (as a daemon or a cron job) in order to perform some mechanical function. In this case, you'd probably want it to keep a record of what it did. Keeping a log file would be the obvious way to go here.

Filehandles

If you're old enough to remember the CB radio craze of the '70s, you might remember that people used nicknames for themselves on the air, and that these nicknames were called "handles." Handles are alive and well in Perl, and like the CB handles of yore, a handle is still a sort of nickname. Database handles and directory handles are two common types, but perhaps the most common is the filehandle. (Yes, it's all one word. For some reason, the creators of Perl seem to like it that way.)

A *handle* in Perl parlance is a token or symbol by which you refer to something external to the program. It is a way of abstracting that thing so that it can be incorporated into Perl's syntax. In a way, a handle is like a variable name in that it is an arbitrary name that is used to represent something else. Unlike a variable name, however, a handle stands for something concrete like a file or directory — not an arbitrary value.

Some functions, such as `print`, allow for filehandles in their syntax. This allows the programmer to direct the output of that command (or the input to it) to come from the file represented by the filehandle.

Opening and closing files

Before you can use a file, you need to open it. By doing this, you place the file in memory, and make the Perl interpreter aware of where it is. You open the file, and create its filehandle at the same time, using the open function:

```
open (MYFILE, /home/joe/myfile);
```

This creates the filehandle MYFILE, and associates it with the file /home/joe/myfile.

Once a file has been opened and a filehandle created for it, you must then close it when you are done. As you might expect, this is done with the close function:

```
close(MYFILE);
```

If you use the same filehandle again in reference to another file, the first file is closed by default. In other words, if you had

```
open(MYFILE, /home/joe/myfile);
some code;
open(MYFILE, /home/joe/myotherfile);
```

/home/joe/myfile would be closed before /home/joe/myotherfile was opened. However, it's a good idea to get into the habit of explicitly closing your files before opening new ones, because it forces you to be aware that it's happening.

Note that when you open a file in this way

```
open(MYFILE, /home/joe/myfile);
```

you are opening the file for *reading*. That is, you are expecting to take input from the file, and not write output to it. You can make this default assumption explicit by using the < character, like this:

```
open(MYFILE, </home/joe/myfile);
```

If you want to open a file for the purpose of writing output to it, you need to use the > character:

```
open(MYFILE, >/home/joe/myfile);
```

If you want to append data to an already existing file, you need to use >>:

```
open(MYFILE, >>/home/joe/myfile);
```

 Opening a file for appending data is especially good for keeping log files.

All well and good, you say, but what if I want to open a file for reading and writing at the same time? In this case, you need to use +> or +<. You should use +>> if you wish to open a file for reading and appending.

20 Min.
To Go

Reading data from a file

Assume that you have the file /home/joe/datafile, that contains this text:

```
first line of text
second line of text
third line of text
fourth line of text
fifth line of text
sixth line of text
seventh line of text
eighth line of text
ninth line of text
tenth line of text
```

Now, consider the following code:

```
#!/usr/bin/perl

$datafile = "/home/joe/datafile";

open(DATAFILE, $datafile);
$line = <DATAFILE>;
print "$line \n";
```

What happens when you run this code? You should get only the first line of text, followed by a blank line, and then your system prompt should come back. Why is this? Let's tackle the blank line first.

When you created the text file, you hit the Enter key after typing each successive line. That placed a newline character at the end of each line. When the interpreter executes the line

```
print "$line \n";
```

it prints that attached newline character, along with the one we've specified. You have two choices for getting rid of the blank line: You could eliminate the newline character from your print statement, but you can't always be sure there'll be a newline on every line, or you could change our input line to

```
chomp($line = <DATAFILE>);
```

Is this starting to look familiar? This looks an awful lot like our old friend:

```
chomp($input = <STDIN>);
```

In fact, the `<STDIN>` token is just a special sort of filehandle that represents the *standard input*.

Now you have another problem to tackle. Why did the program give you only the first line of your data file, and not all of them? It's because you used a scalar variable, `$line`, as your input variable. When you use a scalar in this way, the program assumes that you only want one line of text. In order to get more than one line, you need to use a list:

```perl
#!/usr/bin/perl

$datafile = "/home/joe/datafile";
open(DATAFILE, $datafile);
chomp(@file = <DATAFILE>);

foreach $line (@file) {
        print "$line \n";
}
```

Note that the list context necessitated the use of a `foreach` loop in order to iterate over all the lines in the list. There is actually a simpler way to do this:

```perl
#!/usr/bin/perl

$datafile = "/home/joe/datafile";
open(DATAFILE, $datafile);

while (<DATAFILE>) {
        print;
}
```

In this context, the `while` loop considers its condition met as long as there are more lines remaining in the list. The line itself is passed to the `print` function via the `$_` variable. If you want to make good on your formatting tweaks, you can modify the program slightly:

```perl
#!/usr/bin/perl

$datafile = "/home/joe/datafile";
open(DATAFILE, $datafile);

while (<DATAFILE>) {
    chomp;
```

```
    print;
    print "\n";
}
```

Writing output to a file

Now, suppose that instead of printing each line to the screen, you want to print them to a second file. You need to open another filehandle for writing, and then modify your print statement to print to that filehandle:

```perl
#!/usr/bin/perl

$datafile = "/home/joe/datafile";
$resultfile = ">/home/joe/outfile";   # Note the '>' character.
open(DATAFILE, $datafile);
open(OUTPUTFILE, $resultfile);

while (<DATAFILE>) {
    chomp;
     print OUTPUTFILE;
    print OUTPUTFILE "\n";
}
```

Now, if you look at the file /home/joe/outfile, you will see your output there.

 Be careful using the > character to open a file for writing. If the file you specify already exists and has data in it, the data in the file will be overwritten. If you intend for this to happen, that's fine, but if you don't, you may find that you have destroyed data that you need. When in doubt, use the >> construct to append the new data to the end of the file.

Using filehandles to access processes

One of the interesting features of the open function is that it allows you assign a filehandle to a process. That is, you can run a program, and treat it as if it were a file, reading from it or writing to it. For example, the following bit of code would read from the Unix date program, which outputs the current date and time, and prints the output to the screen:

```
#!/usr/bin/perl

$process = "/bin/date|";

open(PROCESS, $process);

while (<PROCESS>) {
        chomp;
        print;
        print "\n";
}
```

Note the Unix pipe character (|) at the end of the pathname for the date program. This indicates that the output will be *piped from* the process for reading. If we were to place the pipe character in front of the filename, it would indicate that output from our Perl program would be *piped to* the process in question.

**10 Min.
To Go**

File Manipulation Functions

Now that you've seen how to access the contents of files from within a Perl program, it makes sense to take a look at some functions that you can use to manipulate files in other ways. Generally, as regards manipulating files, anything you can do from a system prompt, you can do from within a Perl program using Perl commands that are designed to interface with the operating system.

unlink

You can create files simply by using open to create a filehandle for writing. If the specified file does not already exist, it will be created. In order to remove a file, you must use the unlink function. unlink is used to delete a file or a list of files. If you do not supply a file or a list of files, it will use the value of $_. Suppose that you have a file called /home/me/junkfile that you want to get rid of. In Perl, it is very simple to eliminate it:

```
unlink /home/me/junkfile;
```

You can also supply a variable name:

```
$junk = "/home/me/junkfile";
unlink $junk;
```

As a rule, it's a good idea to unlink files if you don't need them. For example, you might have had the need to create a file to store data for your program to use while it's running, but once the program is done, it doesn't need them anymore. Putting in a few lines at the end of your program to *clean up* is always a good idea.

Whenever you use a function such as unlink, you need to be aware of the permissions on the file you're using. You cannot unlink files in directories for which you don't have write permission.

Never use unlink when running a program as the superuser without being very, VERY sure of what you're doing. Careless, or even slightly inattentive use of this function can do serious damage to your operating system. In fact, it's probably not a good idea to run *any* program as the superuser without being vigilant.

rename

The rename function, as you might guess, changes the name of a file. Its syntax is simple:

```
rename OLDNAME, NEWNAME;
```

If there is already a file with the same name as the new name, it will be overwritten.

chmod

The chmod function does the same thing as the Unix chmod command. That is, it changes the permissions on a file. chmod takes a list of arguments, the first of which must be the numerical permission mode that you wish to switch the file to. (Sorry — Perl's chmod can't use symbolic modes.) For example,

```
chmod 0755, /home/joe/somefile;
```

Look at the Unix man page for chmod if you need to find out how to figure the numerical mode.

chown

Like chmod, chown does the same thing as the Unix command of the same name. It changes the owner of a file. The first argument must be the numerical user ID (UID) of the file's new owner. The second argument must the numerical group ID (GID) of the new owning group. All arguments after that are the names of files to be changed. For example,

```
chown 501, 505, /home/joe/somefile;
```

How and When to die

You have already seen the die function. This function causes your Perl program to abort, and prints an optional error message. The die function is especially useful as an adjunct to the open function:

```
open(HANDLE, /somedir/somefile) or die "couldn't open somefile";
```

This construct prevents the program from going on if the specified file is not available for any reason. This lets you know the reason your program isn't working is that some file isn't available, rather than a bug in the code. (If you hadn't used the die function, the program would produce errors when the expected input is nowhere to be found.)

In general, any time you open a file, especially for reading or appending, you should include a die statement to handle any problems that may be a result of file availability problems.

Done!

SUMMARY

In this session, you learned about file manipulation. You started by learning why you might want to use files as sources of input and destinations for output. You continued by learning how to use the open function to open files and create filehandles. You learned to extract data from files, and to direct output to them. Finally, you learned some appropriate ways in which to use the die function.

QUIZ YOURSELF

1. Explain what a filehandle is, and how they're used. (See "Using Files.")

2. If two filehandles are opened with the same name at the same time, what will happen? (See "Opening and closing files.")

3. How do you extract information from another process? (See "Using filehandles to access processes.")

4. Explain the `die` function, and why you might want to cause your own program to abort. (See "How and when to die.")

Advanced Input and Output: Directory Manipulation

Session Checklist

✔ Using directory handles

✔ Using directory-related functions

✔ Using the filename globbing operator

**30 Min.
To Go**

aving learned how to use filehandles and the functions that manipulate them, you are half way towards being able to make full use of your computer's file system. But while you are able to access individual files, you are still unable to traverse directories, get directory listings, and work with files in groups. Such techniques are the subject of this session.

Directory Handles

In order to manipulate directories, you must assign a directory handle to the directory you want to use. A directory handle works in exactly the same way as a file-handle does, except that you create it using the opendir function.

```
opendir(DIRHANDLE, "/path/to/dirname/");
```

Directory handles have a separate namespace (a way in which names of things are stored) from filehandles, so it shouldn't matter if you have a directory handle and a filehandle with the same name, however, from the point of view of programming style, it's best if you keep them distinct.

Once you've got the directory open, you use the `readdir` function to get the names of the files in that directory. Like many Perl functions, `readdir` behaves differently depending on whether you use it in a scalar or a list context. In a scalar context, it returns the name of the next file in the directory. (In other words, if you had files in your directory named a, b, and so on, the files would be returned in that order.) Used in a list context, `readdir` returns a list of all the filenames in that directory.

Let's take a look at a concrete example of how you might use these functions in a program:

```perl
#!/usr/bin/perl

open(OUTPUTFILE, ">./output");

opendir(MYDIR, "/home/me/mydatadir") || die "we have a problem";
@files = readdir(MYDIR);
closedir(MYDIR);

foreach $file (@files) {
    open (READFILE, $file) || die "couldn't open $file";
    while(<READFILE>) {
        print OUTPUTFILE;
    }
}
close(READFILE); #only need to do this once since each new 'open'
                 #closes the previous one.
```

This program takes the contents of every file in the `mydatadir` directory and dumps their contents into the `output` file. (Note that if your program is in the same directory as your data files, you will also get a copy of your program in your output file.)

What you've done here is to define a directory, open it, read the contents into a list variable, and then use the `foreach` construct to iterate over each list element. Since these list elements are filenames, you can feed them into an `open` statement in order to access their contents. In this way, you can access the contents of these files without actually knowing their names.

Tip

The previous example is typical of the kinds of things that Perl is good at. Though short and simple, it is actually quite powerful. It's well worth your while to get comfortable with it, since you'll probably find yourself writing similar things often.

If you're planning on working on files outside of your immediate home environment, you may want to add a few file tests to make sure that the files you want to work on have the appropriate permissions:

```perl
#!/usr/bin/perl

open(OUTPUTFILE, ">./output");

opendir(MYDIR, "/home/me/mydatadir") || die "we have a problem";
@files = readdir(MYDIR);
closedir(MYDIR);

foreach $file (@files) {
    if ( -r $file ) {
        open (READFILE, $file) || die "couldn't open $file";
        while(<READFILE>) {
            print OUTPUTFILE;
        }
    }
    else {
        print "You do not have read permission on $file";
    }

}
close(READFILE);
```

This saves having to aborting the program if you run into inaccessible files, and also makes it clear that the problem is one of permissions, and not something more fundamental.

**20 Min.
To Go**

Moving Around the File System

Suppose you need to find a certain file, but you don't know what directory it's in. Your system's file finding utility is, for some reason, not behaving properly, and you need to whip up something that will locate this file. The only thing you know about the location of this file is that it is somewhere below your home directory, and it is named lostfile.txt. To make matters worse, you have lots of subdirectories below your home directory, and many of those have sub-subdirectories and so on. (You should probably clean up your home directory, but that's between you and your system administrator.)

In order to find this lost file, we need to create a program that will scan each directory, look for your file, and also look in each subdirectory. The procedure for our program will look something like this:

1. Open directory.
2. Look at first file.
   - 2a. Is this file "lostfile.txt"?
     - 2a-1. If it is, end program.
   - 2b. If it is not, is this file a directory?
     - 2b-1. If it is, open that directory.
       - 2b-1a. Look at first file

And so on. This is a problem that is custom-made for a technique called *recursive programming*. A recursive function is one that calls itself. In order to achieve this, you have to cheat a little, and use a technique we haven't covered yet — the subroutine.

Subroutines are user-created functions, which we will cover more thoroughly in Session 20, but for now, just think of a subroutine as a piece of code that gets a name, and you can use that name in the same way as you use any other function.

Here's the code for the previous procedure:

```perl
#!/usr/bin/perl

sub hunt {  #the 'sub' function lets us create the subroutine

        my $working = shift;       # Take this directory's name from
                                   # the "command line"

        my $start = `pwd`;       # keep track of where we started
                                 # (uses another "cheat" - see below)

        chdir($working) || die "couldn't change to $working";
        opendir(THISDIR, ".");      # open current directory

        my @list = readdir(THISDIR)
```

```
        foreach $file (@list) {
            next if ".";              # ignore current directory
            next if "..";             # ignore parent directory
            if ($file eq "lostfile.txt") {
                print("found ".`pwd`.$file);
                exit 1;               # quit with success!
            }
            elsif (-d $file) {
                &hunt($file);         # this is the recursive
                next;                 # bit.
            }
            chdir($start);
        }
    }

&hunt(".");
```

Never run a program like this as the superuser without being very VERY careful about what it does. If you create a program that traverses the filesystem, and deletes files or directories, you could very easily cripple your operating system.

The "cheat" mentioned in the comments is the backtick (`` ` ``) operator. This operator allows you to execute a system command. Thus the line

```
my $start = `pwd`;
```

assigns the variable $start to the output of the Unix pwd command. This is just a way of keeping track of the directory from which you started. You will meet more of this type of operator in Session 16. (Use the my command to keep any variables created in the subroutine local to that subroutine. You don't want the variable values conflicting with each other when variables with the same name are operating at the same time, which will happen when you program recursively.)

The ampersand character that you see used in &hunt is the way to call your subroutine. When the Perl interpreter sees that character, it knows that it needs to look for the corresponding sub line elsewhere in the program.

This program is recursive because the hunt subroutine calls itself every time it encounters a new directory. If you've never used recursive techniques before, this can seem odd. After all, how can you define something in terms of itself? The fact is, this is entirely possible in Perl. (Nor is this unique to Perl — many languages have the ability to do this.)

Other than these new features, this program is entirely straightforward. It uses simple iteration to go through each file in the working directory by turn.

You have, however, met a new function. The chdir function changes the current working directory to whatever directory is given as an argument. It is important to remember that this function has effects that are relative to whichever directory is being seen as the current directory. For example, the dot character (.) refers to the current directory, and will change when we use chdir. It is also important to remember that when you change the current directory, you need to open it before you can do any reads on it. The initial working directory is always the one in which the program was started.

**10 Min.
To Go**

Creating and Destroying Directories

One thing that you might find especially useful is the ability to create new directories. This is especially true if you have a program that outputs a lot of data to files. It would be useful if you could have a central location for these files.

Creating directories is simple enough. One simply uses the mkdir function. Destroying directories is done with the rmdir function. Note that the directory itself must be empty for rmdir to work.

Suppose you have a program that creates a lot of temporary files. You'd like to place these files in a central location, and then get rid of them when you're done. You could insert these bits of code into your program:

```
$tempdir = "/tmp/junk";
mkdir $tempdir;
opendir(TEMP, $tempdir);
chdir $tmpdir;
open(JUNK, ">junkfile");
```

Now you have your temporary directory and file ready and open for writing. When you're ready to finish up, you can do:

```
chdir "..";
@list = readdir(TEMP);
foreach $name (@list) {
    unlink($name);# deletes the file $name
}
rmdir(TEMP);
```

The reason that you use a `foreach` loop instead of simply unlinking the junk file directly is in case you want to create more than one junkfile. The `foreach` loop iterates over all the files in the directory, unlinking them all.

Again, beware of the danger of this type of thing when operating as the superuser.

Miscellaneous File Manipulating Functions

In addition to `opendir`, `closedir`, `readdir`, `chdir`, `mkdir`, and `rmdir`, there are a few other directory handling functions that you should be aware of.

telldir

The `telldir` function returns a number indicating where in the directory the `readdir` function is.

For example, the code

```
#!/usr/bin/perl -w

opendir(CURR, ".");

while(readdir(CURR)) {
        print (readdir(CURR)."\t".telldir(CURR)."\n");
}
```

produces an output that looks something like

```
.pinerc       852
.addressbook.lu       896
.cddbslave       936
MySQL-3.22.32-1.i386.rpm       996
VMware-2.0-476.i386.rpm       1044
vmware       1076
MySQL-shared-3.22.32-1.i386.rpm       1156
template.txt       1224
mod_perl.html       1276
libapreq-0.31.tar.gz       1332
```

```
.AbiSuite     1384
.cddb    1416
.cycas2     1448
.e-conf     1476
.ee    1504
.fullcircle     1540
.gimp    1572
.Xdefaults     1620
.RealNetworks_RealPlayer_60      1696
.civclientrc     1756
.gnome-pm    1792
.gnucash    1820
.gphoto    1852
```

(This is just an excerpt from the output of the preceding code on the files in my home directory.)

This number can be fed to the seekdir function (described next) to place the pointer at a particular location.

seekdir

The seekdir function takes the position number supplied by telldir and uses it to position the readdir function at particular location in the directory.

For example the code

```perl
#!/usr/bin/perl

opendir(CURR, ".");
seekdir(CURR, 1540);
print(readdir CURR );
print "\n";
```

when run on my home directory produces the output

```
.galeon.gimp.arrow.session.Xdefaults.RealNetworks_RealMediaSDK_60.
RealNetworks_RealPlayer_60.RealNetworks_RealShared_00.civclientrc.
balsarc.gnome.pm.gnp.gnucash.gnupg.gphoto.hpbuilder.icewm.icq.jpil
ot.kmysqladmin.mozilla.ncftp.opera.pan.screem.sitescooper.spruce.t
hemes.wine.xcdroast.esd_auth.gArrow.pref.xchat.xmms.xvpicsBackburn
erBrahmsChoicesGNUstepLaptopMP3MailMy Own FilesMyPilotNew
Folder1NewsPilotRealPlayer7aide.0.7appsautosavebincdbackupeth0expa
ndfontsgifsgmysqlhelph_o@h
```

and so on.

Compare that with the code

```
#!/usr/bin/perl

opendir(CURR, ".");
#seekdir(CURR, 1540);
print(readdir CURR );
print "\n";
```

which has the `seekdir` statement commented out. This version produces

```
...Desktop.emacs.bash_logout.bash_profile.bashrc.kde.kderc.screenr
c.gnome.xsessionerrors.Xauthority.gnome_private.enlightenment.mc.s
sh.ICEauthority.gnome-help-browser.gnome-
desktop.netscapensmail.bash_history.sawfish.xauth.gtkrcntp-
4.0.99i-1.i386.rpmSlashdotlesstif-0.87.0-1.i386.rpmnedit-5.02-2.i3
86.rpm.wpo2000.wpo2000rcDocuments.neditdb.nedit.fetchmailrccore.gf
tpBooks.gimp1.1.ssholdprintingmail.pinerc.addressbook.addressbook.
luevolution.cddbslaveMake-1.00.readmeMySQL-
3.22.32-1.i386.rpm.lokiVMware-2.0-476.i386.rpm.vmwarevmwareMySQL-
client-3.22.32-1.i386.rpm
```

and so on. Both versions are reading the same directory, but are starting in different places.

Globs

When we think of the word "glob" we think of a big ball of something viscous that sticks to things. Such is indeed the case in Perl. When you want to deal with a bunch of files that have a certain thing in common, you can use the *file globbing operator* to stick them all together.

When I speak of the files having "a certain thing in common," I'm talking about the file*names*. For example, if you wanted to move all the files in your home directory that had the .pl suffix, to their own directory, you could do it like this:

```
#!/usr/bin/perl

$perldir = "/home/me/perl";

if ( !-e $perldir ) {
```

```
        mkdir $perldir;
    }

    if ( -e $perldir && !-d perldir ) {
        die "a file named $perldir already exists!"
    }

    @perlfiles = <*.pl>;

    foreach $file (@perlfiles) {
        rename($file, "$perldir\/$file");
    }
```

The use of the asterisk character (*) in combination with the angle bracket operator (<>) creates the filename globbing operator. Essentially, the line

```
    @perlfiles = <*.pl>;
```

means "assign to the list @perlfiles any file that has a name ending with .pl." The asterisk, in other words, stands in for any combination of characters.

Done!

SUMMARY

In this session, you learned how to use Perl to manipulate directories. You started by learning to use the opendir command to create a directory handle. Then you learned how to perform read operations on a directory in order to see the files that are stored there. You learned to change directories using the chdir command. You learned to create and destroy directories, and how to find files that have a common element in their names.

QUIZ YOURSELF

1. What is a glob? What can you use one for? (See "Globs.")
2. How does a directory handle differ from a filehandle? (See "Directory Handles.")
3. Why is it dangerous to run the rmdir command as the superuser? (See "Creating and Destroying Directories.")

Using the Operating System

Session Checklist

✔ Binding processes to filehandles

✔ Using the system and exec functions

✔ Using the fork function

***30 Min.
To Go***

Before Perl got popular as a Web scripting language, it found a niche among system administrators. Because of its freeform style, powerful set of functions, and similarities to other system-oriented languages (such as the various Unix shell environments), Perl allowed system administrators to whip up quick utility programs in minutes. The symbiosis between Perl and people who do systems programming has continued to the present, and has led to a great deal of development on those commands and functions that allow Perl programs to interact with many popular operating systems.

In keeping with the rest of this book, my main focus will be on using Perl with the various Unix and Unix-derived operating systems, however, the techniques derived in this session should apply to all operating systems, with the differences coming mainly in how your particular OS handles particular tasks. If you are looking for information on the particularities of using Perl with your OS, I suggest you look on the World Wide Web. The Web is dotted with pages containing information on almost anything pertaining to Perl.

Pipelines

You have already seen a couple of examples of how to make Perl interact with the OS. The first I want to discuss here is using the open function to access another running process on the machine. Recall the example in Session 14:

```perl
#!/usr/bin/perl

$process = "/bin/date|";

open(PROCESS, $process);

while (<PROCESS>) {
        chomp;
        print;
        print "\n";
}
```

This program uses the open function to create a pipeline to the Unix date program, reads the output of that program, and writes it to the standard output. That you want to read from a pipeline is signified by using the Bourne shell-style pipe character (the vertical bar, |) at the left-hand side of the name of the program you wish to access. If you wanted to write to an external process, you'd put the pipe character on the left-hand side of the program's name.

To what productive use can you put this idea of reading from and writing to a process? Suppose you need to send an urgent message to one of your users, but you don't know when he'll be logged in, and you can't rely on his reading his e-mail right away. You could do something like

```perl
#!/usr/bin/perl

$user = "jerry";

open(READPROC, "/usr/bin/w|");
@wout = <READPROC>;
close READPROC;

foreach $name (@wout) {
    if ($name =~ /$user/) {          # This is a pattern-match.
See
                                      # Session 17.
```

Unix pipes

For those readers who need a refresher, or for those who are coming to Perl from operating systems other than those in the Unix family, a brief tutorial on the concept of pipes might be in order.

A *pipe* in Unixese is a way of communicating between processes. In the Bourne shell, which is one of the most popular Unix command environments, the pipe character to signifies that the output from one command is used as the input to another. Thus it is very common to see Unix commands that look like

```
ls | more
```

which pipes the output of the ls command (the directory listing command — analogous to the dir command in DOS) into the more command, which scrolls through a file page-by-page. If the output of the ls command takes up more than one page, the more command will let you look at it a page at a time.

Another way of using pipes in Unix is the *named pipe*. This is a *file* that uses the output of a process as its content. Using a named pipe, processes can use the output of another program simply by reading from the pipe file.

In Perl, the modifiers used in the open command to signify reading, writing, and piping are, "by an amazing coincidence" (read: "quite deliberately"), the same as the Bourne shell symbols for input and output redirection, and for piping.

```
        open(WRITEPROC, "|write $user");
        print WRITEPROC "call me now!!";
        close WRITEPROC;
    }
}
```

This program scans the output of the Unix w command. If it finds the name jerry in that output, it uses the Unix write command to send him a message. You can set this program up as a cron job to run every five minutes and ensure that Jerry gets his message within five minutes of logging on. Plus, if he ignores it, it will continue to bug him every five minutes. (Heh heh heh.) You could make it less evil by enclosing the whole thing in an `unless` loop that would disable it if the message had already been sent:

```perl
#!/usr/bin/perl

$user = "jerry";
$switch = 0

unless ($switch == 1) {
    open(READPROC, "/usr/bin/w|");
    @wout = <READPROC>;
    close READPROC;

    foreach $name (@wout) {
        if ($name =~ /$user/) {

            open(WRITEPROC, "|write $user");
            print WRITEPROC "call me now!!";
            close WRITEPROC;
            $switch = 1;            #flip switch once
                                    #message has been sent.

        }
    }
}
```

20 Min. To Go

The system and exec Functions

`system` and `exec` are two functions that enable you to start external programs without having to bind their inputs or outputs to a filehandle.

system

The more basic of the two is `system`, which works just as if it were a Bourne shell command prompt.

For example, the program with which you started this session,

```perl
#!/usr/bin/perl

$process = "/bin/date|";
```

```
open(PROCESS, $process);

while (<PROCESS>) {
        chomp;
        print;
        print "\n";
}
```

could be handled much more simply, with the line:

```
print( system("/bin/date") );
```

The `system` command passes the output of the `/bin/date` program to the `print` function via the special variable `$_`.

Even more simply,

```
system("/bin/date");
```

will suffice, because the `system` function will cause the `date` program to have the same standard output (in this case, the terminal screen) as the program that called it. Thus, if the normal behavior of the called program (`date` in this example) is to print to the screen, it will do so from within the Perl program as well. That is, unless you assign the output somewhere else by using, for example, an assignment operator:

```
$date = system("/bin/date");
```

There is a certain pitfall in using shell commands from within Perl, and that is that most shell commands return a value of 0 for success, while most Perl commands return a value of 1. If you have code that is dependent on the return value of a shell command, you'll need to keep that in mind.

exec

The `exec` command is similar to the `system` command, except that there is a difference in the way it operates. When you use the `system` command, the Perl program starts a shell, executes the command, and waits for the shell to finish executing the program. Then the output is passed back to the Perl program, which resumes execution.

By contrast, the exec command replaces the Perl program with the shell command that is called. In other words, once the shell program is started, the Perl program has exited. This is important, because if you try to use an exec in the middle of a program, you will not be able to execute the remainder of the Perl program.

backquotes

Backquotes (sometimes called *backticks*), are equivalent to the system command. Thus, instead of doing

```
$date = system("/bin/date");
```

you could also do

```
'$date = `/bin/date`;
```

The only difference here is that while the system function passes the output of the shell command via the standard output, the backquote function captures the output of the enclosed command as a string.

The backtick character can often be found on the key to the immediate left of the number 1 on most keyboards.

**10 Min.
To Go**

Forking

One interesting way of using the operating system is by using it to clone your Perl program using the fork function. fork makes a *system call*, that is, it interacts with the operating system, not by issuing a shell command, but by issuing a command directly to the OS.

Using fork can be a bit tricky, though because of the way in which it works. Every time you fork a process, the new clone — the *child process* — must have some way to exit. If it doesn't, you will create *zombie processes* that don't ever die. They just sit there, taking up space in your OS's process table, and generally slowing things down.

In addition, certain kinds of careless or malicious uses of fork can rapidly fill up your process table and memory, and crash your system. Consider

```
#!/usr/bin/perl
```

```
while (true) {
    fork;
}
```

Since the expression `true` always returns a true value, the condition in the `while` loop is always true. Thus the preceding code will simply loop and loop, continuing to fork off child processes. In addition, each child process does the same thing. The number of processes increases exponentially until the process table overflows. This is called a *fork bomb*.

 Never write fork bombs; even accidentally, if you can help it. Trust me on this. In the process of writing this session, I created a fork bomb that crashed my computer. Fortunately, most of my work was saved, but I could easily have lost a great deal of work because of it. If you run a fork bomb on your own system, you will have the headache of recovering from a crash. If you run a fork bomb on someone else's system, you will probably make an enemy for life.

In order to use `fork` properly, you need to know a little about process management. Under Unix and its derivatives, each running process receives an identification number called a *process ID*, or PID. When you use a `fork`, the return value of the command is the PID of the child process. Thus you can keep track of the child PID by invoking `fork` in this way:

```
$childPID = fork;
```

A second return value, 0, is given to the child process. Thus you can keep track of which process is which with

```
$childPID = fork;
if ($childPID == 0) {
    # I am the child process.
}
else {
    # I am the parent process.
}
```

unless the `fork` failed, in which case the return value is undefined:

```
if ( !defined( childPID=fork() ) ) {
    die "couldn't fork";
}
```

```
elsif (childPID == 0) {
    # I am the child.
}
else
{
        # I am the parent.
}
```

Once the process has forked, the child process is running independently of, and concurrent with the parent process. If this is the desired behavior, all is well and good, however, if both of these processes are producing output, the outputs may become jumbled together, and generally cause confusion. Thus, it is often a good idea for the parent to wait until the child has done its work, and then resume. Here's an example:

```
if ( !defined( childPID=fork() ) ) {
    die "couldn't fork";
}
elsif (childPID == 0) {
    # I am the child.
    exec(some system command);
}
else
{
        # I am the parent.
    wait;
}
```

The wait function suspends execution of the program until the child process exits. An alternative to wait is waitpid. Whereas wait resumes when any child exits, waitpid only resumes when a specific child exits, thus:

```
if ( !defined( childPID=fork() ) ) {
    die "couldn't fork";
}
elsif (childPID == 0) {
    # I am the child.
    exec(some system command);
}
else
{
```

```
     # I am the parent.
     waitpid($childPID, 0);
}
```

The second argument to waitpid — the 0 — is a flag to the waitpid() system call. Not all systems implement the same flags, so use 0 if the flags don't matter. Read the manual page for waitpid to find out what your system's flags are.

Here's how you might use a fork to modify your program that tells your friend Jerry to call:

```perl
#!/usr/bin/perl

$user = "jerry";

$i = 0;

until ($i == 5) {        # We will bug Jerry only five times.

    if ( !defined( $childPID=fork() ) ) {
        die "couldn't fork.\n";
    }
    elsif ($childPID==0) {

        # I am the child, time to bug our guy...

        open(READPROC, "/usr/bin/w|");
        @wout = <READPROC>;
        close READPROC;

        foreach $name (@wout) {
            if ($name =~ /$user/) {
                open(WRITEPROC, "|write $user");
                print WRITEPROC "call me now!";
                close WRITEPROC;
            }
        }
    exit;                # VERY important. Child process must
                    # exit to avoid forking again, thus
                    # creating a fork bomb.

    }
    else {
```

```
# I am the parent.
waitpid($childPID, 0);
sleep 60;      # process waits sixty seconds between
               # messages.
         $i++;
      }
   }
```

The `exit` statement at the end of the child process section is very important. If you don't have a way for the child process to exit, it will return to the top of the loop, and fork another process off from itself, creating a fork bomb. You need a way to stop it before it can loop again. The `exit` function does exactly what you'd expect it to do — causes the program to exit.

Done!

REVIEW

In this session, you learned several ways to make your Perl program call on functions of your computer's operating system. You learned how to use the `open` function to access pipelines, and how to use the `system` and `exec` functions. Finally, you learned how use functions such as `fork` that access system calls.

QUIZ YOURSELF

1. What is the difference between

   ```
   open(PROC, "/bin/someproc|");
   ```

   and

   ```
   open(PROC, "|/bin/someproc");
   ```

   (See "Pipelines.")

2. How do the `system` command and the backquote operator differ? (See "The system and exec functions.")

3. What is a fork bomb? How can you avoid creating one? (See "Forking.")

PART

III

Saturday Afternoon

1. How can you use command line arguments as data in your programs?
2. What does STDIN represent? How is it most commonly used?
3. Explain the use of the diamond operator.
4. What is flow control? Explain the two different types.
5. What are the two functions for conditional flow control?
6. What are the three functions for iterative flow control?
7. What is meant by the term *native function*?
8. If one function is nested inside another, what is the order of execution?
9. What is the purpose of the chomp function?
10. What is a filehandle?
11. How can you use a filehandle to access a process instead of a file?
12. How does a directory handle differ from a filehandle?
13. Why is it very important to be careful about using the unlink function?
14. What is a pipe?
15. What is the main difference between the system function, and the back-quote operator?
16. How can you avoid creating zombie processes when using the fork function?

PART

IV

*Saturday
Evening*

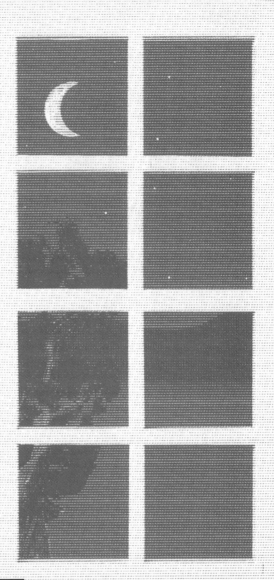

Regular Expressions

Session Checklist

✔ Constructing regular expressions

✔ Using pattern match operators

✔ Using regular expressions and pattern matches in your programs

30 Min. To Go

ne of the areas in which Perl excels is that of handling text. Indeed, Perl is a veritable textual Cuisinart, chopping up lines and paragraphs, extracting some bits, and recombining them in new ways. This is one of the reasons Perl has become so popular for Web-based applications.

What's a Regular Expression?

The core of Perl's text-fu is the *regular expression*. You can think of regular expression as a sort of textual generality. It enables you to describe what a bit of text should look like without actually naming specific text. This sounds rather high-concept, but in practice it makes a lot of sense. Consider: if you stipulate that a certain character, the dot (.) can stand for any other character you can construct expressions based on that idea. The expression h.t would be equivalent to the

words hat or hot. You can extend this idea further. Suppose that the asterisk character (*) will match zero or more of the immediately previous characters. Now you can construct the expression h.*t, which will match hat and hot, and also heat, hoot, heart, or anything else that starts with h and ends with t.

The regular expression operator (*) should not be confused with the filehandle globbing operator, which is discussed in Session 15.

At this point, it should become evident that given a sufficient number of these *wildcard* characters (or *metacharacters*), you can match a simply staggering number of textual possibilities. But it gets even better — you can stipulate character classes (that is, just letters or just numbers), various types of whitespace (spaces and tabs), or position (whether the expression is at the beginning or end of the line). You can specify subsets of characters (e.g., only a, x, or q). You can specify characters of only upper- or lowercase. You can even create expressions that contain other expressions.

Entire books have been written just on the art of creating regular expressions. I won't cover that much material here, but you will get to know the basics of constructing regular expressions, and making use of them in Perl programs.

Constructing Simple Regular Expressions

In the last section, you saw two regular expression operators. You saw the wildcard (.) and the multiplier (*). In this section, you'll see a few more operators, and learn to use them in constructing regular expressions.

Regular expressions are one of the few areas in Perl where the exact format of what you do matters greatly. Things like whitespace, line breaks and the like can really affect the meaning of what you're trying to express.

Character classes

As you saw, the previous dot operator (.), matches any single character. (Actually, that's not strictly true. The dot operator matches any single character as long as it's not the newline character.) The set of characters that is matched by that operator is called a *character class*. The class matched by that operator is a very large one. In many circumstances, you'd probably want to match a more restricted set of characters. Fortunately, there are a few operators to handle those, as we see in Table 17-1

Table 17-1
Predefined Character Class Operators

Operator	Matches
\d	any digit
\w	any word (alphanumeric) character
\s	any whitespace character

In addition, we can negate these classes as seen in Table 17-2:

Table 17-2
Negated Character Classes

Operator	Matches
\D	any nondigit
\W	any nonalphanumeric
\S	any nonwhitespace

In addition to these predefined classes, you can create your own character classes, simply by enclosing a group of characters in square brackets. Thus

```
[aeiou]
```

will match any lower-case vowel, while

```
[aeiouAEIOU]
```

will match any vowel regardless of case.

Like the previous classes, you can negate this class. Do so by placing a carat character (^) at the beginning of the class. Thus

```
[^aeiouAEIOU]
```

will match any nonvowel character.

It is tempting to say here that the class [^aeiouAEIOU] **will match any consonant, but that is not correct. This class will also match numeric and whitespace characters. Remember, when you're creating regular expressions, you're not just dealing with letters, you're dealing with the entire ASCII character set.**

You can use a dash character (-) to indicate a range. Thus

    [a-z]

indicates the entire lowercase alphabet. The class

    [0-9]

is the same as the \d class, and the \w class is the same as

    [a-zA-Z0-9_]

(the underscore character is included in the word class).

By this time, the alert reader has probably wondered how we go about matching the characters that we are using as our operators. What if, for instance, we want to match a period, or a real carat or asterisk? You do that by placing a backslash in front of that character. Thus

    \.

indicates a literal period, while

    *

indicates a literal asterisk. If you want to match a literal backslash,

    \\

is the way to do it.

Multipliers

We have already seen that the asterisk character can be used as a multiplier to match zero or more occurrences of a character. Thus the expression

    B*

will match B, BB, BBB, BBBB, and so on (or no B at all).

A similar operator is the plus sign. The plus sign (+) matches one or more occurrences of the character immediately to its left. Thus

```
B+
```

will match B, BB, and so on.

The question mark character (?) makes the character to its left optional. Thus

```
AB?C
```

will match ABC or AC.

Finally, there is the general multiplier. The general multiplier uses a set of numbers enclosed in curly braces ({}) to indicate that the character immediately to its left should be repeated a certain number of times. Thus

```
B{2,4}
```

will match BB, BBB, and BBBB. If the character on the right is omitted, it means that the maximum number of repeats is unlimited. Thus

```
B{0, }
```

is the same as

```
B*
```

If the comma is omitted, it means "exactly this many." Thus

```
B{10}
```

will match only a string of ten Bs.

Position

**20 Min.
To Go**

Sometimes you need to specify not only *what* to match, but *where* a match should occur. In other words, you may need to specify where on a line a pattern match is to occur.

The carat character (^) indicates that a match needs to occur at the beginning of a line. Thus

```
^Jim
```

would match the line Jim went to the store but not My friend's name is Jim.

The beginning-of-line anchor character should not be confused with the character class negation operator. Even though they both use the carat character, the character class negation operator only occurs within square brackets. Thus,

`[^J]`

is a character class negation, whereas

`^J`

means "Capital J at the beginning of a line."

Similarly, the dollar sign character ($) matches the attached pattern at the end of the line. Thus

`Jim.$`

matches `My friend's name is Jim.` but not `Let's see if Jim is home.`

The final anchor is the word-boundary anchor, \b. This anchor requires that there be a boundary at that position. Thus

`Jim\b`

would match `Jim`, but not `Jimmy`. This can be negated with the \B anchor. This specifies that there must NOT be a boundary there. Thus

`Jim\B`

would match `Jimmy` but not `Jim`.

Alternation

Some times you need to specify an either/or condition. You can do that with the alternation operator, the vertical bar (|). The expression

`Jim|Jerry`

will match either `My friend's name is Jim` or `My friend's name is Jerry`.

Grouping

We can use parentheses to group characters, so that a particular construct is contained in a certain part of the expression. For example:

`(road|foot)race`

will match either `roadrace` or `footrace`. Likewise the expression

```
(a|b)(1|2)
```

will match a1, a2, b1, or b2, whereas

```
a|b1|2
```

will only match a, b1, or 2.

Callbacks

Parentheses can also be used to call back a certain part of a regular expression. This is kind of like attaching a variable name to part of the expression, and then substituting the name in later. To do this, refer to the grouped bit by using an escaped integer. Thus

```
(abc)123\1
```

would match `abc123abc`. If you have a second grouping, you use the next number. Thus:

```
(abc)(123)\1\2
```

would match `abc123abc123`.

Pattern Matching

Now that you know how to construct regular expressions, you need to know how to go about using them in your programs. The first thing to know is that whenever you use a regular expression, you should enclose it between forward slashes, like so:

```
/xyz/
```

This lets the interpreter know that the enclosed text is to be treated as a regular expression, and that the *metacharacters* (operators, anchors and so forth) are to be interpreted in that context. With that in mind, let's look at a simple bit of code. Assume we have a file called sometext.txt, which contains this text:

```
Line one has a haddock
Line two does not have one
Line three does not have a haddock
Line four does
Line five has a haddock
```

and a program that looks like this:

```perl
#!/usr/bin/perl

open(INFILE, "sometext.txt");
open(OUTFILE, ">outtext.txt");

while(<INFILE>) {
    if(/haddock/) {
        print OUTFILE;
    }
}
```

If you run this program, the contents of `outtext.txt` will look like this:

```
Line one has a haddock
Line three does not have a haddock
Line five has a haddock
```

What's happening here, is that each line from INFILE is being passed to the `if` statement via the implicit `$_` variable. Each line is in turn run against the regular expression, which returns `true` if the pattern is matched. For each true match, the line is printed to OUTFILE.

The session here is that you can use a regular expression anywhere you'd use any other type of expression. A match on a regular expression returns `true`, whereas a nonmatch returns `false`.

The binding operator

**10 Min.
To Go**

Another way of using a pattern-match is to bind it to a variable. This is done using the binding operator (=~). This operator is used like so:

```perl
$variablename =~ /regular expression/;
```

Recall this example from Session 16:

```perl
#!/usr/bin/perl

$user = "joe";

$i = 0;

until ($i == 5) {
```

```perl
        if ( !defined( $childPID=fork() ) ) {
                die "couldn't fork.\n";
        }
        elsif ($childPID==0) {

                # I am the child, time to bug our guy...

                open(READPROC, "/usr/bin/w|");
                @wout = <READPROC>;
                close READPROC;

                foreach $name (@wout) {
                        if ($name =~ /$user/) {
                                open(WRITEPROC, "|write $user");
                                print WRITEPROC "call me now!";
                                close WRITEPROC;
                        }
                }
        exit;
        }
        else {
                # I am the parent.
                sleep 5;
                $i++;

        }
}
```

Look closer at this excerpt:

```perl
open(READPROC, "/usr/bin/w|");
@wout = <READPROC>;
close READPROC;

foreach $name (@wout) {
    if ($name =~ /$user/) {
        open(WRITEPROC, "|write $user");
        print WRITEPROC "call me now!";
        close WRITEPROC;
    }
}
```

Here, you have taken the output from your /usr/bin/w process and assigned it to a list variable. You use the foreach statement to iterate over the list elements, assigning each element in turn to the variable $name. Then you use the binding operator to run the value of $name against your regular expression. (In this context, you can think of the binding operator as meaning "contains a match for.") Note that you have substituted a variable containing the value you wish to search for. Putting the variable name inside the slashes tells the interpreter that you wish to interpret the value of that variable as a regular expression.

Substitution

A very powerful use for pattern matching is using it to substitute a new value for the old one. This is done by means of the substitution operator (s). For example,

```perl
s/hello/goodbye/;
```

will substitute the word goodbye wherever the word hello is encountered. Now bring back the fish finder example,

```perl
#!/usr/bin/perl

open(INFILE, "sometext.txt");
open(OUTFILE, ">outtext.txt");

while(<INFILE>) {
    if(/haddock/) {
        print OUTFILE;
    }
}
```

and modify it somewhat to

```perl
#!/usr/bin/perl

open(INFILE, "sometext.txt");
open(OUTFILE, ">outtext.txt");

while(<INFILE>) {
    if(s/haddock/halibut/) {
        print OUTFILE;
    }
}
```

Now the contents of the output file will read

```
Line one has a halibut
Line three does not have a halibut
Line five has a halibut
```

As the lines from INFILE were passed through the if statement, they were oper-
ated on by the substitution operator, thus all haddock were changed to
halibut.

Here's a somewhat more advanced example:

```
#!/usr/bin/perl

open(INFILE, "sometext.txt");
open(OUTFILE, ">outtext.txt");

while(<INFILE>) {
    if(s/ha(\w{2})\w\w*\b/\1/) {
        print OUTFILE;
    }
}
```

Change the sometext.txt text to

```
Line one has a haddock
Line two does not have one
Line three does not have a haddock
Line four does
Line five has a hallway
Line six has a heehaww
```

Now your output will be

```
Line one has a dd
Line three does not have a dd
Line five has a ll
```

This regular expression now searches for the characters ha followed by two of
the same character, followed by at least one word character and then a word
boundary. It then changes the entire pattern to just the two repeating characters,
and prints the line.

A substitution operation can also be bound to a variable, like so:

```
$varname =~ s/reg/exp/
```

This performs the substitution operation, but keeps the value in the variable for later use.

Done!

REVIEW

In this session, you learned how to construct regular expressions using metacharacters. You went on to learn how to use regular expressions in your programs by using their return values, binding them to variables, and using the substitution operator.

QUIZ YOURSELF

1. What is a metacharacter? (See "What's a Regular Expression?")
2. What is the difference between

   `[^Philip]`

   and

   `/^Philip/`

   (See "Character classes.")
3. Write a program that parses a file for the word "bingo." When the word is found, split the line into words, and output the words immediately before, and immediately after bingo. (See "The binding operator.")

Data Transformations

Session Checklist

✔ Using the substr function to extract substrings

✔ Splitting and joining strings

✔ Using assignment to split lists

✔ Transliteration

**30 Min.
To Go**

G iven Perl's facility with text and regular expressions, one of the things that you'll often want to do in your Perl programs is to transform data. That is, you'll sometimes want to take a chunk of text, and make various kinds of changes to it, so that you can use it in ways that wouldn't have been possible with it in its original form.

You saw in Session 17 how to use the s operator to substitute one regular expression for another. This is one kind of data transformation. There are many others, and they all have their uses in different situations.

Finding a Substring

One of the most common operations when dealing with textual data is that of finding a substring. This is, in a sense, what you were doing with the s operator, but in that instance, you were looking for textual patterns. In other cases, you may have no idea what the text will look like, but you might know where it is. You may know, for example, that the interesting part of a certain string might be located exactly fourteen characters from the beginning of the line, and that it is exactly nine characters long. In that case, you can use the substr function to extract it:

```
$substring = substr($string, 14, 9);
```

Thus, if

```
$string = "Now is the time for all good men to come to the aid of
the party.";
```

then the value of $substring would be:

```
e for all
```

Remember that spaces count as characters.

If the value of the second argument — the offset — is a negative number, it is interpreted to be an offset from the end of the string. Thus,

```
$substring = substr($string, -3, 5);
```

will extract the five characters beginning at the third character from the end. Note that the substring still goes from left to right, therefore this particular example will only extract three characters.

Another way you can use the substr function is to replace a substring with another one. For example,

```
$string = "Now is the time for all good men·to come to the aid of
the party.";
```

```
substr($string, 0, 3) = "Later";
```

will produce the output:

```
Later is the time for all good men to come to the aid of the
party.
```

Note that the replacement substring will be shoehorned into the space that you specify using the offset and length.

Splitting and Joining

A related idea is that of splitting a string, and/or joining two strings together. This is done, not surprisingly, with the `split` and `join` functions.

split

Like `substr`, `split` returns a part of a given string, however, there are two important differences. First, instead of returning one chunk of a string, `split` returns a number of chunks, which, when put together form the original string. Second, instead of specifying an offset and length, `split` takes a pattern match and uses that as a delimiter to determine where the string should be split.

If that seems confusing, an example might make it a little clearer. Suppose you have a line of text:

```
$string = "Now is the time for all good men to come to the aid of
the party.";
```

and you wanted it split into individual words. You would use the spaces as delimiters, like so:

```
@words = split(/ /, $string);
```

Now, if you were to do

```
foreach $word (@words) {
    print "$word \n";
}
```

any regular expression could be used as a delimiter; but unless you're doing something horribly complex, you'll probably want to stick to a single character.

The previous snippet could be simplified to:

```
print (split(/ /, @string) . "\n");
```

If you split on a null expression (a regular expression with nothing inside), you can split a string up into individual characters, for example,

```
$string = "Hello.";

@letters = split(//, $string);
foreach $letter (@letters) {
    print "$letter \n";

}
```

would print each letter on a separate line.

join

The `join` function does the opposite of `split`. It joins several strings together into one big string, using an expression as a separator. Thus if you were to do:

```
join(' ', "Now", "is", "the", "time");
```

the resulting output would be

```
Now is the time.
```

Note that in this example, you have used a space as the separator. Similarly, if you were to do

```
join(':', "Now", "is", "the", "time");
```

the resulting output would be

```
Now:is:the:time
```

**20 Min.
To Go**

Splitting Up Lists

Another way of extracting data from a string is to split the elements out of a list and store them individually. There is no function for this, but you can do it implicitly, via assignment. Suppose you have the following list variable:

```
@address = qw(name, street, zip);
```

You can split that list up into its components by doing the following:

```
($n, $a, $z) = @address;
```

Now if you were to

```
print $a;
```

the output would be street.

You can also do this kind of assignment using the split function. Suppose you wanted to get a list of all the usernames on your Unix system. You can do that by parsing the /etc/passwd file. A typical line in /etc/passwd looks like this:

```
nobody:x:99:99:Nobody:/:
```

As you can see, you have a group of fields separated by a colon character. This makes it a perfect candidate for the split function. Here's your program:

```
#!/usr/bin/perl

open(PASS, "/etc/passwd");

while(<PASS>) {
        ($username, $junk) = split(/:/, $_, 2);
        print "$username \n";
}
```

Note that you have added a third argument for your split function. This is a limit, and is a simple integer function. This tells split that you want to have no more than two resulting substrings. By doing this, you can assign the part that you're interested in — the user name — to a variable, and assign the rest to the variable $junk (so named for obvious reasons). By putting the left-hand side of the assignment into a list context, you force each line coming from the /etc/passwd file to be treated as an array, and the values coming from the split function are interpreted as list elements. This causes the values assigned respectively to the scalars on the left.

An Example

You've covered a lot of ground here. The various data-transforming functions and methods are varied and quite flexible. Fortunately, they're fairly easy to use, and make more sense in practice than they do when being discussed.

Here's an example of a program that uses pattern matches and a `split` function to do some interesting things:

```perl
#!/usr/bin/perl

print "Enter your username: ";
chomp($username = <STDIN>);

open(PASS, "/etc/passwd");
@passwd = <PASS>;

foreach $line (@passwd) {
        if($line=~/$username/) {

                ($login, $passwd, $uid, $gid, $realname, $homedir,
$shell) = split(/:/, $line);

                chomp($shell);  # end of line has a \n.

                print "LOGIN ID:\t\t$login \n"
unless ($login eq "");

                print "Your User ID is $uid. \n"
unless ($uid eq "");

                print "Your Group ID is $gid. \n"
unless ($gid eq "");

                print "Your real name is $realname. \n"
unless ($realname eq "");

                print "Your home directory is $homedir. \n"
unless ($homedir eq "");

                print "Your default shell is $shell. \n"
```

```
    unless ($shell eq "");

                last;
        }
}

print "\n";
print "looking for Perl files in your home directory...\n";

opendir(HOME, $homedir) || die "no home directory to open ";

@files = readdir(HOME);

closedir HOME;

foreach $file (@files) {
        open(FILE, "$file");
        while(<FILE>) {
                if(/\#\!\/usr\/bin\/perl/) {
                        print "Found one: $file \n";
                        next;
                }
        }
}
```

Before you read on, see if you can figure out what this program does.

This program prompts you to enter your user name, and then searches the /etc/passwd file for it. When it finds it, it splits the line from /etc/passwd into its component fields, and prints out all of your information, except for your passwd (which is only x anyway since you're displaying good security practices by using shadow passwords). After printing out your user information, it goes into your home directory, opens each file, and looks for a line reading #!/usr/bin/ perl. When it finds one, it prints the name of the file. Thus, it finds all the Perl files in your home directory.

The line that is of particular interest is this:

```
($login, $passwd, $uid, $gid, $realname, $homedir, $shell) =
split(/:/,$line);
```

Each of the scalars on the left-hand side of this statement correspond to a field in an /etc/passwd entry. By splitting the entry on the colon character, you are able to assign each field to its appropriate scalar, and then use the values for whatever purpose you like. You could do the same thing more explicitly like this:

```
@passwd_line = split(/:/, $line);
($login, $passwd, $uid, $gid, $realname, $homedir, $shell) =
@passwd_line;
```

Now, suppose that instead of this section

```
foreach $file (@files) {
        open(FILE, "$file");
        while(<FILE>) {
                if(/\#\!\/usr\/bin\/perl/) {
                        print "Found one: $file \n";
                        next;
                }
        }
}
```

you did this:

```
foreach $file (@files) {
        open(FILE, "$file");
        while(<FILE>) {
                if(s/perl/poil/) {          #EVIL!
                        print "BOOM! \n";
                        next;
                }
        }
}
```

Suddenly, you've transformed this program into a tool of vandalism. You've used the substitution operator to change the word perl to poil. This will cause these programs not to work if you try to run them.

But you're nicer than that. You want to write something that's helpful. So return to your original program, and modify it so that each Perl program found has its name changed to add a .pl suffix if it doesn't already have one:

```
DIVE: foreach $file (@files) {    #We're DIVE-ing for Perls. Get
                                  # it? Ugh.
        open(FILE, "$file");
        while(<FILE>) {
                if(/\#\!\/usr\/bin\/perl/) {
```

```
if ($file =~ /.*\.pl/) {
        next DIVE;
}
else
{
        print ("changing $file to $file" .
"\.pl \n");

        rename ($file, "$file\.pl");
}
        }
    }
}
```

**10 Min.
To Go**

Transliteration

The final data transformation to consider here is that of transliteration.
Transliteration is somewhat different from the transformations you've seen so far,
in that it operates only on text strings, not on regular expressions or variables.

A transliteration is a way of changing all of a certain instance of a string of
characters to a new string of characters. There are many circumstances under
which a simple substitution (using the s operator) can do the same thing, but the
transliteration operator — tr — can also swap two strings, which would be impossible with substitution since the second substitution would undo all the changes
the first one made. Here's a simple example of transliteration in action:

```
$string = "mick and keith";
tr/mk/km/;
```

Now your $string is kicm and meith.

The tr operator can also be used in the same way as the s operator:

```
$string = "mick and keith";
tr/mick/keith/;
```

Now your $string is keith and keith.

If the string you're using as a replacement is shorter than the string it is replac-
ing, the string will repeat to pad out the string to its original number of characters. Thus,

```
$string = "mick and keith";
tr/mick/x/;
```

will yield xxxx and keith. (I like to call this one the *redaction operator*.)

You can also use character ranges such as

```
tr/a-z/A-Z/;
```

and the like.

In addition, there are several modifiers to the tr operator that modify its behavior. The c modifier will cause the replacement to be applied to everything that *isn't* the original string. For example,

```
$string = "mick and keith";
tr/aeiou/x/c;
```

would yield a $string of xixx axx xeixx.

The d modifier suppresses the tr operator's padding behavior. Thus,

```
$string = "mick and keith";
tr/mick/x/d;
```

would make our $string equal to x and keith.

The tr operator can be bound to a variable name in the same way that the s operator is — with the =~ assignment operator:

```
$stones = "mick and keith";
$stones =~ tr/mick/x/;
```

In this way, you can run transforms on a string even if it's not being used as the current value of $_.

Done!

REVIEW

In this session, you learned various ways of dealing with string data. You learned how to extract a substring, how to split a string into component parts, and how to join stings together to make larger strings. You also learned how to split a list variable into its component scalars. Finally, you learned to use the transliteration operator to make substitutions in your text.

QUIZ YOURSELF

1. Explain the difference between the substitution operation and the transliteration operator. (See "Transliteration.")

2. Explain the difference between the `split` and `substr` functions. (See "Splitting and Joining.")

3. Write a program that splits a paragraph of text into lines, and prints the paragraph with a line number in front of each line. (See "Splitting and Joining.)

Session Checklist

✔ Creating formats

✔ Using formats to structure output

✔ Switching formats

✔ Top-of-page formats

30 Min.
To Go

Between data transformations and regular expressions, you've seen a lot of ways to wrangle the content of text. That is, you can take a line of text, find substrings, find regular expressions, work substitutions, and generally perform all kinds of slice-and-dice operations on the text strings. But wouldn't it be nice if you could wrangle the form as well as the content of textual elements? Sure, you could probably manage something along these lines with creative use of regular expressions and print statements, but that would take an awful lot of time and effort. Perl to the rescue once again!

What's a Format?

Simply put, a format is a way of defining how a certain type of output will be presented on the screen or page. It allows the programmer to create a template that will be used as the formal description for whatever output she chooses to plug into it.

A format consists of constant elements, such as titles, column headers, labels, and the like, and variable elements whose values will be substituted into fields, whose form and location you can specify.

How to Create a Format

There are three parts to a format: literal text, variables, and fieldholders. *Fieldholders* are special groupings of characters that tell the interpreter how the variable text is to be displayed. The three elements are grouped together in a *format definition*, which can appear anywhere in your program text. A typical format definition might look something like this:

```
format MYFORMAT =
HEADER1     HEADER2     HEADER3
@<<<<<<<<   @<<<<<<<<   @<<<<<<<<
$datum1,    $datum2,    $datum3
.
```

In this example, MYFORMAT is the name of the format. You will use the name later when you start directing output to the format. The dot on a line by itself indicates the end of the format. The textual elements HEADER1,HEADER2, and HEADER3 are literal text, and will be displayed as shown. The scalars $datum1, $datum2, and $datum3 are variable data, and the strings of characters that look like @<<<<<<<< are fieldholders. In this example, each fieldholder represents a nine-character, left-justified string. The values of our three variables will be loaded into the fields when the format is printed.

Whenever you define a format, the layout you define is considered to be the most important feature. If the value of a variable is too long for the field to which it corresponds, it will be truncated. If it is too short, it will be padded with spaces. Thus, if you define columns as I have done previously, the column format will always be preserved, even if the whole of your data isn't.

Fieldholders

You saw previously that the fieldholder @<<<<<<<< represents a nine-character, left-justified field. Note that there are nine characters (including the @) in the fieldholder, and that the angle brackets are pointing to the left. The number of characters allowed in the field will always match the number of characters in the fieldholder. In a left-justified field such as this one, if the value of the variable to be substituted is shorter than the length of the field, the field will be padded with spaces on the right-hand side of the value.

You can specify a right-justified field by using rightward pointing angle brackets:

@>>>>>>>>

If you do this, the field will be padded with spaces on the left-hand side of the value.

If you use the vertical bar character, like so:

@||||||||

you will create a centered field. The spaces will be padded on both sides of the value so that the value is centered in the field.

Numeric fieldholders are created using the hashmark character:

@######.##

The dot here is interpreted as a decimal point.

You can define a field of arbitrary length by using the construction:

@*

This is used for fields that are expected to take up more than one line. In this instance, the data is presented exactly as it appears in the original string. This is called a *multiline field*.

Finally, you have a constructor that is used to wrap long text. It is called a *filled field*, and it looks like this:

^<<<<<<<<<<<<<<

This is used anywhere you'd like to have multiple lines formatted in a specific way. For example, you might have something like:

Part IV—Saturday Evening

Session 19

```
format CATALOG_ENTRY =

Item: @<<<<<<<<<<<<<    Description: ^<<<<<<<<<<<<<<<<<<<<<<<<
      $item_name                       $item_desc


^<<<<<<<<<<<<<<<<<<<<<<
                                             $item_desc


^<<<<<<<<<<<<<<<<<<<<<<
                                             $item_desc


^<<<<<<<<<<<<<<<<<<<<<<<<
                                             $item_desc


^<<<<<<<<<<<<<<<<<<<<<<<<
                                             $item_desc

.
```

Note that you have multiple references to a single scalar value ($item_desc).
You are assuming that this will be a long string. What happens is that the value of
$item_desc will wrap to the next line when it exceeds the length of the field.
Thus, if you had

```
$item_name = "1999 Strat"
```

and

```
$item_desc = "1999 Fender American Standard Stratocaster. Red.
Alder body, Maple neck, white pickguard. \$699"
```

when printed, the entire output would look like this:

```
Item: 1999 Strat     Description: 1999 Fender American
                                  Standard Stratocaster.
                                  Red. Alder Body, Maple
                                  neck, white pickguard.
                                  $699
```

You can also use the tilde character (~) to make your filled field expandable:

```
format CATALOG_ENTRY = Item: @<<<<<<<<<<<<<    Description:
^<<<<<<<<<<<<<<<<<<<<<<<~~
      $item_name                       $item_desc
```

```
^<<<<<<<<<<<<<<<<<<<<<<<<
                                                          $item_desc
.
```

By placing two consecutive tildes at the end of the fieldholder's first line, you're telling the interpreter "Repeat this until you get a blank line." This way, you can have an item description of any length, and you don't have to worry about running out of space in your filled field.

Using Formats

Now that you know how to create formats, you need to learn how to go about using them in your programs. You do this by using the write function, which takes a filehandle as an argument. By default, the Perl interpreter will automatically use the format that has the same name as the filehande. This allows you to have multiple formats in the same program without having to be overly concerned with which one is being used at any given time.

Let's look at an example:

```
#!/usr/bin/perl

format PASSINFO =
USER            REAL NAME       SHELL         HOMEDIR
@<<<<<<<<       @<<<<<<<<<<<<    @<<<<<<<<     @<<<<<<<<<<<<
$username,      $realname,      $shell        $homedir
.

open(PASS, "/etc/passwd");
open(PASSINFO, ">passinfo.txt");

while(<PASS>) {
        ($username, $passwd, $uid, $gid, $realname, $homedir,
$shell) =
                split(/:/, $_);
        write(PASSINFO);
}
```

This program once again parses the information in the /etc/passwd file, only this time, it prints a formatted list of four columns corresponding to the userID, real name, shell, and home directory for each user on the system. Note that before you can use the write function, you must have a value assigned to each variable that is used in the format. Here, you've done that using the split function.

You can override the default format behavior of the write command by setting the $~ special variable. Suppose you wanted to use your PASSINFO format, but you wanted to print the output to the screen instead of to the passinfo.txt file. You could do so like this:

```perl
open(PASS, "/etc/passwd");

while(<PASS>) {
        ($username, $passwd, $uid, $gid, $realname, $homedir,
$shell) =
                split(/:/, $_);
     $~ = "PASSINFO";
        write;
}
```

Now your program will write to <STDOUT> but will use the PASSINFO format. In a complex program, don't forget to reset the value of $~ like so:

```perl
$~ = "STDOUT";
```

An Example

Here's an example of how you might go about putting formats to practical use:

```perl
#!/usr/bin/perl -w

print q(

    Please select one of the following:

        1. Look up an entry
        2. Add an entry

--> );

$option = <STDIN>;
```

```perl
chomp $option;

if($option eq "1") {
     # Look up an entry
     print "Enter text to search: ";
     chomp($lookup_txt = <STDIN>);
     open (DIRFILE, ".phonebook");
     @lines = <DIRFILE>;
     foreach $line (@lines) {
          if($line =~ /$lookup_txt/) {
               ($name, $num, $street, $city, $state, $zip, $phone)
=
                    split(/:/, $line);
               $~ = "OUTFORMAT";
               write;
          }
     }
     close DIRFILE;

}
else {
     # Add an entry
     print "Name: ";
     chomp($name = <STDIN>);
     print "Street number: ";
     chomp($num = <STDIN>);
     print "Street name: ";
     chomp($street = <STDIN>);
     print "City: ";
     chomp($city = <STDIN>);
     print "State: ";
     chomp ($state = <STDIN>);
     print "Zip Code: ";
     chomp($zip = <STDIN>);
     print "Phone number: ";
     chomp($phone = <STDIN>);

     $addline = join ':', $name, $num, $street, $city, $state,
$zip, $phone;
     open (DIRFILE, ">>/home/joe/share/\.phonebook");
```

```
    print DIRFILE "$addline \n";
    close DIRFILE;
    print "$name added to phonebook file. \n"

}

format OUTFORMAT =

Name:    @<<<<<<<<<<<<<<<<<<<<<<<<<<<<
         $name
Address: @<<<< @<<<<<<<<<<<<<<<
      $num, $street
      @<<<<<<<<<<< @<, @<<<<
      $city,       $state, $zip
Phone:   @<<<<<<<<<
         $phone
```

This program is an interactive phone book program. It stores data in a file named.phonebook in the current directory. Information in this file is of the form:

```
Name:Street number:Street name:City:State:Zipcode:Phone number
```

If the user chooses the first option, she is prompted for some text to search. This text can be any text that appears in the entry. (It could also be a regular expression.) When the search text is found, the entry is printed to the standard output via the `write` function, using the OUTFORMAT format. (If the search text appears in more than one entry, both entries will be printed.)

If the user chooses the second option, she will be able to input a new entry. She will be prompted for each piece of information, and then the program uses a `join` statement to create the entry for printing into the .phonebook file. An alternative way of preparing the information to be saved might be to use another format such as:

```
format SAVEFORM =
$name:$num:$street:$city:$state:$zip:$phone
```

and then using a `write` statement to write that information to the .phonebook file. In this case, it doesn't really matter which method you use, however, if you want your stored information to be highly formatted, the latter method might be more suitable.

**10 Min.
To Go**

Top-of-Page Formats

Top-of-page formats are a special subspecies of format that are intended to be used when you plan to print your output. When writing to a formatted filehandle, the existence of a top-of-page format will cause the Perl interpreter to arrange the output in groups of lines (60 lines by default, but you can change that). If an entry in your format won't fit in the current page's remaining lines, the interpreter will print a form-feed character, and reprint any header-type information that may be contained in the top-of-page format.

Keep in mind that any top-of-page format is related to another regular format, and a top-of-page format cannot function by itself.

A top-of-page format is created by defining a format in the same way that you would for an ordinary format, but the name of a top-of-page format always ends with _TOP. Thus, you could define a top-of-page format for your earlier catalog format like so:

```
format CATALOG_ENTRY_TOP =
Catalog of inventory items.         Page @<
                                        $%
```

Now, whenever you write to the CATALOG_ENTRY format, the output will be broken up into pages, and the header you specified above will be added to each page. $% is a special variable that keeps track of the number of times the top-of-page header has been called, and thus makes a handy page counter.

As I mentioned previously, the default number of lines per page is 60, however, if you need to change that, you can do so by setting the special variable $=. This variable contains the number of lines per page for the current filehandle. You must make sure that the current filehandle is the one to which you want to apply the format. If you set the variable in the wrong place, you could end up changing the value for the wrong format. $= takes the simple number of lines per page as a value. Thus,

```
$= = 50;
```

would set the value at 50 lines per page.

As with ordinary formats, you can change the top-of-page format name so that the top-of-page format being used is a different one. You do that by setting the special variable $^. Thus if you wanted to use a different top-of-page format with your catalog format, you could do this:

```
$^ = "SOMEOTHER_FORMAT_TOP";
```

Done!

REVIEW

In this session, you learned how to create and deploy formats in your programs. You learned how to use fieldholders to position text, and how to use the values of particular variables to fill in your fields. Finally, you learned to use top-of-page formats to format text for printing.

QUIZ YOURSELF

1. Why is there a dot at the end of each format? (See "What's a Format?")
2. What is the significance of the $= variable? Of the $~ variable? (See "Using Formats.")
3. Expand the simple phone book program in this session to include an option for deleting lines and an option for editing lines. (See "An Example.")

Functions II: User-Created Functions and Subroutines

Session Checklist

✔ Creating subroutines

✔ Using subroutines in your programs

✔ Passing data to subroutines

✔ Returning values from subroutines

30 Min.
_To Go_

U p to this point, the vast majority of the programming you've done has been completely linear. That is, it starts at the top of the program and works its way line by line to the bottom. This kind of structure has an attractive simplicity: in order to follow the working of a program, one need only read it top-to-bottom. The downside of this approach is that in practice, you end up repeating a lot of code. Any time you need to do something in the same way that it had been done previously (which tends to happen a lot in programming), you find yourself writing something similar to — or exactly the same as — something you've already written.

Fortunately, Perl lets the programmer define functions and subroutines that can be called from any place in the program. This allows you to avoid duplicating your efforts, since you need only write any given routine once, but you can use it any number of times.

Revisiting the Concept

Let's take a minute to step back from the minutia of actual programming and look at the big picture. Think for a moment about the Perl native functions. What are they, really? They are *reserved words* which, when invoked and given certain types of arguments, produce for us a given type of result. In a very broad sense, isn't that what programs themselves are? While it's true that programs may have a more interactive type of input and output, and are generally more complex, the actual conceptual difference between a function and a program is quite small, and mostly a matter of degree rather than substance.

So you can think of a function as being a sort of prefab miniprogram that you can include within bigger programs. Conversely, you can think of your programs as being a sort of giant metaprogram that is mainly concerned with the manipulation of smaller programs (the functions). In fact, the whole of computer operations can be thought of in these terms. Your computer's processor is a collection of millions of circuits, which are organized into logical arrangements (called *microcode*). These arrangements are abstracted into a command language that the chip's manufacturer publishes. This command language is abstracted into an *assembly language*, which is somewhat more "human friendly," but still controls the operations of the process at a very fine-grained level. Assembly language is then abstracted into somewhat higher-level languages, such as C. When C code is compiled, the compiler basically converts it into machine code so that it can control the processor directly. Then you have Perl, which is interpreted via a program (the interpreter) that is written in C. Thus whenever you write a Perl program, you are actually writing a program that controls a program that controls a program that controls the processor. Phew!

In that context, then, it makes sense that you might write a program whose primary purpose is to be used within a larger program. These programs would not be any different in that respect from the miniprograms that are the native functions, and would be used in the same way. In fact, this is more than just a conceptual possibility. The writing of functions is a VERY common programming practice. It is probably not an exaggeration to say that in programming of any complexity, the writing of functions is the dominant portion of the activity.

Creating Your Own Functions

Now that we've stretched our brain on the theoretical side of functions, let's move on to the relatively easy part — actually writing them.

Nonlinear programming

I said at the top of this session that up till now, all of your programming was done top-to-bottom. With the introduction of subroutines, all this changes. Your subroutines can appear anywhere in the program (though it is common to group them all together at the beginning or at the end), and can include anything that might appear in any program, including other subroutines, or even themselves (in the case of recursive functions — explained later in this session). This greatly expands your bag of programming tricks, but it also forces you to change the way you think about programming. Instead of thinking of the program as a straight line that goes from the top to the bottom, you must now think of is as something of an integrated whole.

Each time you use a subroutine, you find yourself whisked off to a different part of the program, and when the subroutine is finished, you are whisked back to where you left off. If the subroutine invokes another subroutine, you are whisked from the first subroutine to the second, back to the first, and then back to the main part of the program. If the subroutine calls itself, you are whisked from the main program to the subroutine, to a second (and possibly third, fourth, or hundredth) iteration of the same subroutine, and back.

Instead of thinking about your program as a linear succession of steps, you must now think of your program as a machine with many parts that all interact with each other. In order for the whole machine to work, each part must perform its function properly. As a programmer, you must be able to keep all of these relationships in mind. It is not always easy to develop this mindset, but once done, you will find that what you can accomplish with your programs will take a quantum leap.

I have referred to functions that the programmer writes as user-created functions and also as subroutines. These are the same thing, and from this point on, I'll prefer *subroutine* as I believe it is somewhat more descriptive.

One creates a subroutine according to the following format:

```
sub name {
    some code;
}
```

sub is a special word that lets the interpreter know that what comes next is a subroutine definition. name is the name that you give your subroutine. This can be anything as long as it doesn't conflict with any other function's name. (As a matter of practice, though, it's best to name it something descriptive. It may seem cute to name a subroutine harry, but it'll vex you when you forget what harry was supposed to do.) The name is followed by curly braces ({}), inside of which is the code that makes up the function. A simple (and rather useless) example of a subroutine might look like this:

```
sub say_my_name {
    print $name;
}
```

Now, anyplace the say_my_name subroutine is invoked, it will print out the value of the variable $name.

**20 Min.
To Go**

Using the Functions You Create

You use your subroutines in a program in the same way that you use native functions — by creating statements and expressions that use them. The only difference is that in using a subroutine, you must include parentheses after the name of the function, as illustrated in the following:

```
#!/usr/bin/perl

# This is the main part:
$name = "Joe";
say_my_name();

# This is the subroutine:
sub say_my_name {
    print "$name \n";
}
```

When the interpreter reaches a part of a program where a subroutine is called, it immediately skips to where the subroutine is defined, executes that code, and then jumps back to where it left off.

Return values

Like native functions, subroutines have a return value. By default, the return value of a subroutine is the return value of the last statement evaluated within the subroutine. Thus, given

```perl
#!/usr/bin/perl

$name = joe;
print(say_my_name(), "\n");

sub say_my_name {
        print "$name \n";
}
```

the return value of the subroutine will be 1, because the line will have been successfully printed. If you run this program, the output will be:

```
Joe
1
```

If you want to change the return value produced by the subroutine, you can do so using the `return` function:

```perl
#!/usr/bin/perl

$name = joe;
print(say_my_name(), "\n");

sub say_my_name {
        print "$name \n";
        return "done";
}
```

This will produce the output:

```
Joe
done
```

This is a trivial example. The `return` function becomes much more useful when your subroutine actually produces some data. For example,

```perl
#!/usr/bin/perl

$a = 5;
$b = 3;
print(add_a_and_b(), "/n");

sub add_a_and_b {
    $c = $a + $b;
    return $c;
}
```

returns the value of the addition operation.

Passing arguments to functions

Many Perl native functions take arguments. The print function, for example takes as arguments the data it is supposed to print, as well as (optionally) a filehandle that tells where to print it. Arguments make a function much more useful in that they can modify the behavior of the function in response to certain conditions.

Your subroutines can also take arguments. As you saw previously, when you invoke a subroutine, you follow the name with parentheses. If you place anything inside these parentheses, it is interpreted as an argument, and is assigned to a special variable — the list variable @_.

The @_ variable is local to the subroutine. That is, it exists only within the subroutine, so that each subroutine in your program can have its own @_ variable without conflicting with other subroutines.

Consider the following:

```perl
#!/usr/bin/perl

print( add_us(2,3), "\n");

sub add_us {
    $result = $_[0] + $_[1];
    return $result;
}
```

Remember that the scalar values $_[0] and $_[1] correspond to the first two elements of the list @_. This means that you can pass any two values to the subroutine, and they will be added here. Try modifying the program to make it a little more general:

```perl
#!/usr/bin/perl

print "We need two numbers to add together. \n";
print "Enter the first number: ";
chomp($a = <STDIN>);
print "Enter the second number: ";
chomp($b = <STDIN>);

print("The result is: ", add_us($a,$b), "\n");

sub add_us {
    $result = $_[0] + $_[1];
    return $result;
}
```

You can think of the @_ variable as being a sort of subroutine-specific version of the @ARGV variable. Just as the @ARGV variable lets you pass arguments to the program when you run it, the @_ variable lets you pass arguments to the subroutine when you call it.

Whenever possible, you should try to get data in and out of your subroutines using arguments and return values rather than global variables. The reason for this is that at some point, you might want to extract your function and use it in other programs. If you've used global variables in your subroutine, you'll have to change them to suit each and every program you write, whereas using arguments and return values, you should simply be able to plug them in anywhere you need them.

**10 Min.
To Go**

Private variables

When you write subroutines, it's usually a good thing to keep the variables in a given function separate from the variables in other functions, and the variables pertaining to the program as a whole. This helps you to keep organization within your program. Note in the last subroutine shown in the previous section that the variable @- exists only within that function. When a variable is thus limited to a single function it is called a *private* variable. Other functions have their own @_ variables, but they never conflict because the Perl interpreter knows that they are meant to be private.

Such is not the case with variables you define in your subroutines. In the absence of any indication to the contrary, the interpreter will assume that they are the same as the variables that are used in the rest of the program. That is, the interpreter will assume that they are *global* variables.

If you want to create a private variable, you do so by using the my function, like so:

```
my $varname = value;
```

When the interpreter sees the word my, it knows that the variable is not intended to exist outside the function in which it is defined. You can have variables with the same name in other functions, or within the main structure of the program and they will be kept separate.

Recursive Functions

Recursive functions are functions that call themselves. A general example of a recursive function might be:

```
sub I_Am_Recursive {
    I_Am_Recursive();
}
```

Those of us trained in the language arts may well balk at the idea that a function can be part of its own definition, but from a functional point of view, there is no reason why a function can't be recursive. In fact, the only thing that differentiates a recursive function from a nonrecursive function is the requirement that a recursive function must have some sort of ending condition built in. This is not so much a formal requirement as a practical one. The previous general case has no ending condition, and therefore will continue to call itself forever. The ending condition is needed to avoid these kinds of infinite loops.

You have already met one recursive function, and it is worth calling it back for another look:

```
#!/usr/bin/perl
sub hunt {

    my $working = shift;        # Take this directory's name from
                                # the "command line"

    my $start = `pwd`;
```

```
chdir($working) || die "couldn't change to $working";
opendir(THISDIR, ".");   # open current directory

my @list = readdir(THISDIR)
foreach $file (@list) {
    next if ".";        # ignore current directory
    next if "..";       # ignore parent directory
    if ($file eq "lostfile.txt") {
        print("found ".`pwd`.$file);
        exit 1;         # quit with success!
    }
    elsif (-d $file) {
        hunt($file);    # this is the recursive
        next;           # bit.
    }
    chdir($start);
}
}

hunt(".");
```

Note the way the recursive part of this function works. If the file found is not your target file, but is a directory, the function calls itself to work on the directory. The end condition here is implicit. The function will stop calling itself when there are no more subdirectories to be examined. Good uses of recursive programming often have these sorts of implicit end conditions, whereas you might cast a somewhat more suspicious eye on recursive functions for which you have to jump through hoops in order to construct an end condition.

Good Style Using Subroutines

The use of subroutines is generally considered to be good programming style, at least in contrast to huge files with repeated chunks of code. However, when you use subroutines, try to keep a few things in mind:

- Make the subroutines as general as you can so that they can be applied in varying situations.

- Make subroutines logical and clear in terms of how they process arguments and in terms of the values they return. Before you start writing a subroutine, think about the kinds of input it'll handle and the kinds of data you want it to output. Do you want the return value to be Boolean (simple success or failure); or do you want it to compute or transform some data?

- Make sure that wherever a subroutine calls another subroutine, the subsequent subroutine does what you think it's going to do. That is, if you change a subroutine that is called somewhere else, go back and check the calling function to make sure you haven't accidentally broken it.

- Use private variables wherever possible.

- If you write a recursive function, make sure you have an end condition.

Done!

REVIEW

In this session, you learned how to create subroutines. You learned how to incorporate subroutines into your program, and how to use them to manipulate data. Finally, you learned how to program effectively using subroutines.

QUIZ YOURSELF

1. Why is it often a good thing to create your own functions? (See "Revisiting the Concept.")

2. Describe the function of the @_ variable. (See "Passing arguments to functions.")

3. What is a recursive function? How are recursive functions used? What is the danger inherent in using recursive functions? (See "Recursive Functions.")

PART

IV

Saturday Evening

1. What is a regular expression?

2. When creating regular expressions, how are character classes created?

3. Construct a regular expression that will match all three of these phrases: 1) "Firetruck", 2) "fit as a buck", and 3) "flick" but will not match "folk."

4. Given:

   ```
   $string = "Hello to all my friends";
   $frag = substr($string, -2, 4);
   print $frag;
   ```

   what will be the output?

5. Given a list, what is the easiest way to assign its contents to separate scalars?

6. How does transliteration differ from simple substitution?

7. What is the difference between a fieldholder that looks like this:

   ```
   @<<<<<<<<<
   ```

   and one that looks like this:

   ```
   @>>>>>>>>>
   ```

8. Explain the significance of a filled field line with two tilde characters at the end.

9. What is the meaning of the special variable $~? How is it used with formats?

10. What is the difference between a subroutine and a function?

11. What are the advantages of using subroutines in your programs?

12. Explain the significance of the special variable @_.

☑ Friday

☑ Saturday

☑ **Sunday**

PART

V

Sunday Morning

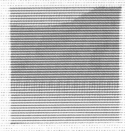

Getting and Installing Packages and Modules

Session Checklist

✔ Learning about packages and modules

✔ Installing packages and modules using the CPAN interface

✔ Installing packages and module without CPAN

30 Min.
To Go

I t has been remarked that Perl is a language for lazy programmers. That isn't to say that Perl programmers are incorrigible slackers who never do any work (really!), but rather that Perl is designed so that common and repetitive programming tasks can be handled with minimal effort. Perl hackers have taken this idea to heart, and a frequent brand of one-upmanship in the Perl community is to accomplish a task using a shorter program than your neighbor.

From a certain perspective, this has less to do with actual laziness than with a certain admiration for the beauty of efficiency. The shorter the program, the less energy put into writing. Using less energy to accomplish a given task implies greater efficiency. Greater efficiency means there's more energy to be used for other tasks. So the so-called laziness of the Perl hacker is just a disguise for getting as much done as possible in the shortest amount of code.

Among the types of inefficiencies that Perl hackers abhor, duplication of effort ranks right up there. One will often hear Perl hackers speak disdainfully of "reinventing the wheel." After all, the wheel has already been invented. If we had to reinvent it every time we wanted to use one, we wouldn't get much done.

In practice, the Perl programmer's disdain for duplication of effort manifests in the idea that if someone else has already solved a particular problem, you are better off using their solution than you are in coming up with a solution of your own. The flip side of this is, if you come up with a solution to a problem that is either new, or better than the existing solution, the Perl community would be awfully happy if you shared it with the world. Sharing solutions is the basic idea behind Perl's package and module infrastructure.

What Are Packages and Modules?

Packages and modules are two different forms of abstracting subroutines. A package creates a separate namespace for variable and subroutine names. Recall that when you created subroutines in your programs, you tried as much as possible to use local variables and to keep the subroutines from interfering with each other and with the program as a whole. Packages give an explicit way to do this.

By declaring a package, all of the variables and all of the subroutines in the package will be local to that package. In order to use them, you must name the package explicitly. You would use a package where you had a large number of subroutines and wanted to keep them separate from the main part of the program. That way, a subroutine could have a variable named $norbert, and the main part of the program could also have a variable named $norbert, and there would be no conflict between the two.

A module is a special kind of package. A module has been gussied up with a few special magical incantations to make it portable. That is, any module can be used in any program, as long as you follow a couple of simple procedures.

The best thing about modules is that there are lots of them already in existence. Modules are the means by which Perl programmers share their code, and there are a huge number of modules that exist to perform a mindboggling assortment of tasks.

Each module provides a set of subroutines that you can use exactly like you would use native functions, except that the functions contained in the modules generally have a very specific purpose.

For example, later in this section, we'll be looking at the DBI module. This is a module that provides a set of functions specifically designed for talking to database programs (DBI stands for *database interface*). This module provides, for example, the dbi->connect function, which makes a network connection to a database.

Fun with CPAN

Because modules are such a big part of Perl, the standard Perl distribution comes with a handy program that helps you find and install them. The program is called CPAN, so called because it uses the Comprehensive Perl Archive Network (CPAN). CPAN is a repository of many modules contributed by many authors. You can visit the CPAN Web site at www.cpan.org.

Using CPAN, you can connect directly to a CPAN repository site (there are several), download, and install modules all from a single interface. Obviously, your computer needs to be connected to the Internet in order for this to work.

CPAN has two modes — an interactive mode, and a noninteractive mode. In this session we will only be concerned with the interactive mode. If you want to learn how to use the noninteractive mode, read the CPAN perldoc **page (**perldoc **CPAN).**

To start the CPAN interface, type

```
perl -MCPAN -e shell
```

at a system prompt.

The -MCPAN **syntax is the way that Perl lets you invoke modules on the command line. The CPAN interface is provided by the CPAN module, which should have been installed when you installed the main Perl distribution. If invoking the CPAN interface in this way doesn't work, you may not have installed the CPAN module, in which case, you'll have to download and install it manually (see the next section for how to do that.)**

You should get a CPAN prompt that looks like this:

```
cpan>
```

If you have problems doing this, you may need to have superuser privileges in order to access some of the resources needed for the CPAN program to work. Become root if you can. If you can't, ask your system administrator what you can do.

The first time you use CPAN, you may need to configure the program before you can use it. If you see a screen that looks like this:

```
CPAN is the world-wide archive of perl resources. It consists of
about 100 sites that all replicate the same contents all around
the globe. Many countries have at least one CPAN site already. The
resources found on CPAN are easily accessible with the CPAN.pm
module. If you want to use CPAN.pm, you have to configure it
properly.

If you do not want to enter a dialog now, you can answer 'no' to
this question and I'll try to autoconfigure. (Note: you can
revisit this dialog anytime later by typing 'o conf init' at the
cpan prompt.)

Are you ready for manual configuration? [yes]
```

Then you will need to configure the program. Even if you don't get this screen automatically, it's still a good idea to configure the program. To do this type

```
o conf init
```

at the cpan> prompt.

Once you've done that, CPAN will ask you a series of questions with a default option in square brackets at the end. To accept the default option, simply press the Enter key. To change the option, type the new value and press Enter. The questions are fairly well explained by the program so we won't go into them here, except to say that you will need to know the pathnames of certain programs on your system. These are fairly easy to find using the which command. Once you've finished the configuration program, the cpan> prompt will return, and CPAN will again be ready for action.

Getting Information

**20 Min.
To Go**

The first thing you'll probably want to do is to use the CPAN program to get information about particular modules. This is done using any of the display commands shown in Table 21-1.

Table 21-1
CPAN Display Commands

Command	Action
a	Authors
b	Bundles
d	Distributions
m	Modules
i	Any

Authors returns a list of authors of various modules. Bundles are prepackaged bundles of modules that you might need for a particular purpose. For example, if you wished to do a lot of work with XML, you might install Bundle::XML, which contains a lot of modules designed for XML processing. Distributions are package files, usually in tar.gz format. Modules returns a list of modules, and the i option will return any author, bundle, distribution, or module that suits the search criterion. Any of these display commands can take a string or regular expression as an argument. Thus

```
cpan> i DBI
```

returns the following:

```
Bundle        Bundle::DBI    (T/TI/TIMB/DBI-1.18.tar.gz)
Module        DBI            (T/TI/TIMB/DBI-1.18.tar.gz)
2 items found
```

For more information about the bundle, you can do

```
cpan> b DBI
Bundle id = Bundle::DBI
    CPAN_USERID  TIMB (Tim Bunce <dbi-users@perl.org>)
    CPAN_VERSION 1.03
    CPAN_FILE    T/TI/TIMB/DBI-1.18.tar.gz
    MANPAGE      Bundle::DBI - A bundle to install DBI and
required modules.
    CONTAINS     Storable Net::Daemon RPC::PlServer Getopt::Long
DBI
```

```
INST_FILE    /usr/lib/perl5/site_perl/5.005/i386-
linux/Bundle/DBI.pm
    INST_VERSION 1.03
```

If you don't know exactly what module you're looking for, you can use the search engine at search.cpan.org. This site has the modules broken down into categories as well as a searchable database.

In addition, there are a couple of options that seek to advise you on modules you may want to update or install. These are the r option, which gives you suggestions on modules to reinstall, and the u option, which gives you a list of uninstalled modules.

Installing Packages

The meat of the CPAN program, however, is its ability to download and install modules, bundles, and the like. The commands for doing that are shown in Table 21-2.

Table 21-2
CPAN Installation Commands

Command	Action
get	download
make	make (implies get)
test	make test (implies make)
install	make install (implies test)
clean	make clean
look	open subshell in these dists' directories
readme	display these dists' README files

Each of these commands, except for look and readme is a step in the compilation and installation process. Note that many of them imply the previous step.

Thus `get` downloads a module, while `make` downloads and compiles the module, and `test` downloads, compiles, and tests the module. The easiest way to install any module, bundles or distribution is simply to use the `install` command. This takes care of all the steps necessary to download, build, and install any given module, bundle, or distribution.

In the case of bundles, an entire sequence of modules will be downloaded and installed. For example, giving the command

```
cpan> install Bundle::DBI
```

will download and install a good many modules related to database processing. After giving the command, you need do nothing while the modules are installed. (This can take a while depending on the size of the package, and the speed of your network connection. If it's slow, you might want to have something else to do while the process runs.) Once you've installed everything you need to, give the command q and you will quit the CPAN program.

**10 Min.
To Go**

Installing Modules Without CPAN

If for any reason you are unable or unwilling to use the CPAN program, there is an alternate method for installing modules. This method is similar to compiling and installing other kinds of software.

As with CPAN, the first thing you need to do is find the package you want to install. You can do this by using the search engine at `search.cpan.org`. Once you've found the particular module you're looking for, you can download it. If you're using the search engine, you can download the package directly from that page. If not, use one of the CPAN FTP mirror sites. They are listed at `www.perl.com/CPAN-local/SITES.html`.

Once you've got the package, unpack it using the command

```
tar xvfz modulename.tar.gz
```

where *modulename* is the name of the module's tarball. Once the file is extracted, move into the directory created by the unpacking process, and list the contents of the directory. There should be a file called README in this directory. Read this file carefully. It will explain the proper procedure for installing the module, with any special considerations that you need to take into account.

Notwithstanding the contents of the README file, as a general procedure at this point, do the following:

1. Give the command `perl Makefile.pl`. A bunch of messages should scroll up the screen. If you need to provide any information at this point, you will be prompted for it. This step creates a configuration file called `Makefile`, which is used as a script for the remainder of the installation process.

2. Give the command `make`. This may or may not be necessary depending on exactly how the package is constructed, but it won't hurt anything if you do it when you don't need to.

3. Give the command `make test`. This will run the packages various self-tests. If there are any problems, they should manifest at this point.

4. Give the command `make install`. This command will place the module in the appropriate directory for use in your Perl programs.

Once you've done these steps, your module should be installed and ready to be used.

Done!

REVIEW

In this session, you learned to install packages and modules for use in your Perl programs. You started by learning how to get information about modules from `search.cpan.org`. Then you learned to install the modules using Perl's built in CPAN interface. Finally, you learned to install modules without using the CPAN interface.

QUIZ YOURSELF

1. What is CPAN? (See "Fun with CPAN.")

2. Explain each component of the command

   `perl -MCPAN -e shell`

   (See "Fun with CPAN.")

3. Explain the procedure for installing a package from a tarball. (See "Installing Modules Without CPAN.")

Using Packages and Modules

Session Checklist

✔ Learning why to use modules

✔ Meeting the conditions for using modules

✔ Using the require and use functions

✔ Using module functions

30 Min.
To Go

Why Use Packages and Modules?

There are several reasons why modules and packages offer advantages to you, the programmer:

- **Less work for you:** Using packages from the CPAN archive allows you to take advantage of a lot of useful functions that have been written by other programmers, saving you the trouble of having to write them yourself. A further advantage here is that the modules in the CPAN archive have been used and tested by others, so that you can be assured that they work.

- **More functions for you:** The module system has made Perl a truly extensible language. The extensions represented by modules create a "bigger" Perl — one that is able to handle complex tasks with relative ease.

- **Interfaces to other languages:** Many of the modules that are available are designed to allow you to use other languages' functions in your Perl program. For example, the DBI module (which we'll look at in a bit more depth in Session 23) allows you to talk to database servers in their native language — Structured Query Language (SQL). By embedding your SQL calls within a Perl program, you can then use Perl functions to manipulate the data returned by the SQL calls. The Perl/Tk module allows you to use the Tk toolkit to create graphical applications.

- **Platform independence:** Many modules are designed to provide a set of functions that operate in a consistent way on different operating systems. Functions originally written on a Macintosh system that might need to be rewritten to work properly can often be rewritten using modules so that they will operate exactly the same way regardless of the operating system.

- **Better program organization:** When writing a large piece of software, it is often best to move subroutines out into their own package. This allows you to keep the main program small and streamlined. This is conceptually helpful in that the simpler you can keep the main program, the more clearly you'll be able to think about it. Moving the bulk of the programming detail into packaged subroutines also forces you to organize your data in a neater fashion. Variables that are local to subroutines stay in the subroutines and do not get confused with global variables.

- **Easier reuse of code:** If you had created a package for one program, you might find that some of the functions you had written are useful in something else you're working on. Using those functions is as simple as calling the module in the current program. (This is another aspect of the first advantage, "less work for you.")

- **The ability to share your code:** One of the things that makes Perl such a vibrant and robust language is the contribution of programmers all over the world sharing their code. If you believe that something you've written might be useful to others, modules give you a convenient way to make it available to others to use. (You might even consider donating it to CPAN.)

Using Modules

Once you've got a module installed, it's ready to be used. In order to use the module in your own program there are two things you have to do: You have to declare that you're intending to use that particular module, and then you have to actually use the module's functions in your program.

@INC

In order to import the functions of external modules into your program, two conditions must be met. First, the module must reside in a directory whose full path name is included in the special variable @INC. If you want to see what the current value of @INC is on your system, use this command:

```
perl -e 'print @INC;'
```

The value should look something like this:

```
/usr/lib/perl5/5.00503/i386-linux/usr/lib/perl5/5.00503/usr/
lib/perl5/site_perl/5.005/i386-linux/usr/lib/perl5/site_perl/5.005
```

The interpreter looks for modules in these directories. If you're using modules from CPAN, it is almost certain that when you installed the module it was placed in one of these directories. If you're using a module of your own creation, you should either place it into one of these directories, or else modify @INC to include the name of the directory where you put it. You can do that with the command

```
perl -I /home/joe/mymods
```

Or, you can do it from within your program with a command like

```
push(@INC, "/home/joe/mymods");
```

which would add the directory at the end of @INC, or

```
unshift(@INC, "/home/joe/mymods");
```

which would add it at the beginning.

Using push or unshift in this way will affect the value of @INC only for the duration of your program. The basic value of @INC is built into the Perl interpreter when it is compiled.

use and require

The second condition that must be met is that you must explicitly declare in your program that you intend to use that module. You can do this using either the use or the require command. Both of these will incorporate the module's code into your program. The difference between the two has to do with the way in which the module's code is incorporated into your program.

require is the simpler of the two. It simply loads the module code into memory and provides access to the subroutines. use on the other hand allows for a good deal of initialization and symbol table manipulation before your code is actually executed.

Which should you use? It depends on what you're doing. If you're intending to use a simple set of functions — perhaps a module that you're writing yourself — use require. It's much easier on system resources. On the other hand, if you're using a CPAN library with advanced functions, use use. It will make sure that all of the functions are initialized properly.

**20 Min.
To Go**

Using Module Functions in Your Programs

Once you've made the module declarations that you need for your program, it only remains to use the functions in your program. The functions you'll need to use will vary from module to module. The first step, then, is to read up on your module, and see how it's used. You can do this by reading the perldoc pages. For example, if you wish to see the documentation for the IO::Socket module (which provides certain interesting network functions), give the command

```
perldoc IO::Socket
```

Object-oriented programming

Many Perl modules make use of object-oriented programming techniques. Perl has a syntax to handle this, and fortunately it's not much of a difference from normal Perl programming.

Object-oriented programming, or OOP, has become very trendy in recent years, and there are plenty of good reasons for that. Unfortunately, the jargon that has grown up around it can be confusing to a novice. Talk of objects, classes, methods, and so forth can be enough to make you wonder why you got interested in programming in the first place.

If you are familiar with another object-oriented language such as C++ or Java, then you already know how OOP techniques work. If you're not, here's what you need to know to do simple OOP in Perl.

An *object* is nothing more than a big chunk of data. You can think of it as a sort of compound variable made up of other variables. The values of the various variables control aspects of its behavior. You don't have to grapple directly with the object. Rather, you manipulate it by means of a *method*. A method is a kind of function that the module's (and hence, the object's) programmer has created precisely for the purpose of manipulating the object.

A method is invoked by means of the *arrow operator* (->). For example, if I wanted to call a method called foo on an object called bar, I might do it like this:

```
$handle = bar->foo;
```

In addition, a method might take *arguments*, which are often attributes that we wish to ascribe to the object. Thus,

```
$handle = bar->foo(arg1, arg2, arg3);
```

is often seen.

Once the method has been called, the variable to which the result has been assigned is often a *handle* (like a filehandle or a directory handle) for referring to that object. For example, here's how you connect to a database using the DBI module (we'll cover DBI in more detail in Session 23):

```
$dbh = DBI->connect("database", "username", "password");
```

The connect method is one that is used to create a new database handle object, and so is called directly from the DBI class. $dbh is a *database handle*, and is now the object upon which you will call further methods. Thus, if you want to prepare an SQL statement to be sent to the database you would do:

```
$sth = $dbh->prepare("some SQL statement");
```

Now you have a second object handle, $sth, which refers to the given SQL statement. You can execute that statement on the database sever by doing

```
$sth->execute;
```

Once you've done that, you have means of extracting the data that the database returns.

The point of all this is that despite the fact that OOP terminology often seems difficult, it actually makes it easier to deal with complex operations.

Once you've looked at the methods and functions that the module provides, you can simply include them into your programs as if they were native functions.

Here's an example of a program that makes use of the LWP::Simple module:

```
#!/usr/bin/perl

use LWP::Simple;
$location = "http://www.weather.com/weather/local/02136";
getprint $location;
```

The LWP module provides functions for making Web connections. It is very simple to write Web client software in Perl using LWP. In this example, you connect to www.weather.com, and download the page giving local weather information for the 02136 Zip code. The getprint function simply gets the page residing at the desired URL, and prints it to standard output. The getprint function is described in the perldoc page for LWP::Simple:

```
getprint($url)
         Get and print a document identified by a URL. The
         document is printed to STDOUT as data is received from
         the network.  If the request fails, then the status
         code and message are printed on STDERR.  The return
         value is the HTTP response code.
```

**10 Min.
To Go**

Other functions from the LWP::Simple module are shown in Table 22-1.

Table 22-1
LWP::Simple functions

Function	Arguments	Action
get	URL	Fetches and returns the desired URL
head	URL	Fetches and returns headers for document desired
getprint	URL	Fetches and prints the desired URL
getstore	URL, filename	Fetches desired URL, and stores it in a file
mirror	URL, filename	Same as getstore but checks date of last modification

Unfortunately, there really is no substitute for reading the documentation to learn how a Perl module is used, however, if its use is a simple set of functions as with LWP::Simple, simply learning what each function takes as an argument, and what it returns will go a long way towards helping you understand how to use them.

Once you know how to use them, you can integrate them into native Perl without too much effort. For example, using the LWP get function, you can assign the contents of a Web page to an array like so:

```
@webpage = get($url);
```

In this instance, you are simply assigning the return value of the get function (the Web page) to the @webpage variable.

A wealth of information about Perl modules can be found in the two-volume *Perl Module Reference* (O'Reilly & Associates, 1997). Some of this information is a bit outdated, since new modules, and new versions of modules are being created all the time, but the basics are there, and there is a lot of information about the functions provided by each module.

Done!

REVIEW

In this session, you learned about the advantages to of using Perl's built-in module system. You learned to use the require and use functions to import modular functions into your program. Finally, you learned to use the modular functions to extend the range of your programming toolkit.

QUIZ YOURSELF

1. Researching and learning to use modules is a lot of work. In light of this, what advantages are to be gained from using Perl's module system? (See "Why Use Packages and Modules?")

2. Explain the function of the @INC variable. How can its value be changed? (See "Using Modules.")

3. Use the LWP module to get the latest headlines from www.cnn.com. (See "Using Module Functions.")

A Case Study: The Database Interface Module

Session Checklist

✔ Installing the DBI module

✔ Connecting to a database server

✔ Getting data from the database server

✔ Applying DBI to real world situations

**30 Min.
To Go**

I n the last session, I described how to use modules in fairly general terms. Although I did offer a few examples, I thought it might be best to take a more in-depth look at a single module. The module that I've chosen is the Perl DBI module. DBI stands for Database Interface, and true to its name, the DBI module is used to allow Perl programs to access database servers without having to code all the particulars of database functions yourself.

Using Perl to Access a Database

The DBI module provides a set of functions for making network connections to database servers, and using their functions. It does all this regardless of the particular database server being used. You can use almost any database — Oracle, Sybase, Postgres, Informix, MySQL, or any database using the ODBC programming interface.

What's a database?

A database is really nothing more than a way of organizing data so that related pieces of information can be associated and recalled. Remember your /etc/passwd file? This is a very simple kind of database. The file contains a line for each user on the system and each line contains various pieces of information related to that person. This sort of thing is known as a *flat file database*. However, it is also possible to construct databases where each piece of data may be related to many other things. These sorts of multidimensional databases are often of substantial complexity and require special software called *database servers* to keep track of how the information is organized.

Database servers operate much like any other kind of server. They listen on a network port, and respond to incoming connections. Once connected to a server, a client may make any number of additions, deletions, or updates to the data, or may simply request certain pieces of data by making *queries*. When given a query, the server locates the proper data, constructs a response, and sends it back to the client.

While the various database servers may differ in the way they deal with things like administrative tasks, when it comes to the data almost every popular database speaks a language called *Structured Query Language*, or SQL. SQL is not nearly as complex as a full featured programming language such as Perl. It contains only functions and syntax for interacting with database servers, and not general programming features. Nevertheless, it is possible to get quite complex with SQL given sufficient imagination.

One of the functions of the Perl DBI module is to make it possible to embed SQL statements within Perl code. This gives you the strong database handling of SQL, but the ability to use Perl to handle your data — the best of both worlds!

What kinds of data go in databases? Almost anything. Databases can handle text, binary, or numerical data in just about any form.

For this session, I will assume that you have a database installed on your local machine. If you don't, I would recommend the excellent MySQL server. MySQL is available free of charge at www.mysql.com, and binary packages are available for many platforms. You may need to spend some time reading the server's documentation, so that you can get it up and running properly. Once you've done that, create a user called `perl` and give it full permissions on the system. In addition, create a database called `perl`. In that database, create a table called `perl_table`, and populate it like this:

```
COLUMN1            COLUMN2            COLUMN3
value1-1           value1-2           value1-3
value2-1           value2-2           value2-3
valie3-1           value3-2           value3-3
```

Installing the DBI Module

**20 Min.
To Go**

You can install the DBI module in either of the ways that I described in Session 21. If you choose to install it using the CPAN interface, you need only invoke the CPAN shell:

```
perl -MCPAN -e shell
```

Then at the `cpan>` prompt, type

```
install DBI
```

The CPAN interface program will download and build the module for you. Alternatively, you can download the DBI package from one of CPAN's mirror sites.

In addition to installing the DBI module, you should also install the DBD (Database Driver) module that corresponds to the database server you're using. (You won't need to use DBD functions in your program, but the DBI module needs DBD in order to know how to talk to the database server.) For example, if you're using the MySQL server, you should install the DBD::mysql module, like so:

```
cpan> install DBD::mSQL
```

(The MySQL driver is included in the mSQL package.)
This installation will ask you several questions when it installs:

```
Which drivers do you want to install?

    1)   MySQL only
    2)   mSQL only (either of mSQL 1 or mSQL 2)
    3)   MySQL and mSQL (either of mSQL 1 or mSQL 2)
```

```
4)   mSQL 1 and mSQL 2
5)   MySQL, mSQL 1 and mSQL 2
```

```
Enter the appropriate number:   [3]
```

If you're only planning on running MySQL, choose 1.

```
Do you want to install the MysqlPerl emulation? You might keep
your old
Mysql module (to be distinguished from DBD::mysql!) if you are
concerned
about compatibility to existing applications! [y]
```

Answer yes to this.

```
Where is your MySQL installed? Please tell me the directory that
contains the subdir 'include'. [/usr]
```

You can probably just hit Enter here.

```
Which database should I use for testing the MySQL drivers? [test]
```

Enter is fine, here, too.

```
On which host is database test running (hostname, ip address
or host:port) [localhost]
```

Again, Enter.

```
User name for connecting to database test? [undef]
```

Enter your MySQL username here. (You should have created this when you set up MySQL.)

```
Password for connecting to database test? [undef]
```

Enter your MySQL password here.

On the username and password questions, you can accept undef **as a username, and the installation program will perform the various tests as an anonymous user. This is handy if you don't have all your MySQL account data set up, although it does skip some tests that require administrative privileges.**

Once you've got these modules installed, you're ready to go to work.

Using DBI Methods and Functions

As you saw in Session 21, the DBI module uses object-oriented syntax. The module provides methods for creating database and statement handles that you can use to send SQL statements to the database.

A tutorial on the SQL language is outside the scope of this book. It should be largely evident from the statements themselves what they do. Their purpose is to illustrate the use of the DBI module, and not to teach you the language.

Connecting to a database server

The first method that you need to learn is the DBI->connect method. This method establishes a connection to the database server, and creates a database handle for you to use as a target for your SQL statements. The DBI->connect method works like this:

```
$dbh = DBI->connect($database, $username, $passwd);
```

The variables that the DBI->connect method takes as arguments are just what their names imply. They can either be defined before being passed as arguments, or they can be stated directly. The $database variable needs to be explained a bit. This value needs to be in the format:

```
dbi:driver:database=<database name>:host=<hostname>
```

The format will vary a bit from database to database. This is the proper format for MySQL. To find out about other databases, read their DBD perldoc pages, for example, perldoc DBD::oracle, to find out the specific syntax for an Oracle database.

Thus, an example of a connection statement might look like this:

```
$dbh = DBI->connect("DBI:mysql:database=perl:host=localhost",
"perl", "e492a") || die "couldn't connect to database";
```

Or, you might prefer a cleaner look:

```
$database = "dbi:database=perl:host=locahost";
$username = "perl";
$password = "e492a";
```

```
$dbh = DBI->connect($database, $username, $password) || die
"couldn't connect to database";
```

Once this statement is executed successfully, your program is connected to the database server, and the $dbh variable becomes a *handle object*. One interesting feature of this handle object is that you can create more than one of them at a time, for example:

```
$dbh1 = DBI->connect("DBI:mysql:database=perl:host=localhost",
"perl", "e492a") || die "couldn't connect to database";

$dbh2 = DBI-
>connect("DBI:mysql:database=A_DIFFERENT_DATABASE:host=localhost",
"perl", "e492a") || die "couldn't connect to database";
You can then direct statements to either $dbh1 or $dbh2.
```

You don't have to use $dbh **as the name of your database handle object. Any scalar variable name will work equally well.**

Creating SQL statements

Once you've established a connection to a database, you can begin to execute statements using the connection. This is done using two methods, prepare, and execute.

The actual SQL statement is created using the prepare method. This method is called on the database handle like so:

```
$sth = $dbh->prepare($sql_statement);
```

So, an example of preparing a statement might look like this:

```
$sth = $dbh->prepare("SELECT * FROM perl_table");
```

This statement would simply fetch all the data from the table called perl_table. In calling this method, you create another object handle. $sth is the statement handle, and it refers to the particular statement you're creating.

Once the statement is prepared, it can be executed. The execute method is called on the statement handle:

```
$sth->execute;
```

Once the Perl interpreter executes this line, the SQL statement is sent to the database server.

Handling the data

Now that you've executed an SQL statement, you need a way to deal with the data that the database server sends in return. The DBI module contains a lot of methods and functions for doing this. We will look at one of the more simple methods, fetchrow_array. The fetchrow_array method is called on the statement handle. Once called, it fetches a row of data from the statement handle, and reads it into an array. A simple example of using this might be:

```perl
while ( @row = $sth->fetchrow_array() ) {
    print @row;
}
```

This will simply print out each row of data associated with the statement handle.

Here's an example of a full-fledged program using the database you created at the beginning of the session:

```perl
#!/usr/bin/perl

use DBI;

# Gather some information from the user:
print "Enter your MySQL username: "
$username = <STDIN>;
print "Enter your MySQL password: "
$password = <STDIN>;

# Connect to the database

my $dbh = DBI->connect(DBD:mysql:database=perl:host=localhost,
$username,
    $password) || die "Couldn't connect to database";

print "Database connection established."

# Prepare statement
```

```perl
my $sth = $dbh->prepare( "SELECT * FROM perl_table" );

# Send statement to database

$sth->execute || die "Couldn't execute statement";

# Print out the data

my @row
while ( @row = $sth->fetchrow_array() ) {
     print "@row \n";
}
# One more thing: we need to disconnect from the database server
# when we're done:

$dbh->disconnect;
```

If you've done everything right, the output of this program should be

```
value1-1 value1-2 value1-3
value2-1 value2-2 value2-3
value3-1 value3-2 value3-3
```

Let's add a little more sophistication to your program:

```perl
#!/usr/bin/perl

use DBI;

# Gather some information from the user:
print "Enter your MySQL username: "
$username = <STDIN>;
print "Enter your MySQL password: "
$password = <STDIN>;

# Connect to the database

my $dbh = DBI->connect(DBD:mysql:database=perl:host=localhost,
"$username", "@password") || die "Couldn't connect to database";

# Prepare statement
```

```
my $sth = $dbh->prepare( "SELECT * FROM perl_table" );

# Send statement to database

$sth->execute || die "Couldn't execute statement";

# Print out the data

$i=1;
my @row
while ( @row = $sth->fetchrow_array() ) {
    $~ = "DISPLAY";
    write;
    $i++;
}

$dbh->disconnect;

format DISPLAY =

          COLUMN 1       COLUMN 2       COLUMN 3
ROW $i    @<<<<<<<<<     @<<<<<<<<<     @<<<<<<<<
          $row[0]        $row[1]        $row[2]
.
```

In this instance, we get the username and password from the user interactively. Also, once we've got the data, we are able to use our standard array handling syntax to handle each element of each row separately. This allows us to write our data to a format. The output of our program should look like this:

```
          COLUMN 1       COLUMN 2       COLUMN 3
ROW 1     value1-1       value1-2       value1-3

          COLUMN 1       COLUMN 2       COLUMN 3
ROW 2     value2-1       value2-2       value2-3

          COLUMN 1       COLUMN 2       COLUMN 3
ROW 3     vaule3-1       value3-2       value3-3
```

Once you've fetched the data out of the database and into a variable in your program, the data is just the same as any other data you might have. You can do anything with it that you might do with any other data.

Practical Applications

What can you do with this sort of thing? Take a look at the popular Web site at slashdot.org. This site contains news stories and comments from readers on those stories. This site is written in Perl and uses a MySQL database to hold all of its information. Any time a story or a comment is posted, Perl functions format it for storage in the database, and whenever a reader wants to look at the comments, Perl functions fetch them out and incorporate them into the Web page.

You'll learn more about using Perl to generate Web pages in the Sunday Afternoon section of this course.

In addition to stories and comments, Slashdot uses Perl functions and the database to hold all of its user, author, and administrator information, as well as moderators' ratings of comments, reader's display preferences, and so on.

Slashdot is a tremendously complex Web site; and it's used by thousands of people. Yet all of this traffic and information is handled by Perl functions. This is just one example of what can be accomplished by the creative handling of data with Perl.

If you're interested in seeing how Slashdot does what it does, the Perl code that runs the site is available at slashcode.com.

And of course, the Perl DBI is just one of a multitude of modules that are available for use. There are modules for network programming, graphics, operating system interfaces, textual interfaces, Internet functions, scientific data handling, and so forth. If it's a reasonably common programming chore, somebody's probably written a module for it.

All of this may seem a little overwhelming. After all, how are you supposed to keep track of all the functions in all the modules that are out there? The answer is, you're not. Pick and choose only what you need, and learn about functions as you need to use them. Before long, you'll be surprised at what you know.

Done!

REVIEW

In this session, you learned the basics of Perl's Database Interface (DBI) module. You learned to install the module, and configure it for use with your database server. You learned to connect to the server and execute SQL statements on the server using Perl commands. You learned how to fetch data out of the server, and process it.

QUIZ YOURSELF

1. In addition to the DBI module, you had to install one of the DBD modules. Why? (See "Installing the DBI Module.")

2. What is an *object method*? How is one invoked? (See "Using DBI Methods and Functions.")

3. Why is the name of the DBI module invoked in the statement:

    ```
    $dbh = DBI->connect;
    ```

    (See "Using DBI Methods and Functions.")

Creating Your Own Packages and Modules

Session Checklist

✔ Learning why to create modules

✔ Creating a simple module

✔ Using your module

✔ Using BEGIN and END statements

✔ Keeping your variables in their places

**30 Min.
To Go**

I n the foregoing sessions, you have seen how modules can be used to provide functions that, in their absence, you'd have to code yourself — possibly at prohibitive levels of effort. In this session, I'll show you how to create your own packages and modules.

Why Create a Package or Module?

By this point, you should see the reasons why creating your own modules might be appealing. By creating a module, you need only write a given subroutine once in order to be able to use it in any number of programs. If the programming you do tends to relate to a common area, having a core set of functions can make each program a breeze to write.

Another possible reason to use modules is to maintain the simplicity of a program. Often when creating a large or complex program, it helps to maintain the focus when the subroutines are moved into a file of their own. This keeps the size of the main file down (although the module file can get quite large), and keeps the logical structure of the main program in the foreground. In addition, it helps to keep the number of variables in the main program to a minimum, as most of the variables become local to the subroutines in the module.

Finally, you may be motivated by altruism. If your subroutines are sufficiently general (that is, if they apply to tasks beyond the single program you've designed them for), other programmers may find them useful. By packaging them as a module, you can make it very simple for other programmers to use them.

Creating a Module

Creating a module is a slightly more complicated affair than writing a program, but is still fairly simple.

Declare your package to be a package (or not)

The first step in creating your package is an optional one. If you want your package to be a full-fledged module, as opposed to a simple collection of subroutines, you need to declare that your package is a package. This is done, not surprisingly, using the package function. This should be the first line of your package file, after the Perl interpreter invocation:

```
#!/usr/bin/perl

package mymod;
```

Note that in declaring the package in this way, you are making an implicit assumption that a file called mymod.pm will exist in one of the directories included in the value of @INC. You can also specify subdirectories of any of the @INC directories using a double colon. Thus,

```
package MINE::mymod;
```

will assume that a file called mymod.pm resides in a directory called MINE, which is a subdirectory of one of the @INC directories.

If you choose to declare your package in this way, there are some additional requirements that you must meet before your package is ready to be used. Just because you have declared your package does not mean that its subroutines can be automatically used in your programs in exactly the same way as Perl native functions. In order to use one of your module's functions, you must name it explicitly. Thus if you have a function in your module called `foo()`, you must invoke it in your program as `mymod::foo()`.

You can get around this by exporting your functions. In order to do this, you need to use the Exporter module, like so:

```
#!/usr/bin/perl

package mymod;

require Exporter;
@ISA=qw(Exporter);
@EXPORT=qw(&foo);
```

Any functions that you wish to export need to go inside the list of values for the `@EXPORT` variable. The `@ISA` variable is used to tell the interpreter where to look for methods that are not listed in the current package. In this context, you're telling the interpreter that the Exporter module will tell it how to handle the values belonging to the `@EXPORT` variable. (If that seems confusing, don't worry — just be aware that `@ISA` needs to appear whenever you use the Exporter module.)

Note that you have preceded the name of your subroutine with an ampersand — `&foo`. This explicitly tags the name `foo` as a subroutine.

You may be wondering at this point why, if this is an optional step, you would want to bother with it. The answer is, that in addition to subroutines, you can also export variables, and (if you're into the OOP thing) methods and classes. You can also use other variables to tag subroutines, variables, and so forth as optionally exported or not exported. In this way, you can keep the internal parts of the module from being accidentally messed up by being used wrongly in a program. For now, though, you don't really need to worry about that. Just be aware that that using the exporter gives you a lot more control over the structure of the package.

Invoke any other modules you need to use

As with the Exporter module in the previous step, you are allowed to use other modules within your modules. If you do this, of course, you will need to have those other modules installed before yours will work. It is important to be aware of this if you decide to share your module with others. You may want to include a list of dependencies as a comment in your module.

Declare any variables that are local to the package

If you have any variables that will be used in more than one subroutine in the package, this is the place to declare them. You should make sure that these variables are declared outside of any particular subroutine, because any variable declared inside a subroutine will be local to that subroutine. When declaring variables, make sure that you keep them local to the package by using the my function, as in:

```
my $var = 0;
```

That is, unless you plan to export them. If you plan to export them, you need to make sure they're included in the @EXPORT list.

Create your subroutines

This is the main part of the package. Put your subroutines here. They can be in any order.

Define a return value.

Your package needs to have a return value. If it does not, you will get an error when you try to run your program. Put a line like this at the end of your module:

```
return 1;
```

**20 Min.
To Go**

A Simple Module and Program

Here's a quick and very basic example of a module and a program that uses it:
First the program:

```
#!/usr/bin/perl

    require mymod;          # Use 'require', because we're not
using
                            # package declarations yet.


mymod_func;
```

Now the module:

```
#!/usr/bin/perl

sub mymod_func {
        print "This is my function. \n";
}

return 1;
```

Now, when you run the program, it should give the output:

```
This is my function.
```

If you wanted to make the module a little more formal, it could look like this:

```
#!/usr/bin/perl

package mymod;

use Exporter;
@ISA=qw(Exporter);
@EXPORT=qw(&mymod_func);

sub mymod_func {
    print "This is my function. \n";
}

return 1;
```

Now you can use either `require` or `use` in the program when you invoke the module. Note that each function you wish to export needs to go in the @EXPORT list. Thus, if you had two functions,

```
@EXPORT=qw(&mymod_func1, &mymod_func2);
```

BEGIN and END Blocks

It's time for me to own up to a little fib I told at the beginning of this book. When I told you that Perl is an interpreted language, and not a compiled language, I was only telling half the truth. In fact, Perl is *both interpreted and compiled*. The Perl interpreter is also a compiler. While it's true that you don't have to compile your programs as you do with, say, C, it is also true that every time you run a Perl program, the Perl code gets compiled into a kind of shorthand called *bytecode*.

One of the things that this lets you do is to give instructions to the compiler in the course of your program that affect the way the program is compiled. Such is the case with the BEGIN statement. A BEGIN statement looks like a subroutine, but what it actually does is to have the enclosed code compiled before anything else happens. Thus if you have some code that everything else depends on, it's often a good idea to put it in a BEGIN block.

The opposite of the BEGIN block is the END block. The END block is compiled last, just before the program exits. It is primarily used for housekeeping chores such as removing temporary files. Here's an example of a program using BEGIN and END blocks:

```perl
#!/usr/bin/perl

print "This is the main phase of the program. \n";

END {
    print "This is the cleanup phase. \n";
}

BEGIN {
    print "This is the beginning phase of the program. \n";
}
```

When you run this code, what you will get for output is

```
This is the beginning phase of the program.
This is the main phase of the program.
This is the cleanup phase.
```

Although BEGIN and END blocks can be used anywhere in any program, they become especially important in the context of modules because they can be used to force your subroutines to be evaluated prior to the running of the main part of the program. This ensures that your subroutine names are recognized by the interpreter when the main part of the program starts to run. So, a slightly more formal version of the module you created previously might look like this:

```
#! /usr/bin/perl

package mymod;

use Exporter;
@ISA=qw(Exporter);
@EXPORT=qw(&mymod_func);

BEGIN{

    sub mymod_func {
        print "This is my function";
    }
}

return 1;
```

Alternately, anything you want to have happen before the program exits should be put inside an END block. The END block will execute even before a program is halted with a die statement, so anything that needs to be cleaned up will be cleaned up.

Keeping an Eye on Your Variables

**10 Min.
To Go**

Once you start using packages, modules, and subroutines in earnest, your variables can quickly start to get out of hand. It is important that you keep track of these beasties so they don't clobber each other. You have seen that you can restrict a variable's area of influence by using the my function, but I think it's important that you get a clear idea of good practices with regard to variable organization.

A quick guide to variable scoping

Every Perl variable has an attribute called *scope*. A variable's scope is considered to be that part of a program in which the variable can be seen. If you create a variable on its own with no qualifiers, it is said to have *global scope*. In other words, that variable is recognized throughout the entire program. (It should be noted that even global variables are somewhat restricted in their scope since they are not recognized outside of the program in which they were created. If you want that to happen, you need to export them.) Let's say you create a variable called $globvar. You do that, as you've seen, by having a line like:

```
$globvar = "somevalue";
```

The advantage of a global variable is that it can be handled from anywhere in the program. If you refer to it at any point, the value of that variable will be available. The disadvantage to this is that you have to be careful about how you refer to it. A careless operation could cause the variable's value to be changed from what you intend it to be. Another disadvantage is that you cannot name any other variable the same thing that you have already named a global variable. If you do that, the first variable will be replaced with the second.

Using my to limit scope

In complex programs, there are often times when you might want to give a certain variable the same name as another variable. Maybe the variable serves the same function, only in a different part of the program. The problem is, if you're using a modular programming style, there's no guarantee that subroutines will be called in the proper order necessary to preserve the correct values of a certain variable. In cases like this, we may find that we want to fence off part of the program in order to keep a variable inside. This is the mission of the my function.

my restricts a variable to that block of code in which it was defined. If the variable was defined on a line outside any block, the variable will be restricted to the program as a whole. Essentially, this is the same as a global variable, except that you wouldn't be able to export it. If a my variable is invoked inside a sub statement, the variable will not be recognized outside of that subroutine. This is also true of any conditional or iterative construct.

Here are some examples of mys usage:

```
sub somefunc {
    my $localvar = 0;
    # $localvar is recognized here
    some code;
}

# localvar is not recognized here.
```

or

```
while (something) {
    my $localvar = 0;
    # localvar exists only inside the loop
}
```

or

```
foreach $var (@list) {
    my $localvar = $var;
    #localvar exists only during array processing
}
```

It should be noted that the my function restricts the variable to only the *innermost* block to which it belongs. For example:

```
foreach $var (@list) {
    my $localvar = 0;
    # $localvar exists here;
    while (something){
        my $innervar = 0;
        # both $localvar and $innervar exist here
    }
    # $localvar exists here, but $innervar does not
}

# neither $localvar nor $innervar exists here
```

In addition to the my function, there is also the local function. local is used to temporarily replace the value of a global variable with a value that exists only as long as the local statement is in effect. For example:

```
$var = 0;

# $var = 0 here.

sub something {
    local $var = 1;
    # $var = 1 here.
}

# $var = 0 here.
```

This is really not considered good programming style. If you want to do this sort of thing, you should consider how you could do it by restructuring the program and using my variables. However, there are times when only local does what you need. A good example of such a time would be when you want to temporarily override the value of one of Perl's built-in variables.

It is important to keep on top of your variables when creating complex programs. If you need to keep a list of what's what, go ahead and do so. As a rule, you should only give variables as much scope as they need to have. If you have a legitimate use for a global variable, go ahead and make one, but if it doesn't really need to be global, localize it.

Done!

REVIEW

In this session, you learned how to create modules. You learned how to declare your packages using the package function, and how to use the Exporter module to export your functions for use in programs. You learned to create BEGIN and END blocks in order to have code executed before or after the rest of your program. Finally, you learned the importance of keeping an eye on the scope of your variables.

QUIZ YOURSELF

---

1. When creating packages of subroutines, is it always a good idea to use the Exporter and package function, thus turning your collection into a full-fledged module? Why or why not? (See "Declare your package to be a package (or not).")

2. What does the BEGIN token do? Why would you use it in a module? (See "BEGIN and END Blocks.")

3. What is scope? Why is it important? (See "A quick guide to variable scoping.")

The Standard Library

Session Checklist

✔ Deciding which modules to install

✔ Looking at modules in the standard library

✔ Looking at a few nonstandard modules

**30 Min.
To Go**

Now that you understand the ins and outs of using packages and modules, you need to know what kinds of modules are available for use. While it is possible to use search.cpan.org to find any given module, that's not necessarily going to help you if the module you need is part of the Perl Standard Library.

Which Modules Do You Need?

The basic Perl distribution comes with a good number of packages and modules already installed. Some of these are so basic to the functioning of any even moderately complex Perl program that it would be almost impossible to run a decent system without them. Others are not quite so basic, but are popular enough that the

Perl developers thought it was worthwhile to include them in the basic Perl package. All of these packages are part of the Standard Library.

In addition there are certain modules that, while not necessarily so popular as to necessitate their inclusion in a default installation, are useful enough that the odds are great that you will find yourself installing them at some point.

Why not just install everything? That's one strategy. If you've got the disk space on your computer, and the processor speed to handle searching large directories every time you try to load a module, you may well want to install everything. On the other hand, what are the odds that you're actually going to use the Math::Spline module? In practice, you'll end up installing a combination of modules that you think may be useful, along with those that are required in order to make something else run.

Case in point: I have a lot of less-used modules on my system because at one point I worked for the people who develop the code that runs the Slashdot Web site. My job made it necessary for me to actually run the Slashcode on my computer, so that I could look at the way it works. Before I was able to run the Slashcode, I had to install a whole set of modules that the Slashcode developers had used in the course of their work. Fortunately, all these modules were packaged in a bundle, so that I merely had to give the command `install Bundle::Slash` at the `cpan>` prompt in order to install them all. Now that I no longer need to run that code, I have no need for those modules, but there's no point in removing them from my computer. They're not doing any harm, and who knows — I might need them again some day.

But I probably won't. Most casual Perl programmers will make do just fine with modules that installed by default, and a few of the more popular downloadable modules.

The Standard Library

Those modules that come packaged with the Perl distribution are known as the *Standard Library*. These are modules that you should not have to install because they are already on your system. While many of them are quite useful, you may find that you never even look at certain others. Some of the modules are only useful to Perl developers. Others will not interest you if you never do any network programming.

Check out your system

Perl automatically keeps a log of every module installed on your system. To see this log, simply give the command

```
perldoc perllocal
```

at a system prompt. You should see a bunch of entries that look more or less like this:

```
Wed Nov 22 14:37:27 2000: Module the Apache::DBI manpage

    o    installed into: /usr/lib/perl5/site_perl/5.005

    o    LINKTYPE: dynamic

    o    VERSION: 0.10

    o    EXE_FILES:
```

This tells you the date and time of installation, the name of the module, and some information about it.

An Abridged Guided Tour

**20 Min.
To Go**

Let's take a look at some of the modules that are available as part of the standard library as well as a few of the more useful nonstandard modules. (The following are short descriptions only. For the full scoop, read the module's perldoc page.)

Note

Although I refer to all of the following as "modules," some of them are, in fact *pragmas*. A pragma is an instruction that you give that changes the behavior of the Perl compiler. Pragmas are used in much the same way as modules, so they are generally grouped together. You can tell them apart because pragmas usually begin with a lower case letter, whereas modules begin with a capital letter.

General programming tools

General programming tools are exactly what their name implies they are – tools that help you write programs.

Benchmark

The Benchmark module contains functions for seeing how fast given pieces of code will run. Some of its functions and methods are

- timethis: Runs a piece of code several times.
- timethese: Runs several pieces of code several times.
- timeit: Runs a piece of code to see how long it takes.
- new: Creates a new benchmark object.

Config

The Config module enables access to the Perl executable's configuration information. Here's a sample script that will print out this information:

```
#!/usr/bin/perl

use Config;
use Config qw(myconfig config_sh);
print myconfig();
print config_sh();
```

Env

The Env module enables access to your system's environment variables. These variables are stored in a hash called %ENV. You can see these environment variables by running this program:

```
#!/usr/bin/perl

use Env;
use Env(PATH);
print $PATH;
```

English

The English module allows you to use "English" names for special variables. These names are the same as the names used by the Unix awk program. For example, in Perl, the return value from the previous function is stored in the variable $_. Using the English module, we could use the name $ARG for that variable.

lib

The lib module enables you to manipulate the module search path variable, @INC, as your program is being compiled.

Shell

The Shell module enables you to run Unix shell commands inside your Perl program without having to use a system command or backquotes. For example, you could use the cat command like this:

```
#!/usr/bin/perl

use Shell;

$file = cat("<somefile");
print $file;
```

strict

The strict module forces you to use certain safe programming practices. For example, when the strict module is in effect, you must declare your variables in this way:

```
#!/usr/bin/perl

use strict;

use vars qw($foo, $bar, $baz);
```

subs

The subs module enables you to predeclare your subroutine names so that you can use them without parentheses even before they are defined. For example, in a program not using subs, you would have to invoke a subroutine as

```
mysub();
```

Using subs, you can do

```
use subs qw(mysub);
```

```
mysub;
```

vars

You have already seen the use of the vars pragma in conjunction with the strict pragma. vars allows you to predeclare your global variables.

File and directory access tools

These modules enable you to have easy access to the files and directories residing on the computer upon which your Perl program is running Cwd. The Cwd module makes it easier to get the name of the current working directory. Cwd has several functions that manipulate the current working directory in a number of ways. The most basic function provided by this module is the getcwd function. It works like this:

```
#!/usr/bin/perl

use Cwd;

$current_dir = getcwd;
```

DirHandle

The DirHandle module provides object-oriented methods for dealing with directory access. This is simply an alternative to the normal procedural functions, such as opendir.

File::Basename

The File::Basename module provides functions for manipulating files and path names. The fileparse function splits a pathname into its component parts, thus

/home/joe/somefile.pl becomes the path, /home/joe/, the base name some-file, and the suffix .pl. Thus:

```
($path, $base, $suff) = fileparse('/home/joe/somefile.pl',
'\.pl');
```

Note how the suffix has been specified.

In addition to fileparse, File::Basename also provides basename, which returns only the name of the file, and dirname which returns only the path part.

File::Copy

The File::Copy module enables you to use simple syntax to make copies of files, or to move them. For example,

```
#!/usr/bin/perl

use File::Copy;

copy("File1", "File2")
move("OldFileName", "NewFileName);
```

FileHandle

The FileHandle module is similar to the DirHandle module, in that it provides object methods as an alternative to the standard procedural methods for dealing with filehandles. For example,

```
#!/usr/bin/perl

use FileHandle;
$fh = new FileHandle;
$fh->open("< filename");
```

associates the handle object $fh with the file filename. This is similar to

```
#!/usr/bin/perl

open(FH, "<filename");
```

Except that the file handle is associated with a scalar object-variable rather than an explicit filehandle. The main advantage of this is that you can use object-oriented methods to manipulate the filehandle. In addition, the module provides a set of methods that can be called on the handle object.

Network programming tools

These modules give you additional functions and methods that you can use to create network-enabled programs.

**10 Min.
To Go**

Net::Ping

The Net::Ping module checks to see if a remote host is online. It does this by using object-oriented methods. For example,

```perl
#!/usr/bin/perl

use Net::Ping;

$host = "some.hostname.or.IP";
$pinger = Net::Ping->new();  # create "ping object" $pinger
print "$host is alive. \n" if $pinger->ping($host);
$pinger->close();
```

Socket

The Socket module enables you to create TCP or UDP sockets and creates a socket handle for them to be manipulated. For example,

```perl
#!/usr/bin/perl

use Socket;

socket(HANDLE, $proto);
```

creates a socket handle called HANDLE, using the protocol specified in $proto. $proto needs to be set with a statement like

```perl
$proto = getprotobyname('tcp');
```

Once the socket is created, it can be opened using the connect (for TCP) or send (for UDP) functions.

> **Note** There is actually quite a bit of technical networking stuff involved in using Socket. If you are familiar with the C language's socket.h library, the Perl Socket module is more or less the same. If you're new to network programming, you might want to take a look at the IO::Socket module instead.

Sys::Hostname

The Sys::Hostname module provides the hostname function, which attempts to get the name of the local host by every possible method. This is something that can be used if the native function gethostbyname doesn't work. For example,

```
#!/usr/bin/perl

use Sys::Hostname;
$host = hostname;
print "$host \n";
```

should print out your computer's name.

Nonstandard but useful modules

As I mentioned before, there are a huge number of modules that are not considered part of the standard library. Some of these are fairly esoteric, but many of them are quite common. Here are some of the most useful of the more common ones.

DBI

We covered this one in some detail in Session 23. DBI provides a set of object methods for interacting with database servers.

IO::Socket

The IO::Socket module provides an object-oriented interface for dealing with network programming. It is a good but easier to use module than the plain Socket module, and is a good choice for people who are new to network programming. IO::Socket enables you to create socket handle objects that can be controlled by assigning certain attributes to them, and by calling methods on them. An example of some typical socket creation code might look like this:

```
#!/usr/bin/perl

use IO::Socket;

$mysock = IO::Socket::INET->new(PeerAddr=>'www.example.com',
                                PeerPort=>'http(80)',
                                Proto => 'tcp');
```

Now you can manipulate data through this socket by simply calling functions and methods on the handle.

Net

If the IO::Socket module seems a bit too low-level for you, there are a whole slew of modules that are part of the NET package. These modules provide interfaces to just about any networking function you can think of. For example, the Net::Telnet module creates a *Telnet object handle* that allows you to create a Telnet connection and interact with it. Net::FTP does the same thing, only it creates an interface to the Internet's File Transfer Protocol. Similarly, Net::DNS gives you a set of methods and functions for interacting with the Domain Name Service.

This should give you an idea of just some of what is available. If you are interested in learning more about what modules are out there for your programming pleasure, I suggest you browse search.cpan.org, or, alternatively, get your hands on a copy of the *Perl Module Reference* (O'Reilly & Associates, 1997). The latter is a two-volume set, and unless you're planning on doing a lot of modular programming, the cost will probably be prohibitive. However, you might be able to find a copy at your local library or on the desk of your local Perl guru.

Done!

REVIEW

In this session, you learned about some of the more common modules and pragmas found in the standard Perl library. Beginning with general programming tools, you moved on through file and directory access tools into networking tools. Finally, you looked at some nonstandard but useful modules.

QUIZ YOURSELF

1. What is a pragma? How can you tell the difference between a pragma and a module? (See "An Abridged Guided Tour.")

2. Which module would you use for very finely grained network programming? Why? (See "Network programming tools.")

3. What is the best way to find out what methods and functions are provided by a module? (See "Which modules do you need"?)

Session Checklist

✔ Creating references

✔ Managing lists of lists using references

✔ Using references to manage anonymous lists and hashes

✔ Creating and using references to anonymous subroutines

✔ Using braces to keep your code organized

**30 Min.
To Go**

I n this session, we will examine the final aspect of the core of the Perl language — references. References are an alternative way of passing data between functions in which the data itself is not is not passed, but rather an indirect pointer is created.

What Is a Reference?

References are one of the more slippery topics in Perl. Essentially, a reference is a pointer to something else. Whereas an ordinary variable says "This thing, here," a reference says, "That thing, over there." References are created using the backslash operator, and stored in a simple scalar variable. Thus,

```
$ref = \$var;
```

creates a reference, $ref, to a scalar variable, $var. $ref itself does not contain the value of $var, rather it contains the *address* (location in memory) of $var. For example, if you had the program

```
#!/usr/bin/perl

$var = "foo";
$ref = \$var;
print "$ref \n";
```

you would get output that looks something like

```
SCALAR(0x80e4ae8)
```

In order to use the reference to extract the value from $var, we must *de-reference* it. This is done using the dollar sign, like so:

```
#!/usr/bin/perl

$var = "foo";
$ref = \$var;
print "$$ref \n";
```

Now, your output will be foo.
Likewise, you can create a reference to an array:

```
#!/usr/bin/perl

@list = ("foo", "bar", "baz", "hejaz");
$ref = \$var;
print "@$ref \n";
```

Notice that to de-reference your array, you had to use the @ symbol. You could also access a single member of the array like this:

```
print "$$ref[0] \n";
```

It should be clear at this point that if you wish to de-reference a variable, you do so by prepending the symbol of the type of variable that it is to the scalar name of the reference. Thus, for a hash:

```
#!/usr/bin/perl
```

```
%hash = ("foo" => "bar"        # NOTE: the "=>" operator is exactly
                               # the same as a comma. It makes
        "baz" => "hejaz")      # hashes easier to read.
$ref = \$var;
print "%$ref \n";
```

Again, to access a single element:

```
print "$$ref{baz} \n";
```

gives us hejaz — the value corresponding the key baz.

References and Complex Data Structures

And now a question arises: Why would anyone want to do this? After all, it's simpler to say

```
$var;
```

than it is to say

```
$$ref
```

and it is part of Perl's philosophy to avoid unnecessary complexity. The answer has to do with the ability to create complex data structures. Back in Session 8, you learned that you could create lists of lists. Thus:

```
#!/usr/bin/perl

@list_1 = ("foo", "bar", "baz", "hejaz");
@list_2 = ("whee", "poit", "ptang");
@listoflists = (@list_1, @list_2);
print "@listoflists \n";
```

would give you the output

```
foo bar baz hejaz whee poit ptang
```

The problem arises in trying to access a single element of that list. You may know that poit is the second value in @list_2 (that is, $list_2[1]), but how that relates to its position in @listoflists may be open to question. (Yes, in this case you know it, but what happens when you start using push, pop, and shift functions on it?) It would be ideal if you could simply treat @listoflists as a multidimensional array, and access poit as something like $listoflists[1,1], but you can't. You can, however, do it using a list of references to lists, like so:

```
#!/usr/bin/perl

@list_1 = ("foo", "bar", "baz", "hejaz");
@list_2 = ("whee", "poit", "ptang");

$ref_1 = \@list_1;
$ref_2 = \@list_2;

@listofrefs = ($ref_1, $ref_2);

print "${$listofrefs[1]}[1] \n";
```

This will give you the desired output. Moreover, it will always give you the value of the second element in the second list, no matter what operations have been worked on the lists. Voilá! Multidimensional arrays.

Note the grouping here. Inside the brackets is a simple scalar that contains the value of the second term in @listoflists. That is, $listoflists[1], which is $ref_1. Outside the brackets, you have on the left the de-referencing symbol. This reconstitutes your array, @list_2, and on the right, you have the element of @list_2 that you're after. Whenever you do something like this, you must take care to keep an eye on where your brackets are in order to make sure that you're de-referencing what you think you're de-referencing.

A simpler way of doing multidimensional arrays is by doing it implicitly. You can use square brackets to implicitly create a reference to an array, like so:

```
$ref = [2, 3, 4];
```

In this case, $ref is a reference to an anonymous array (that is, an array without a name). De-referencing a single element can be done in this way:
$elem = $$ref[1];

If you group these anonymous arrays inside another array, you can create a named array of anonymous arrays, like so:

```
@multidim = (["a", "b", "c"],
             ["larry", "curly", "moe"],
             ["itchy", "scratchy", "poochie"]);
```

Now, if, for example, you wanted to access the second value of the second row (curly), you could do so like this:

```
$rowcol = $multidim[1][1];
```

Since you created implicit references by using square brackets around your anonymous lists, the Perl interpreter knows enough to perform the implicit de-referencing operation when it sees the multiple index numbers.

Likewise, you can use similar techniques to create hashes of anonymous hashes:

```
%dogs = (
    Spot => {
        breed => "Labrador Retriever",
        color => "black",
        owner => {
            name => "Jane Smith",
            address => "123 Elm St.",
            phone => "(617) 555-1212",
        }
    },

    Blackie => {
        breed => "Dalmatian",
        color => "Spotted",
        owner => {
            name => "John Brown",
            address => "456 Pine St.",
            phone => "(617) 555-1414"
        }
    }
}
```

Now, you can access Blackie's owner's address like so:

```
print $dogs{'Blackie'}{'owner'}{'address'};
```

Again, the multiple keys tell the interpreter that it needs to do the implicit de-referencing.

Subroutine References

In addition to variables, references can also be created to anonymous subroutines. This is a somewhat less formal way of going about subroutines. You create subroutine references implicitly by assigning a anonymous subroutine to a scalar variable name, like so:

```
$subref = sub {
        some code;
};
```

Note the semicolon here. This is necessary because the code block is part of an assignment statement. This wouldn't ordinarily be necessary in a named subroutine. Once you've created a subroutine reference, you can de-reference it like so:

```
&$subref;
```

If there are arguments to be passed to your subroutine, they are simply enclosed in parentheses:

```
&$subref(arg);
```

Symbolic References

The references discussed previously are known as *hard references*. That is, when a reference is created, it exists, and things that access that reference are accessing the thing it refers to, only without calling by name.

But, what happens if we call something using a reference that hasn't actually been created? When this happens, we create a *symbolic reference*, which is really just another name for something. If that seems a bit confusing, perhaps an example will clear it up:

```
#!/usr/bin/perl

$name = "var";
$$name = "hello there";
print $var;
```

The output of this program will be hello there. Did you see what happened? The variable $var was never explicitly assigned. As if that weren't affront enough, you did a de-reference on $name ($$name), which was never a reference. What happened here?

When you de-referenced $name, you told the interpreter that you wanted to use the value of $name as a *fake reference*. It created the scalar $var out of the value of $name, and then treated the de-reference as if it were a de-reference of a reference that actually existed, thus assigning the value hello there to the implicitly created $var.

If you had done

```
@$name = (something);
```

we would have instead created a list variable called @var instead of a scalar.

This can be a little dangerous. The Perl interpreter assumes that you know what you're doing when you throw de-references around. It is very easy to intend to use a hard reference, but accidentally use a symbolic reference. To guard against this, you can use the strict pragma. You can even restrict the strict pragma to references by doing this:

```
use strict 'refs';
```

This will tell the compiler not to use symbolic references, and you will get an error if you do so. If you need to use a symbolic reference in some portion of your program, you can turn off the strict refs pragma by giving the command:

```
no strict 'refs';
```

This will countermand the effects of the use statement, but will only be in effect in the innermost block in which it is defined. Thus,

```
#!/usr/bin/perl

use strict 'refs';

# no symbolic refs here

sub something {
    no strict 'refs';
    # symbolic refs okay here
}

# no symbolic refs here
```

**10 Min.
To Go**

Keeping Things Organized — Using Braces

When you start getting into references, it's easy for your code to become messy. This is more than just an aesthetic problem. Messy code is disorganized code. It's harder to read, and harder to debug. The messier your code is, the more likely it is that you will have serious problems with it.

The solution to the messy code problem is to keep things organized. Perl lets you do this in various ways by using quotes and curly braces to block off particular parts of code.

You saw earlier that you could combine a reference and a scalar variable like so:

```perl
#!/usr/bin/perl

@list_1 = ("foo", "bar", "baz", "hejaz");
@list_2 = ("whee", "poit", "ptang");

$ref_1 = \@list_1;
$ref_2 = \@list_2;

@listofrefs = ($ref_1, $ref_2);

print "${$listofrefs[1]}[1] \n";
```

In the `print` statement, the curly braces serve to keep the scalar part, `$listofrefs[1]` separate from the de-reference, `${}[1]`. Braces can be used this way in general. For example, the statement

```perl
print ${var};
```

is the same as

```perl
print $var;
```

This becomes useful if you have a variable name that could be confused with something else. Suppose that you have a variable called `$shift`. `shift`, of course, is the name of a Perl native function, and so using it as a variable name can get you into trouble because the interpreter considers that name to be a *reserved word*. You can get around this problem by referring to the variable as `${shift}`. (Although you really should just change the name of the variable.) If you really did mean to use the function `shift`, you can signal that by adding something that makes it clear that you mean the function, and not just an identifier, such as:

```
${ shift() }
```

Here, the parentheses show that you're talking about a function. You could get the same effect with an argument:

```
${ shift @list };
```

That last one is especially useful if @list is a list of references! Consider:

```
#!/usr/bin/perl

@list_1 = ("foo", "bar", "baz", "hejaz");
@list_2 = ("whee", "poit", "ptang");

$ref_1 = \@list_1;
$ref_2 = \@list_2;

@listofrefs = ($ref_1, $ref_2);

while (@listofrefs) {
        foreach $val ( @{ shift @listofrefs } ) {
                print "$val \n";
        }
}
```

Here, you use the `shift` **function to give the next reference in** @listofrefs, **and then, using braces, you de-reference that value, and feed the resulting value to the** foreach **loop, effectively iterating over all the values in the all the arrays referred to by the values in** @listofrefs.

This is also useful when you want to jam the value of a variable right up next to some other text, but you don't want the adjacent text to be considered part of the variable. Thus:

```
$bug = "Spider";
print "${bug}man";
```

would output Spiderman. There are, of course, other ways of doing this, such as

```
print ($bug . "man");
```

But, you may find that the former gives your statement a better flow. As the two previous examples show, the braces can be used either inside or outside quotation marks.

You can also use braces to make a de-reference clearer, as in

```
print ${$ref};
```

or

```
print @{$ref};
```

To a certain extent, using braces for organization is a matter of personal taste; however, your goal should always be to make your code as clear as possible. Try to look at your code with an objective eye and identify places where a reader could become confused. When you find these places, do what you can to disambiguate your code. Perl's syntax is somewhat freeform, but you should not use that as an excuse to be sloppy. If you can't sufficiently clarify your code using braces, leave a comment.

Done!

REVIEW

In this session, you learned to create references and to use them to pass data indirectly. First you learned to create references using the backslash operator, and to de-reference them by prepending the referent's data type character ($, @, or %) to the reference. You learned to use references to manage lists of lists. You learned to create references to anonymous lists and hashes by implication. You learned to create anonymous subroutines using references. You learned to use symbolic references. You learned to suppress the use of symbolic references using the strict pragma. Finally, you learned to use braces to keep things organized.

QUIZ YOURSELF

1. If you know that the reference $ref is a reference to an array, what it proper way to de-reference it? (See "What Is a Reference?")

2. To what does the expression $$ref[1][1] refer? (See "References and Complex Data Structures.")

3. Why would you want to create an anonymous array? (See "References and Complex Data Structures.")

PART

V

Sunday Morning

1. What is the difference between a package and a module?
2. Why, in general, is it preferable to use Perl's built in CPAN interface to install modules?
3. What is the significance of the special variable @INC?
4. What is the difference between the use and require functions?
5. What is a *method*?
6. When installing the DBI module, why is it also necessary to install one of the modules in the DBD family?
7. What is wrong with the following code?

   ```perl
   #!/usr/bin/perl
   use DBI;
   $dbh = DBI      ->
   connect("DBI:mysql:database=perl:host=localhost",
                   "perl", "e492a") || die "couldn't connect to
   database";
   $dbh->execute("SELECT * FROM table);
   ```

8. Which DBI method is used to fetch a row of data into an array?
9. Is Perl an interpreted or a compiled language? Explain.
10. What is the function of the BEGIN command?
11. What is a variable's *scope*?
12. What is the Perl Standard Library?

13. How can you find out which modules are installed on your system?

14. What is a *pragma*?

15. What is the function of the IO::Socket module?

16. What is a reference?

17. What is a symbolic reference?

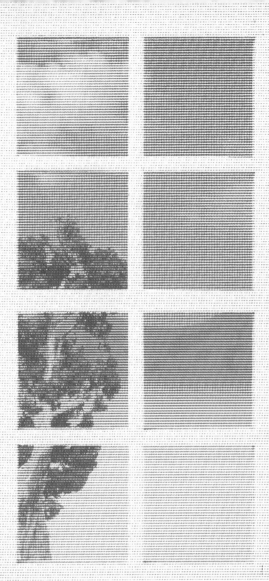

Introduction to Web Programming

Session Checklist

✔ Reviewing HTML

✔ Going beyond static HTML

✔ Making the Web useful

✔ Understanding the CGI

**30 Min.
To Go**

Programming for the Web has evolved along with the Web itself. Initially, the Web was a mass of static pages that would show every user the same content. As more people started using the Web and developers realized the importance of allowing the user to interact with sites, dynamic Web pages came into existence. Many of these dynamic pages use the Common Gateway Interface (CGI) to accomplish this. This session begins by reviewing the Hypertext Markup Language (HTML), the language that dictates how the content of a Web page will be displayed.

A Quick HTML Refresher

Hypertext Markup Language (HTML) is made up of a series of tags that are placed within the content of a document to define how it should be displayed to the user.

In this way, HTML is less of a programming language and more of a method of formatting content.

HTML tags are of two types. The first type can be thought of as a switch. The tag turns on the formatting and must be turned off with another tag. The closing tag looks just like the beginning tag except that the first character after the tag bracket is a slash (/). For example, this following code section shows two sentences. The first sentence, being between the <B> and </B> tags, is boldface. The second sentence is not.

```
<B>I am boldfaced.</B> I am not boldfaced.
```

The other type of HTML tag is the sort of tag that requires no closing tag. These tags are generally used to set the attributes of the area, or to insert an image as shown here.

```
<IMG src="http://www.someurl.com/image.jpg">
```

Note that there is no </IMG> tag.

While there are many HTML tags, three main tags are necessary to create an HTML document. The first is the tag that signifies to the Web browser that the document is an HTML document. This tag is <HTML>, and it generally appears on the first line of a HTML document. At the end of the HTML content of the page, a </HTML> tag is required to signify the end of the HTML content. The second main tag is the <HEAD> tag, which creates the header of the document. The header contains all of the information that is not displayed in the page itself. A closing tag of </HEAD> is required at the end of the header content. The final necessary tag is the <BODY> tag. It is used to set the body of the document off from the other parts of the document.

Using just these tags, here is the skeleton of a Web page in the source code shown here.

```
<HTML>
  <HEAD>
    <TITLE>I am the title of the document</TITLE>
  </HEAD>
  <BODY>
    I am the body of the document.
  </BODY>
</HTML>
```

However, this HTML document has defined no text color, no background color, and none of the general attributes of the page. There are additional attributes to the <BODY ...> tag that are used to accomplish this, by setting their values to the color name or to the hex value.

- <BODY bgcolor=?> sets the background color.
- <BODY text=?> sets the text color.
- <BODY link=?> sets the text color of a link.
- <BODY vlink=?> sets the text color of visited links.
- <BODY alink=?> sets the text color of a link on click.

Here is the HTML skeleton slightly fleshed out with a few lines to set the background color, the text color, and the link text colors.

```
<HTML>
  <HEAD>
    <TITLE>Example HTML Document</TITLE>
  </HEAD>
  <BODY bgcolor="white" text="black" link="red" vlink="blue"
   alink="green">
    I am the body of the document. I am black text on a white
    background.<BR>
    <A href="http://www.foo.com/">I am an unvisited link</A><BR>
  </BODY>
</HTML>
```

The image in Figure 27-1 shows how this document appears in a Web browser.

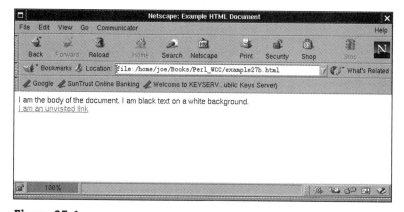

Figure 27-1
The document as displayed in a browser.

The foundation of HTML documents is made up of hyperlinks, which are used to navigate between documents. The tag to create a hyperlink is

```
<A href="URL">name to click</A>
```

This displays "name to click" in the document in the color defined in the body attribute section, or if that has not been set, to the default colors specified in the Web browser. The format for an e-mail hyperlink is basically the same as the previous one, but with the `mailto:` specified as shown here.

```
<A href="mailto:someuser@foo.com">name to click</A>
```

A final type of hyperlink is used when you want to link to somewhere else on the current document. This requires two separate tags:

- To create the target location: `<A name="NAME">name of location</A>`
- To create the link to the target location: `<A href="#NAME">name to click</A>`

Other useful HTML tags format the text within the document. Boldface, italic, underline as well as horizontal separators and line breaks help to format the text. Tags for formatting text and paragraphs may be viewed in Table 27-1.

Table 27-1
Character and Paragraph Formatting Tags in HTML4.01

Tag	Function
`<PRE></PRE>`	Create preformatted text
`<H1></H1>`	Create the largest headline text
`<H6></H6>`	Create the smallest headline text
`<B></B>`	Create boldface text
`<I></I>`	Create italic text
`<U></U>`	Create underline text
`<TT></TT>`	Create typewriter-style text
`<STRONG></STRONG>`	Emphasize the text
`<EM></EM>`	Emphasize the text
`<CITE></CITE>`	Create a citation (usually italic)

Tag	Function
`<FONT size=? ></FONT>`	Set the size of the font, from 1 to 7
`<FONT color=? ></FONT>`	Set the color of the font, in name or hex value
`<FONT face=? ></FONT>`	Set the font typeface to use, if possible
`<P></P>`	Create a new paragraph
`<P align=? >`	Align paragraph to left, right, or center
` `	Insert a line break
`<DL></DL>`	Create a definition list
`<DT>`	Precede a term
`<DD>`	Precede a term definition
`<OL></OL>`	Create a numbered list
`<LI></LI>`	Precede each item in the list, adds a number if within `<OL></OL>` or adds a bullet if within `<UL></UL>`
`<UL></UL>`	Create a bulleted list
`<HR>`	Insert a horizontal rule

Finally, HTML has tags to create forms for user input. However, the bare HTML simply gives the appearance of a form. In order to make functional forms, a CGI program is necessary. We'll cover that at the end of this session. For now, the HTML tags to create the appearance of a form within an HTML document are shown in Table 27-2.

Table 27-2
Form Tags in HTML4.01

Tag	Function
`<FORM></FORM>`	Create a form
`<SELECT multiple name="NAME" size=x></SELECT>`	Create a scrolling menu that displays x items in the menu at once
`<OPTION>`	Set off each item in the menu

Continued

Table 27-2   *Continued*

Tag	Function
`<SELECT name="NAME"></SELECT>`	Create a drop-down menu showing only the top item at once
`<TEXTAREA name="NAME" cols=x rows=y></TEXTAREA>`	Create a textbox x characters wide and y lines high
`<INPUT type="checkbox" name="NAME">`	Create a checkbox, follow with text
`<INPUT type="radio" name="NAME" value="z">`	Create a radio button, follow with text
`<INPUT type="text" name="NAME" size=x>`	Create a single-line text area of length x
`<INPUT type="submit" value="NAME">`	Create a submit button
`<INPUT type="image" border=0 name="NAME" src="image.jpg">`	Create a submit button using image.jpg
`<INPUT type="reset">`	Create a reset button that sets all forms in the document back to defaults

Here is the HTML skeleton, more fully fleshed out as a form to collect poll information about favorite ice cream flavors. The document uses a single-line text area, radio buttons, a scrolling, multiple-select menu, and a large text area.

```
<HTML>
  <HEAD>
    <TITLE>Example HTML Document</TITLE>
  </HEAD>
  <BODY bgcolor="white" text="black" link="red" vlink="blue"
   alink="green">
    <FONT color=#000000 face="Arial, Helvetica, sans-serif">
    <H1>Example HTML Document with Forms</H1><BR>
    <!-- create a form  (Note: This is an HTML comment!)-->
    <FORM>
      <!-- create the single line text space form -->
      <BR>
      <P>Please enter your name:
```

```
          <INPUT type="text" name="username" size="20"></P>
          <!-- create radio buttons for gender selection -->
          <P>Please select your gender:<BR>
          <INPUT type="radio" name="gender" value=0>Male<BR>
          <INPUT type="radio" name="gender" value=1>Female<BR>
          </P>
          <!-- create a scrolling box that displays 4 choices at once
            -->
          <P>Please select your favorite flavors of ice cream:<BR>
          <SELECT multiple name="icecream" size="4">
            <OPTION>Vanilla
            <OPTION>Chocolate
            <OPTION>Strawberry
            <OPTION>Butter Pecan
            <OPTION>Mint Chocolate Chip
            <OPTION>Coffee
            <OPTION>Chocolate Chip Cookie Dough
          </SELECT></P>
          <!-- create a text box for comments to be sent to user -->
          <P>Please enter any comments you have in the box below.
            Thank you.</P>
          <TEXTAREA name="comments" cols=50 rows=4>
          Please enter the comments here.
          </TEXTAREA>
          </P>
          <!-- create the submit and clear buttons -->
          <INPUT type="submit" value="submit">
          <INPUT type="reset">
        </FORM><!--end of form content -->
        <A href="mailto:someuser@foo.com">someuser@foo.com</A>
      </BODY>
    </HTML>
```

In a Web browser, this HTML document with forms now looks as shown in
Figure 27-2.

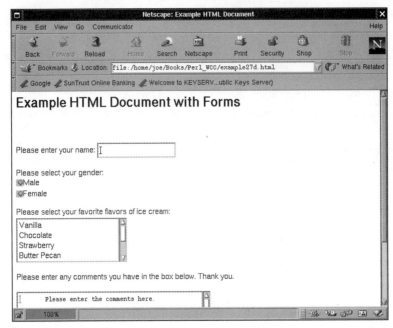

Figure 27-2
The form as it appears in the browser.

Now that you can create static HTML documents, let's go beyond static HTML.

Beyond Static HTML

**20 Min.
To Go**

Today, Web sites are steadily changing from collections of static HTML documents into interactive sites. These sites require dynamic content and cannot rely on static HTML alone.

There are two main ways to implement dynamic content within a Web page. The first method uses the Common Gateway Interface (CGI) and a server that re-serves a page to a client upon execution of the CGI program. The second way to implement dynamic content is to use Dynamic Hypertext Markup Language, or DHTML. DHTML is not really "dynamic HTML," it is simply a way of putting HTML together with Cascading Style Sheets (CSS), the Document Object Module (DOM), and JavaScript or VBScript. DHTML is a fairly new development without defined standards, while CGI is a de facto standard that has been around for many years.

In the CGI implementation of dynamic content, the server handles the processing work and displays the dynamically created page to the user. While this has costs in terms of network traffic and server processing time, it is handled by the server and follows a standard, so it is compatible with the software of most users.

However, in the DHTML implementation of dynamic content, the user's Web browser handles the processing of the dynamic portion. The server does not play a part in processing the dynamic content. But, different Web browsers handle DHTML content differently, most notably in the DOM. The DOM is how the browser recognizes the HTML elements within the JavaScript (or VBScript). This means that the developer must either write separate code for every Web browser or attempt to write compatible code across all platforms.

Interactive sites are not used for entertainment only. The ability to interact with users in real time enables Webmasters to make their sites useful in many ways.

Making the Web Useful

A common goal of Webmasters is to create functional sites that users enjoy using. In order for sites to be useful as well as engaging, the user must be able to interact with the content of the site. With dynamic content in Web sites, the user is given the ability to interact with the content of the site. Common examples of useful sites that use dynamic content include online shopping sites, search engines, and online technical support sites.

Consider a man who needs a software package immediately. He travels to a Web site specializing in software, types the package he is looking for into the site's search tool, and decides to purchase the software package for immediate download. He selects the option to buy the software package, and is then prompted for his contact and account information. After this information is verified, he downloads the software to his computer. Upon installation, he encounters a problem. Instead of calling the technical support line of the software developers where he is sure to be on hold for hours, he accesses their Web site. At their site, he searches for his specific problem, and the site dynamically presents him with the possible solutions, and ignores solutions to unrelated problems.

In this example, dynamic content is accessed at least three separate times (searching for the software package, ordering it, and searching for his problem). By implementing dynamic content in Web sites, the Web is becoming more useful. Perl scripts using the Common Gateway Interface are one main way dynamic content is implemented on the Web today.

**10 Min.
To Go**

The Common Gateway Interface

The Common Gateway Interface (CGI) is a de facto standard for interfacing external applications with other servers. As we have discussed, HTML documents alone are static. To create pages that contain dynamic content, we use CGI programs executed in real time, and output dynamic information.

For example, if a user is shopping at an online bookstore and wishes to search for *Perl Weekend Crash Course*, the page that displays the textbox to type the phrase into is contained in a static HTML document. However, once the user submits the query, a CGI program must execute. The CGI program must query the book databases, retrieve the query response, and display it to the user.

Since a CGI program is executed on the system every time a user submits a form, there are a couple of points to keep in mind. First, the program should process very quickly. If it does not, the user will be stuck staring at nothing while it processes. Secondly, certain precautionary measures must be taken to prevent harmful things to happen to the system. In general, the Web server will require that all CGI programs reside in a specified folder on the system. This keeps average users from creating CGI programs, unless they have access granted by the system administrator.

Since Perl is a scripting language and therefore does not require a compile of the source code to create executable code, Perl CGI programs are called CGI scripts. If a CGI program were written in C, the source code would have to be compiled and then the executable placed in the proper folder, and it would not be called a CGI script.

CGI scripts written in Perl can perform powerful functions in a short time, serving the user dynamic content efficiently.

Done!

REVIEW

Hypertext Markup Language (HTML) is the language that defines how the content of a Web page is displayed. However, HTML alone can only define a static document. Static documents, by definition, are not interactive. The current push towards interactive sites online necessitates that sites implement dynamic content. The Common Gateway Interface (CGI) and dynamic HTML (DHTML) are the two main ways that dynamic content is created today. CGI is a de facto standard for interfacing external applications with data servers. The external application is presented to the user, generally as an HTML document with forms. The user uses the forms and upon submission of the form, a CGI program runs and re-serves the user another HTML document based upon the submitted form information. CGI scripts written in Perl serve dynamic content efficiently to the user.

Quiz Yourself

1. List five tags for formatting characters in HTML. (See "A Quick HTML Refresher.")

2. Create a static HTML document to poll the user on pet ownership using checkboxes and a pull-down menu. (See "A Quick HTML Refresher.")

3. Compare and contrast DHTML and CGI-implemented dynamic Web content. (See "Beyond Static HTML.")

4. List three sites that you find useful. Select one of the sites and analyze how often it utilizes dynamic content to facilitate (See "Making the Web Useful.")

5. Outline the steps that a CGI program executes after a user submits a poll. (See "The Common Gateway Interface.")

Passing Data via CGI

Session Checklist

✔ Extracting data from HTML forms

✔ Using GET and POST

✔ Parsing and processing form data

**30 Min.
To Go**

You use HTML forms to give the user an easy way to input data. HTML forms also make it easy to collect this data. The data is extracted from the HTML form, sent to the CGI via GET or POST, and lastly, parsed and processed. This session begins with a discussion on how to extract information from HTML forms.

Extracting Data from HTML Forms

Once you have created an HTML form to collect input from the user, you need a way to access the user's input. If you recall from the previous session, each section of the form has a certain *name value* associated with it. Consider this snippet of HTML from the HTML forms example in Session 27.

```
<P>Please select your favorite flavors of ice cream:<BR>
<SELECT multiple name="icecream" size="4">
  <OPTION>Vanilla
  <OPTION>Chocolate
  <OPTION>Strawberry
  <OPTION>Butter Pecan
  <OPTION>Mint Chocolate Chip
  <OPTION>Coffee
  <OPTION>Chocolate Chip Cookie Dough
</SELECT></P>
```

In the `<SELECT multiple name="icecream" size="4">` tag shown previously, the name associated with this select is `icecream`. `icecream` is called the key of this select. When a user submits this form, and has selected `Vanilla` as her favorite ice cream flavor, the value of the key is set to `Vanilla`. This is called a key-value pair, which looks like this:

```
icecream=Vanilla
```

Later in this session, I'll show you how this data is sent to the CGI program, and how to parse and use it.

Another method of extracting data from HTML forms is to use the environment variables. CGI has a set of environment variables that the Web server sends to every CGI program run. Our CGI program can parse these variables and use the data they hold. The environment variables are contained in a hash called %ENV.

A table of the variable names and the associated values is shown in Table 28-1.

Table 28-1
CGI Environment Variables

Variable Name	Value
SERVER_ADMIN	E-mail address for the server's Webmaster
SERVER_NAME	Server's fully qualified domain name
SERVER_PORT	Port number the server is listening on
SERVER_SOFTWARE	server software you're using
SCRIPT_FILENAME	full pathname of current CGI
SCRIPT_NAME	pathname relative to document root
REQUEST_METHOD	GET or POST

Variable Name	Value
REQUEST_URI	Pathname of requested document/CGI relative to document root
REMOTE_ADDR	IP address of visitor
REMOTE_HOST	Hostname of the visitor (if reverse DNS is allowed; otherwise same as IP)
REMOTE_PORT	Port the visitor is connected to the server on
REMOTE_USER	Visitor's username (for .htaccess protected pages only)
QUERY_STRING	Query string (set by GET; see "GET and POST" section later in this session)
HTTPS	"on", if the script is called through a secure server
HTTP_COOKIE	The visitor's cookie, if one is set
HTTP_HOST	Hostname of the server
HTTP_REFERER	URL of the page that called the script
HTTP_USER_AGENT	Browser type of the visitor
DOCUMENT_ROOT	Root directory of the server
PATH	System path the server is running under

Some servers set additional environment variables; the server documentation will specify these. Also, not every environment variable is set for every CGI. QUERY_STRING is only set when GET is the method used to send the form data (see "GET and POST" later in this session). REMOTE_USER is only set for password-protected pages using a .htaccess file.

The %ENV hash is automatically created and populated for every CGI. In order to print out the IP address of the visitor, you would use:

```
print "IP of visitor: $ENV{'REMOTE_ADDR'}\n";
```

You can create a simple Perl CGI script to print out each environment variable. This script will be useful later, to verify that the correct items are being sent from the HTML form.

```
#!/usr/bin/Perl
print "Content-type:text/html\n\n";
print <<END;
<HTML>
<HEAD><TITLE>Environment Variables</TITLE></HEAD>
<BODY>
END
  foreach $var (sort(keys %ENV)){
    print "$var = $ENV{$var}<BR>\n";
  }
print "</BODY></HTML>";
```

Doing this assumes that you have access to a Web server that can serve pages generated by a CGI script. When you process data from a Web form, the standard output is considered to be the user's browser. Thus when you use print **statements in this way, the data will be printed to the browser.**

Now that you can extract data from the HTML forms, you need to know how to send it to your CGI program.

GET and POST

There are two ways to send data from an HTML form to a CGI program: GET and POST. GET and POST are methods that determine how the form data is sent to the server.

The GET method sends the input values from the form as part of the URL. The variables are also saved in the QUERY_STRING environment variable. The POST method sends the input values from the form as an input stream to the program.

The QUERY_STRING can be set in a few different ways. One way is to set it using HTML forms that utilize the GET method. Take the Ice Cream survey from Session 27. Change the <FORM...> tag to:

```
<FORM action="environ.cgi" method="GET">
```

When the user submits the form (by clicking on the submit button), the user's Web browser will call the environ.cgi CGI program and use the GET method. The form will put the form data (basically, the settings of all the controls in the form) into the URL the browser uses to call the CGI script, as well as saving it into the QUERY_STRING environment variable. If you now take the Ice Cream survey and submit it, two things will happen. First, the URL in the web browser location bar looks similar to:

```
http://www.foo.com/ch28/environ.cgi?username=foo&gender=1&icecream
=mint+chocolate+chip&comments=what+a+great+idea
```

Secondly, the QUERY_STRING shown in the browser's address window is set to the same content displayed after the question mark (?) in the above URL. It looks like:

```
QUERY_STRING = username=foo&gender=1&icecream=Mint+Chocolate+Chip&
                comments=what+a+great+idea
```

Note that the key-value pairs associated with the form are separated by an at sign (&). I'll show you how to parse this within the CGI in the next section. Also note that any spaces in the input have been changed to the plus sign (+), and similar changes have been made to other special nonalphanumeric characters, using a percent sign (%) as an escape character. This is called URL encoding.

GET is not a secure method, so passwords and other sensitive data should not be sent using the GET method. The data is passed through as part of the URL, so it shows up in the Web server's log file, which is generally readable by most users. Private information should be sent using the POST method. (Although the POST method doesn't display the information, it is still sent over the Internet in clear text. This may be okay for very basic data, such as your name, but should not be used for very sensitive data, such as a credit card number.)

The POST method sends the data to your CGI as an input stream. This means that your CGI must first get the stream and store it in a string that you can easily manipulate later. In order to save the input stream into a string, copy the STDIN into a buffer the length of the content, as shown here:

```
read(STDIN, $buffer, $ENV{'CONTENT_LENGTH'});
```

Once you have the form data stored in a string, you can easily parse and process it.

Parsing and Processing Form Data

Once the data has been sent to your CGI script, you must parse and process it. This will allow you to pass dynamic information to the user, compute the current standing of a poll, and handle database searching and other functions.

Splitting on ampersands

When a form uses the GET method for many key-value pairs, it sends it in a string that separates the key-value pairs with an ampersand (&). Your CGI script must separate these pairs in order to use this data. This can be done using Perl's split function. The split function allows you to split a string into an array of strings, breaking on a specific character. The Perl code to split up your QUERY_STRING into an array of key-value pairs, called @pairs, looks like this:

```
@pairs = split (/&/, $ENV{'QUERY_STRING'});
```

You have created an array called @pairs that contains the key-value pairs contained in the QUERY_STRING. This will make parsing these values easier later.

URL Decoding

As we have discussed, a Web server URL-encodes the data sent from the HTML forms to the CGI. In order to use this information, you must decode this data. Using Perl's commands for substitution and transliteration, you can easily decode the URL-encoded data.

You can use this line in order to translate every + back into a space:

```
$value =~ tr/+/ /;
```

In order to convert the hex pairs back to their equivalent ASCII character, use the pack() function along with regular expressions:

```
$value =~ s/%([a-fA-F0-9][a-fA-F0-9])/pack("C", hex($1))/eg;
```

Often, it is easier to simply save all of the values from the submitted form into a hash:

```
$FORM($key) = $value;
```

Putting It All Together

The following CGI script saves the form data from the input stream into a string, stores it, decodes it, and prints out each value. This can be quite useful in debugging a script.

```
#!/usr/bin/Perl
print "Content-type:text/html\n\n";
@icecream=read(STDIN, $buffer, $ENV{'CONTENT_LENGTH'});
@pairs = split (/&/, $buffer);
foreach $pair (@pairs){
    ($key, $value) = split(/=/, $pair);
    $value =~ tr/+/ /;
    $value =~ s/%([a-fA-F0-9][a-fA-F0-9])/pack("C", hex($1))/eg;
    if ($key eq "icecream") {
        push(@icecream, $value);
    }
    else {
        $FORM{$key} = $value;
    }
}
print <<END;
<HTML>
<HEAD><TITLE>POST output</TITLE></HEAD>
<BODY>
<H1>Results from POST</H1><BR>
END
foreach $key (keys(%FORM)){
    print "$key = $FORM{$key}<BR>";
}
foreach $icecream (@icecream){
    print "icecream = $icecream<BR>\n";
}
print "</BODY></HTML>";
```

Let's take your ice cream survey HTML and modify it such that you use a POST rather than a GET, and print out the form data that is sent. Do this by setting the action to call the previous form.cgi, and to set the method to POST.

```
<FORM action="form.cgi" method="POST">
```

Open the ice cream survey in your Web browser, and fill out the survey. Figure 28-1 shows form just before submission.

Submit the form. It will POST the data to form.cgi, which will print the content out in the Web browser, as shown in Figure 28-2.

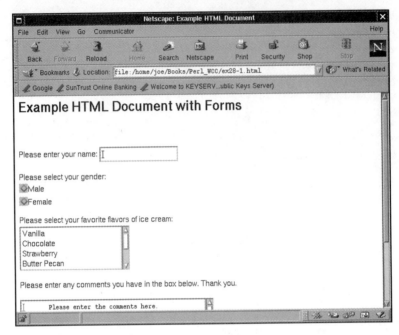

Figure 28-1
The ice cream survey as rendered in a browser.

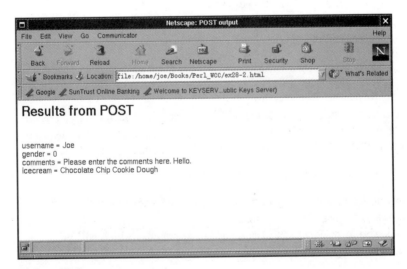

Figure 28-2
The survey's results

**10 Min.
To Go**

Making the CGI Useful

While it's helpful to see the data that the user posted was properly sent to your CGI, printing back to the user what she posted is not very useful. In order to make your survey functional, you want to tabulate the results. You also want to e-mail the comments to the Webmaster.

In order to do this, you will use parts of `form.cgi` (shown previously) to save the form data into an easy-to-manipulate hash. You will also add sections to e-mail the comments to the Webmaster, and a section to display the survey results to the user after submission. These sections can be used to accomplish other manipulations of form data.

There are three parts you must implement in order to display the survey results to the user. You must collect his survey results, tabulate those results along with the existing results, and then display the final tabulation to the user.

First, you create a file to hold all of the survey information. The file is a plain-text file of data. Each line is a separate record. This is called a flat-file database.

In general, CGI programs are not allowed to create files themselves. Therefore, you must create the flat-file database yourself in the folder where your CGI is, and set the permissions to be world writeable:

```
touch icecreamsurvey.out
chmod 666 icecreamsurvey.out
```

Next, you write the posted information to this file. You must first open the file, and then lock it so that no other CGI POST can write while you are

```
open SURVEY_DB or die "Couldn't open $SURVEY_DB_FILE for writing:
$!.\n";
flock (SURVEY_DB, 2);
```

Use a variable to set the filehandle of the flat-file database within your script. If the filehandle changes in the future, you only have to change it at one place within the script. Previously, you set SURVEY_DB **to** `icecreamsurvey.out`, **and you used** SURVEY_DB **to call the file.**

In the chance that someone wrote to the file as you were locking it, you set the file pointer to the end of the file. The `seek` command is used to set the location of the file pointer. `seek` is of the form

```
seek(filehandle, offset, whence);
```

where offset is the number of bytes to offset of the pointer relative to whence. Whence is one of the following:

* 0: beginning of file
* 1: current file position
* 2: end of file

Therefore, in order to set your file pointer to the end of the database file, you use:

```
seek(SURVEY_DB, 0, 2);
```

Now that the file is open and locked, and the file pointer is at the end of the file, you can write the data to it. You write one post as a single line within the file, so each line is a record in the database. The attributes associated within each record are delimited by pipes (|). In this example, your database file will look similar to this:

```
username | gender | icecream | comments
```

In order to write the data to the file, you print each element to it, as shown here:

```
print SURVEY_DB "$FORM{'username'}|";
print SURVEY_DB "$FORM{'gender'}|";
foreach $icecream (@icecream) {
  print SURVEY_DB "$icecream,";
}
print SURVEY_DB "|";
print SURVEY_DB "$FORM{'comments'}\n";
```

The ice cream section includes a foreach that prints out every element in the @icecream array. This is because the user can select more than one type of ice cream. You want each selection in the database.

Now, you must close the file, which releases the lock so that other posts to the CGI can add their information.

```
close(SURVEY_DB);
```

The database is now being updated. This means that you have a database to pull information from in order to calculate the results. This involves opening the file, reading it into an array, closing the file, and iterating through every line, incrementing the counters for the results.

Opening and closing the file use the same syntax as above. In order to read an entire file into an array, use:

```
@data = <SURVEY_DB>;
```

Once the data has been copied into the array, you can close the file. This minimizes the time the file is held open. Now that you have read the database into the array, you read it line by line, and update the information of variables you use as counters.

```
foreach $i (@data) {
        chomp($i);
        ($username, $gender, $icecreamtype, $comments) = split
          (/\|/,$i);
     # increment total user count
        $total_user++;
     # etc...

}
```

Other information can be calculated by accessing the stored information and using Perl to increment variables. Once the results have been tallied, you can post the results to the user by simply printing out HTML with embedded Perl.

```
print <<END;
<HTML>
<HEAD><TITLE>Results of Ice Cream Survey</TITLE></HEAD>
<BODY>
<H2>Ice Cream Survey Results</H2><BR>
    <B>Total visitors:</B> $total_user<BR>
    <BR><BR>
    <P>Thank you for submitting! If you have any additional
comments, please e-mail the webmaster, <A
href="mailto:webmaster\@foo.com">webmaster\@foo.com</A>
    </BODY></HTML>
END
```

Once you put these parts together, you can write the data to the database file, read from the database file, compile the current results, and print the results to the user. Now you can e-mail the comments to the Webmaster.

In order to e-mail the comments to the Webmaster, there are a few pieces of information that you need to know. First, you need to know the path for sendmail on the server that your CGI resides on (which sendmail or whereis sendmail should yield the location of sendmail). Second, you need to know the address to mail the comments to.

First, open a pipe to the mail program. The pipe causes all of the output you print to the filehandle to be fed directly to the mail program.

```
$mailprogpath = '/usr/sbin/sendmail';
open (MAIL, "|$mailprogpath -t") or die ("Can't access
  $mailprogpath\n");
```

Next, you set the recipient address to the Webmaster.

```
$recipient_addr = "webmaster\@foo.com";
```

Now that you have a pipe open to the mail program, you simply send it the information that you would like it to mail to the Webmaster. First you set the header information (To, From, Subject):

```
print MAIL "To: $recipient_addr\n";
print MAIL "From: $FORM{'username'} via Ice Cream Survey\n";
print MAIL "Subject: Comments on Ice Cream Survey\n\n";
```

You end the header information by placing an additional newline character at the end of the Subject line. Now, everything printed to MAIL will be part of the body of the e-mail. To send the name of the person who was surveyed and their comments, use

```
print MAIL "$FORM{'username'}\n\n";
print MAIL "$FORM{'comments'}\n\n";
```

Now that you have printed the name of the person who was surveyed along with his comments, you are finished with the message, and must close the input stream:

```
close(MAIL);
```

You are now able to decode posted form data and manipulate it for various uses. You can store it in a flat-file database, and use Perl to parse the database file and compile statistical information from that database. You can also print results to the user. By using any combination of these abilities, you can accomplish almost everything you would like to with form data.

Done!

REVIEW

To extract information from HTML forms, information is sent to the CGI in the form of key-value pairs. Key-value pairs set a specified variable name (*key*) to the value that the user specified. These key-value pairs are then sent to a CGI program using either GET or POST. GET sends the pairs from the form as part of the URL, as well as saving them in the QUERY_STRING environment variable. POST sends the pairs from the form as an input stream to the program. When GET and POST send this data, they URL-encode it. When the CGI receives the information, it must un-encode it. Once the data is decoded, the CGI program can manipulate the data. CGI programs are often used to collect information, save it to a database, compute results, and to post information back to the user.

QUIZ YOURSELF

1. Describe what a key-value pair is. (See "Extracting Data from HTML Forms.")

2. What are GET and POST? How is GET different from POST? (See "GET and POST.")

3. Using the HTML document to poll pet ownership created in Session 27, write a CGI program to list what percentage of the people polled have certain types of pets. (See "Parsing and Processing Form Data.")

4. Name three items that have to be URL decoded after the form data has been submitted. (See "Parsing and Processing Form Data.")

5. Write a document with associated CGI to allow the user to e-mail you comments. (See "Parsing and Processing Form Data.")

The CGI.pm Module

Session Checklist

✔ Using shortcuts to HTML generation

✔ Understanding CGI module functions

✔ Processing form data

✔ Benefiting from smarter HTML

30 Min.
To Go

The CGI.pm library module uses objects to create HTML forms and parse their contents. CGI.pm includes functions that enable you to create HTML documents quickly. By generating HTML this way, the value of previous queries is used to initialize the form. This preserves the state of the form. CGI.pm also provides functions to parse and interpret queries sent to CGI scripts.

Shortcuts to HTML Generation

CGI.pm includes many functions that can generate HTML easily. Before you use these functions, you must select which mode you wish to use. CGI.pm can be used in either function-oriented mode or object-oriented mode.

Function-oriented vs. object-oriented

In function-oriented mode, you import the CGI functions into your script's name-space, and then call them directly. An example of a simple function-oriented script is shown next:

```
#!/usr/bin/Perl
use CGI qw/:standard/;
print header(),
start_html(-title=>'Function-Oriented Generation',
            -BGCOLOR=>'red',
            -author=>'user@foo.com'),
h2('Function-Oriented Generation'),
'This has been generated using CGI.pm in function-oriented
 mode.',
end_html();
```

In this script, you import the :standard set of function definitions, which include the HTML generation functions.

In object-oriented mode, we use CGI; and communicate with CGI.pm using a CGI object. This object contains all of the information about the current CGI trans-action, including values passed to the CGI. An object-oriented version of the script above may look like this:

```
#!/usr/bin/Perl
use CGI;
$query = new CGI;
print $query->header(),
      $query->start_html(-title=>'Object-Oriented Generation',
                          -BGCOLOR=>'red',
                          -author=>'user@foo.com'),
      $query->h2('Object-Oriented Generation'),
      'This has been generated using CGI.pm in object-oriented
       mode.',
      $query->end_html();
```

Note that in this instance of the script, we create an object $query and use the arrow operator to de-reference it, then call the function in CGI.pm. The examples of code in this session will use the object-oriented mode.

HTML header creation

CGI.pm includes the `start_html()` function you used in the examples above. It creates an HTML header and the opening `<BODY>` tag. Other parameters are available, including the character set of the browser, and a parameter to turn the page into an attachment. The available parameters are listed in Table 29-1.

Table 29-1
HTTP Header Parameters in CGI.pm

Parameter	Definition
-expires	Specify when to expire the CGI script.
-type	Specify the content-type of the document.
-cookie	Ask the browser to return a cookie during all transactions with the script.
-charset	Control the character set of the browser.
-attachment	Turn the page into an attachment.
-nph	Generate a valid header for use in scripts in which the header is not parsed.

The syntax for utilizing multiple parameters is shown in the example below:

```
print $query->start_html(-title=>'Title of the Document',
                         -author=>'user@foo.com',
                         -meta=>{'keywords'=>'keyword1
                            keyword2'},
                         -BGCOLOR=>'black',
                         -TEXT=>'white');
```

Ending an HTML document

To end an HTML document by printing `</BODY></HTML>`, CGI.pm offers the function:

```
print $query->end_html;
```

Other HTML tags

Unpaired tags such as <BR> and <HR> can be created using the syntax:

```
print $query->br;
```

This prints out the text <BR>.
Paired tags such as <B> and <H3> can be created using the syntax

```
print $query->b("This is in boldface.");
```

You can also nest tags as shown here:

```
print $query->h3("I am a ", query->b("header"), "of size 3");
```

While most of the tags are represented in lowercase, there are a few exceptions due to conflicts with other Perl functions.

- <TR> must be specified with Tr or TR.
- <param> must be specified with PARAM().
- <select> must be specified with Select().
- <sub> must be specified with Sub().

Tags with attributes can be written syntactically in one of two ways. You have already seen the first type in the previous examples using start_html. An example may look like this:

```
print $query->img {-src=>'foo.gif',
                    -align=>'right'};
```

The dashes in front of the attributes may be removed. This is the other syntactic method:

```
print $query->img {src=>'foo.gif',
                   align=>'right'};
```

Sometimes an attribute has no argument. In this case, set the attribute to undef as shown here:

```
print $query->table({border=>undef});
```

This creates the tag <TABLE border>.

Form tags

Using CGI.pm to create forms uses the same syntax as the HTML tags specified previously, but there is one point to keep in mind. The default values that you specify for the form are only used the first time the script is invoked. The values present in the query string — even if blank — are used otherwise. There are two ways to change the value of a field from its previous value:

- Call param() to set it
- Use the -override parameter. -override forces the default at all times.

To start a form, call startform(), which returns a <FORM> tag with the optional method, action, and form encoding. The code for creating a form fits the syntax shown next:

```
print $query->startform($method, $action, $encoding);
```

Between the start of the form and the end of the form, you'll want to insert textfields, textareas, menus, and the like. The syntax is the same as with the other functions to create HTML tags.

For example, to create a textfield, the code looks similar to

```
print $query->textfield(-name=>'field_name',
                        -default=>'start',
                        -size=>2,
                        -maxlength=>24);
```

The preceding code will output this HTML:

```
<TEXTFIELD name="field_name" size="2" maxlength="24">
start
</TEXTFIELD>
```

To create a scrolling list, call scrolling_list() as shown here:

```
print $query->scrolling_list(-name=>'scrolling_list_name',
                             -values=>['foo', 'bar', 'baz',
                                       'qux'],
                             -default=>'foo',
                             -size=>2,
                             -multiple=>'false',
                             -labels=>\%labels);
```

In this case, you set the name of the list to be `scrolling_list_name`.

This means that the values are passed along with that key. The possible values are `foo`, `bar`, `baz`, and `qux`, with `foo` set as the default. Only two are displayed to the user at a time, as set in the size. Multiple is set to `false`, so the user can only select one at a time. `labels` enables you to assign the labels that the user will see. In this example, we'll assume that the associative array `%labels` has already been created.

CGI.pm provides an easy way to create HTML documents by simply calling functions. This enables you to import information and create dynamic HTML. Often, however, you only wish to do simple things with your script, so allocating an object and then discarding it is wasteful. In these cases, you can import CGI modules instead.

**20 Min.
To Go**

CGI Module Functions

In the instance that you have a script that you just want to use to read parameters or collect form data, it is wasteful to allocate an object and then discard it. Instead of doing this, you can import CGI module functions into your namespace. I touched on this briefly when comparing function-oriented mode to object-oriented mode. Common syntax for importing methods looks similar to

```
use CGI qw(:standard);
```

Now, instead of accessing your CGI object to print, you can do it directly, like this:

```
print start_html(-title=>'Module Functions'),
    h2('More on Module Functions'),
    "Foo. CGI Module Functions.",
    end_html();
```

In this case, state is maintained through the use of a CGI object that is created automatically. This object can be accessed directly by referring to it as

```
$CGI::$Q;
```

You can also import method names themselves into the current namespace. The syntax for this is

```
use CGI qw(header start_html h2 b end_html);
```

Note that the method names do not have a preceding colon (`:`), unlike the previous example. `:standard` is an export tag, or method family. These are distinguished from methods by the preceding colon. The syntax for importing more than one export tag is

```
use CGI qw(:cgi :html);
```

The nine method families defined in CGI.pm are listed in Table 29-2.

Table 29-2
Method Families in CGI.pm

Method Family	Description
:cgi	CGI protocol tags
:form	HTML Form tags
:html2	HTML2 defined tags — br(), p(), head()
:html3	HTML3 defined tags — tables, frames, etc.
:netscape	Netscape extensions — blink(), center()
:html	All HTML shortcuts — html2, html3, netscape
:multipart	Multipart MIME type elements
:standard	Html2, form, and cgi families
:all	All methods

By importing only the necessary CGI module functions into your namespace, you utilize less space. By importing only a family of methods, you make your scripts less wasteful.

**10 Min.
To Go**

Processing Form Data

By using CGI.pm and the CGI object, the query string is automatically parsed and stored. When you wish to process the form data, you need to retrieve the values stored in the object.

Earlier, I showed you how to create a textfield using CGI.pm. The sample code to create a textfield is repeated here.

```
print $query->textfield(-name=>'field_name',
                        -default=>'start',
                        -size=>2,
                        -maxlength=>24);
```

At the time that the form this is a part of is processed, you'll want to extract the data from this textfield. To do this, use

```
$value = $query->param('field_name');
```

This puts into $value the value in $query where the key is field_name. The param() function is used with CGI.pm to set as well as to retrieve data from the CGI object.

This format for extracting data from the object works for every key-value pair stored in the object. The key is the name associated with the form element.

For example, we created a sample scrolling list previously. Recall,

```
print $query->scrolling_list(-name=>'scrolling_list_name',
                             -values=>['foo', 'bar', 'baz',
                                        'qux'],
                             -default=>'foo',
                             -size=>2,
                             -multiple=>'false',
                             -labels=>\%labels);
```

In this instance, the key associated with this list is scrolling_list_name. The selection made by the user will be stored in the CGI object as scrolling_list_name=user_selection. To extract the user_selection from the CGI object, use:

```
$selection = $query->param('scrolling_list_name');
```

The syntax for extracting the data associated with this scrolling list is exactly the same as the syntax for extracting the data associated with the textfield.

However, there is one difference. If the user was allowed to select multiple options from this list, the values returned from the CGI object would be a list, and you would have to use an array to store the list. It would look like this:

```
@selection = $query->param('scrolling_list_name');
```

A rule of thumb is to know whether you are retrieving a single object back, as in a textfield or a standalone checkbox, or if you may be receiving multiple objects back from a single form element, as in a multiple select list or a group of checkboxes. If you could be receiving multiple elements, you extract them into an array. If it is only a singular element, a string will suffice.

Smarter HTML

The CGI.pm module offers functions to assist in making smarter HTML. CGI.pm provides access to various HTTP session variables and cookies.

HTTP session variables

`Accept()` is one of the useful HTTP session variables that you can access through CGI.pm. `Accept()` returns a list of the MIME types that the remote browser will accept.

While generally you would not find an entire list useful, if you pass the method a single argument like

```
$query->Accept('text/html')
```

`Accept()` returns a floating-point value that corresponds to the browser's preference for this type. `0.0` indicates that the browser doesn't want to handle this type, and `1.0` indicates that the browser is ready and willing to handle textHTML.

Another useful HTTP variable that CGI.pm provides is `http()`. `http()` returns the list of all HTTP environment variables when called with no arguments. If `http()` is called with the name of an HTTP header field like `HTTP_ACCEPT_LANGUAGE`, it will return its value.

HTTP session variables function similar to CGI environment variables. Used well, HTTP session variables enable you to handle users using different browsers, languages, and network connections. By using this information, you can adapt your HTML documents accordingly.

Cookies

Cookies are used to manage state within a browser session. You can create and read from cookies using modules specified in CGI.pm. Cookies, much like the key-value pairs in a CGI query string, are made up of name-value pairs.

You can create cookies and send them to the browser in the HTTP header. The browser then stores the cookie on the client machine, maintains a list of cookies, and returns them to the CGI script during later interactions with the particular Web server.

To create a new cookie, use `cookie()`. There are many parameters you can set for each cookie, however. For example, if you are an online bookstore using cookies, you may wish to create a cookie to save the last book viewed by the user. If a week passes before the user returns, you do not care about the last book viewed. Your cookie may look like this:

```
$cookie = $query->cookie(-name=>'last_book_viewed',
                         -value=>'name_of_book',
                         -expires=>'+7d',
                         -domain=>'foobooks.com');
```

You send this cookie to the browser by way of the HTTP header as shown here:

```
print $query->header(-cookie=>$cookie);
```

There are additional parameters that may be used with cookie(). These are detailed in Table 29-3.

Table 29-3
Cookie Parameters in CGI.pm

Parameter	Definition
-name	Name of the cookie (required)
-value	Value of the cookie (required)
-path	Partial path for which the cookie is valid
-domain	Partial domain for which the cookie is valid
-expires	Period of validity for the cookie
-secure	If true, cookie is only used within secure session

Through the use of HTTP session variables and cookies, you are able to write smarter HTML. HTTP session variables offer a way to tailor content to the user's browser type, language, and other variables. The cookies assist in holding the state from a previous visit.

Done!

REVIEW

The CGI.pm module offers access to many functions useful when writing CGI scripts for the Internet. CGI.pm uses objects to create HTML forms, hold the data, and parse the contents. By using the CGI.pm functions to generate HTML documents in Perl, the forms are initialized with the most recent query, preserving the state of the document. The CGI object used with CGI.pm functions is easier to parse and interpret than GET's query string and POST's input stream. With CGI.pm, you can import only the necessary methods into your namespace, which makes the script less wasteful. Through the use of HTTP session variables and cookies, you can create HTML documents that are smarter, tailored to the user, and that contain information about the most recent visit.

Quiz Yourself

1. What are the main differences between function-oriented mode and object-oriented mode? (See "Shortcuts to HTML Generation.")

2. Write a Perl script that generates an HTML document that includes a textfield and at least 4 other HTML elements using only functions in CGI.pm. (See "Shortcuts to HTML Generation.")

3. Using the document created in question 3, write the code to extract the textfield data from the CGI object. (See "Processing Form Data.")

4. Describe what cookies are used for and use Perl to write code to create a cookie to be used with a search engine CGI script. (See "Smarter HTML.")

Apache and mod_perl

Session Checklist

✔ Installing Apache Web server

✔ Controlling server-side processing

✔ Understanding the downside of CGI

✔ Giving Apache some Perl muscle

✔ Programming with mod_perl

**30 Min.
To Go**

Throughout this afternoon, we have talked about implementing HTML documents and Perl CGI scripts on Web servers. However, we have not discussed Web servers in detail. Apache is currently the most popular Web server used today, and it supports a number of features other than simply serving HTML content. Apache supports the use of server-side includes (SSIs): directives placed directly in HTML documents that the server computes on the fly. Apache also supports integration with Perl in the mod_perl project, which enables you to access the Apache API through Perl. In instances where CGI scripts are not the proper solution, SSIs and mod_perl offer other options.

The Apache Web Server

A Web server is a program that runs on a computer and serves up Web sites. The Web server waits for a request from a visitor for an object, and replies by sending these objects to the visitor. These objects include HTML documents, images, sounds, and video.

The Apache Web server is one of the fastest and most robust Web servers. The Apache Software Foundation (ASF) maintains Apache at http://www.apache.org/.

Apache is a very reliable Web server, used by 60 percent of the Web server market at the time of this writing. Apache is incredibly reliable and supports many features in its main core of functions. Also, since Apache is open-source, other developers have written modules that support other features. In the chance that there is not a module that supports a feature you would like, due to Apache being open-source, you can write the feature yourself. Since Apache dominates the Web server market, support is relatively easy to find.

Basics of installation

Apache can be built and installed in many different ways. There are three main ways that Apache is installed: binary installation, through an operating system package, and directly from the source.

Binary installation involves obtaining a precompiled source for your specific operating system. This means that you must use a Linux binary on your Linux machine, and a Solaris binary on your Solaris machine. It also means that if a binary for your OS doesn't exist, you have to install using a different method. Binaries are generally preconfigured, which means that you lose some flexibility in being able to alter Apache to your specifics. Lastly, binaries are generally a couple of versions behind the current source, so you lose the benefit of having new feature sets and recent bug fixes.

Package-specific binaries for Apache also exist in a form usable by package managers like Red Hat Package Manager (RPM) and Debian's Package Manager. These are basically identical to a binary, however they are configured to play well with other RPMs and provide an easy-to-manage way to install, update, and remove packages. Packages are generally less flexible than binaries, and often times it is difficult to tell where a package will be installed. However, packages do provide an easy installation route if you do not want any special configurations, or if you are simply trying to get your feet wet, and plan to do a fully customized installation later.

The third installation option involves downloading the Apache source and compiling it directly on the Web server. While this may sound a bit frightening, the

Apache developers have made the installation an easy one. Compiling the source offers the most flexible installation as well as the most up-to-date source.

If you simply wish to get Apache up and running as quickly as possible without any special configurations, using a binary or a package is the easiest way to install Apache. However, if you require some special configurations and want more control over the installation, compiling the source is the best method of installation.

Apache can do more than simply serve up HTML documents. In the rest of this session, I'll discuss various ways to harness Apache's power through the use of server-side processing and mod_perl.

Server-Side Processing

**20 Min.
To Go**

Server-side processing is a process whereby bits of data evaluated by the server to serve dynamic content to the user without serving an entire page using a CGI program. Server-side includes (SSI) are one main way to add server-side processed dynamic content.

Server-side includes (SSI) are directives placed directly in HTML pages and are evaluated on the server as the page is delivered. They enable you to add dynamic content to a page without making the entire page dynamic. The decision of whether to use SSI depends on how much dynamic content is being served. If only a part of a page needs to show dynamic content, then SSI is a good way to do this. If most of the page is generated dynamically, however, CGI programs are more likely a better solution.

Configuring Apache for SSI

In order to configure Apache to permit SSI, you add the following directive to your httpd.conf or .htaccess file:

```
Options +Includes
```

Next, you need to tell Apache which files should be parsed for SSI content. You don't want to tell Apache to parse every HTML file for SSI directives, as this will slow down the server significantly. However, you may wish to configure Apache to parse every .shtml file for SSI directives. Tell Apache

```
AddType text/html .shtml
AddHandler server-parsed .shtml
```

However, this means that you have to rename all pages with SSI directives to .shtml files, and change all links to those pages. Another method you can use to configure Apache to parse for SSI directives is to tell Apache to parse all files with the execute bit set. This way, you simply have to make all files with SSI directives executable.

In order to set Apache to parse executable files for SSI directives, set

```
XBitHack on
```

Now that you have configured Apache to handle SSI, let's discuss how to write SSI directives.

SSI directives

SSI directives are formatted like HTML comments. If SSI is not enabled on the Web server, it will ignore the directives and they will be served as part of the HTML document. If SSI is enabled, the directive will be replaced with the calculated value.

The basic syntax of an SSI directive looks like this:

```
<!-- #element key1=value1 key2=value2 ... -->
```

One common use of SSI is to add the current date and time to an HTML document:

```
<!-- #echo var=DATE_LOCAL -->
```

This echoes the value of DATE_LOCAL. DATE_LOCAL is one of many standard variables. SSI supports the set of environment variables available to CGI, as well as allowing you to define your own variables using set.

You can change the format the date is printed in by using the config element and the timefmt key as shown here.

```
<!-- #config timefmt="%d, %Y" -->
<!-- #echo var=DATE_LOCAL -->
```

Another common use of SSI is to print the last modified date of a file. This is shown here:

```
Last modified: <!-- #flastmod file="index.html" -->
```

The problem with this method is that it requires you to edit the file every time you add this directive to a page. A better way would be to use the variable LAST_MODIFIED, which will populate the directive with the last modified timestamp of the file:

```
Last modified: <!-- #echo var="LAST_MODIFIED" -->
```

SSI can also be used to include the results of a CGI program. If you wanted to show the results of your ice cream survey from earlier this afternoon within a HTML document, you could use the following directive:

```
<!-- #exec cgi="/cgi-bin/surveyresults.pl" -->
```

While managing a site, often times you'll wish to standardize the appearance of each of the pages within your site. You can use SSI to include a common header and/or footer within a site. To do this, create a file that includes all of the code you would like in your footer. The include element can be coupled with either the file key or the virtual key. The file key requires that the file path be relative to the current directory, and cannot include the / or ../ character sequences as part of the file path. The virtual key specifies a URL relative to the file being served, and must exist on the same server:

```
<!-- #include virtual="/common/footer.html" -->
```

SSI can also execute commands in the shell using the exec element:

```
<!-- #exec cmd="ls -l" -->
```

This means that any code embedded in the exec element will be executed. This can be incredibly dangerous. However, you can configure Apache to allow SSI, but disallow the exec element by adding

```
Options +IncludesNOEXEC
```

Through the use of SSI, you can embed dynamic content that is processed by the Web server at the time of serving.

The Downside of CGI

While I spoke about the benefits of CGI this afternoon, there are always downsides to every upside. CGI programs are no different. CGI programs have a high runtime overhead, pose a certain security risk, and often require multiple interactions between the client and the server.

Sites that utilize CGI programs to deliver dynamic content must execute the CGI script every time and serve the dynamic content to the user every time the site is accessed. On a high-traffic site, this can cause the Web server to slow significantly.

Since CGI scripts are executed on the server, they can access privileged server information if the script is careless. A rogue user could exploit a CGI script and gain access to a server without permission or take down a Web server with a well-placed denial of service (DoS) attack. If you program well, and are careful with privileged access, this should not be a problem. If you find it necessary to access secure information through your script, you can set the script to be `suid`, and use `suidperl`. CGI scripts can be written securely, however the threat still exists.

Often, you use a CGI script to handle multiple levels of interaction between a user and the Web server. An example of this would be a site with a survey script that would serve a survey question and form. After posting to this script, the server re-serves the page to site visitors, but with the updated survey results. The original document is served through the use of a CGI program, the POST/GET of the survey selection by the user is another interaction the server must handle, and the final results are served through a CGI program. Other scripts involve many more interactions between the client and the server. Again, on a high-traffic site, this can significantly slow down the Web server. It also increases the likelihood that a level of interaction will fail.

While CGI programs are fast and fairly easy to implement on low-traffic sites, on high-traffic sites and sites concerned with security, they may not be the correct solution to dynamic content question. However, you have the ability to integrate Perl with Apache in a robust, secure way. In a situation where Perl CGI scripts do not seem like the proper solution, mod_perl may be the answer.

Giving Apache Some Perl Muscle

10 Min. To Go

Perl and Apache are strong alone, but if you integrate them, you can make them stronger yet. If you link the Perl runtime library into the Apache server and provide an object-oriented interface to the server's API, you can give Apache some Perl muscle. Mod_perl enables you to do this.

Mod_perl gives additional power and speed. It gives access to the Web server and enables you to intervene at any point in the process. This enables you to customize the processing of authentication, logging, and other phases. Mod_perl has a very low runtime overhead, unlike CGI. In fact, mod_perl can replace CGI programs entirely, and run existing CGI programs transparently.

The easiest way to compile mod_perl support into Apache is to run mod_perl's `Makefile.pl`, which will configure the mod_perl module into Apache. Once this is complete and mod_perl is linked into `httpd`, you can run it with the `-l` switch, which will list the compiled-in modules.

Existing perl CGI scripts should continue to run, though they may require an adjustment if `write()` is used. In developing new CGI scripts, it is best to use CGI.pm, as mod_perl and CGI.pm have no conflicts.

Mod_perl runs within an http child process, therefore with the userID and groupID specified in the `http.conf` file. Generally, this user and group should only be able to access world-readable files. However, different mod_perl scripts run using the same Perl interpreter instance. This means that a rogue mod_perl script can redefine the Perl objects and change how the other mod_perl scripts act. You can turn on tainting checks by including the directive `PerlTaintCheck On` in the `httpd.conf` file. This will help to avoid using bad data passed to your mod_perl script.

An interesting difference between Perl CGI scripts and mod_perl scripts is that CGI scripts start up a new Perl interpreter every time they run whereas Mod_perl scripts reuse the same Perl interpreter. This means that some mod_perl variables will survive from script to script. While this can be useful at times, it can also be a debugging nightmare. I'll discuss this in more detail in the next section. Now that you have an idea of what mod_perl can do and how it works, let's see mod_perl in action.

mod_perl in Action

Programming in mod_perl is not that different from programming in Perl. However, there are a few instances where mod_perl and Perl act differently. This section offers samples of code and comments about common errors that Perl programmers run into when programming in mod_perl and in porting old CGI scripts.

The most common problem that Perl programmers run into when writing mod_perl scripts is that sometimes a script will work, and other times it will not. This is generally a problem that can be solved by running `httpd` in single process mode. Since mod_perl uses the same Perl interpreter, global variables can exist from one script to another unless you change them. The first step in debugging problems where a script works sometimes but not other times it by running the Web server in single process mode.

To handle the request parameters in a way very similar to CGI::params, you can use the code snippet shown here:

```
my $stuff = Apache->request;
my %params = $stuff->method eq 'POST' ? $stuff->content : $stuff->args;
```

This assumes that the variables are in the form of key-value pairs.

Often, it is useful to be able to redirect a POST request to another location. Mod_perl allows you to do this quite simply. It involves reading in the data, then setting the method to GET, populating args() with the data, and passing it along to the next location.

```
use Apache::Constants qw(M_GET);
my $stuff = shift;
my $content = $stuff->content;
$stuff->method("GET");
$stuff->method_number(M_GET);
$stuff->headers_in->unset("Content-length");
$stuff->args($content);
$stuff->internal_redirect_handler("/final/location/here");
```

If you wish to redirect but still preserve the environment variables, you can do this by using an `internal_redirct()` by calling `subprocess_env()`. This will preserve the environment variables, though it does prefix them with `REDIRECT_`.

If you wish to print out your environment variables similar to the way you handled it in Session 28, you can use

```
package MyEnvVar;
use Apache;
use Apache::Constants;
sub handler {
  my $stuff = shift;
  print $stuff->send_http_header("text/plain");
  print map {$_ => $ENV{$_}\n"} keys %ENV;
  return OK;
}
1;
```

This is the code. We must then configure it as:

```
PerlModule MyEnvVar
<Location /envvar>
    SetHandler perl-script
    PerlHandler MyEnvVar
</Location>
```

A common problem that new mod_perl programmers run into is that they notice that the server tends to hang when they are attempting to read a form. This occurs because the `$r-&gt;content` method reads `application/x-www-form-urlencoded` data directly and does not save a copy. If you then call it again, the server will hang. The "Accessing the Apache API via mod_perl" FAQ at `http://perl.apache.org/faq/mod_perl_api.html` provides sample code for converting the request from a POST to a GET.

There is a plethora of additional information about mod_perl on the Internet. To get additional information about specific issues, travel to `http://perl.apache.org/`. This is the official mod_perl site, and it has information about issues like security and porting, as well as many code samples. It also includes links to other sites that may have information about what you are looking for. It is the best starting point for mod_perl resources.

Done!

REVIEW

The Apache Software Foundation provides the Apache Web server, a very robust server supported on many different platforms. The Apache Web server offers the ability to use server-side processed content in the form of server-side includes. SSIs are used to insert small sections of dynamic content into HTML documents. SSIs should be used instead of CGI in HTML documents that have relatively little dynamic content. Apache also supports integration with Perl in the form of mod_perl. Mod_perl links the Perl runtime library into Apache to gives you an object-oriented interface to the Apache API. Apache and Perl together are incredibly powerful.

QUIZ YOURSELF

1. What are the benefits of installing Apache from a binary? The disadvantages? (See "The Apache Web Server.")
2. Describe a situation where the use of SSIs would be preferable to the use of CGI. Describe a situation where the use of CGI would be preferable to SSI. (See "Server-Side Processing.")
3. List three problems with the use of CGI programs. (See "The Downside of CGI.")
4. What is mod_perl? (See "Giving Apache Some Perl Muscle.")
5. Create and implement a counter for a Web page using mod_perl. (See "mod_perl In Action.")

PART

VI

Sunday Afternoon

1. What is HTML? How does HTML present documents on the Web?

2. What does the <FORM> tag do?

3. What does CGI stand for? In brief, how does it work? Give an example of how it might be used.

4. What is a danger associated with CGI?

5. What are GET and POST? How do they differ?

6. What is the read function? What is its use in CGI applications?

7. Why might it be to your advantage to use the Perl CGI module to create your HTML documents?

8. What does the start_html method do? What is represented by the arguments it takes?

9. Why does the CGI module have a function-oriented mode as well as an object-oriented mode?

10. What is a cookie?

11. What is an SSI?

12. What is mod_perl? How does it improve the performance of an Apache Web server?

APPENDIX

Answers to Part Reviews

Friday Evening Review Answers

1. There are several tools available to help find whether certain software packages are installed on a Unix system. The most common is the which command. This command will return the full path names of any files that match its argument, so for example, to search for the Perl executable, one would give the command which perl. On a Linux system, the command locate can also be used to find a particular file. The downside of locate is that it will return the names and paths of any directory that contains the text string that it is given as an argument. Thus, locate perl will return not only /usr/bin/perl but any other directory or file that has the name perl anywhere in the path.

2. Perl is likely to be installed on any Unix or Unix-derived system. Thus, Linux, FreeBSD, OpenBSD, AIX, Solaris, or any other Unix-type system is likely to have Perl installed. Indeed, Perl is such an integral tool in these environments that it is difficult to imagine a working installation that did not have it.

3. The source code for the Perl distribution is available from a number of places, including www.perl.org, or any of its mirrors. The source code compiles on a wide variety of platforms. Binary distributions of Perl for Linux and Windows are available from www.activestate.com. Binary distributions for Macintosh are available from www.macperl.com.

4. Installing from source code gives you the ability to tailor your installation to your environment. In addition, you can install Perl on a Unix system from source code even if you don't have superuser privileges, provided that you have sufficient disk space allocated to your account. The disadvantages are a higher degree of complication, and the need for a certain amount of previous experience with the procedure. Also, on a Windows system, installing from source code may be problematic if you do not have the appropriate compiler installed.

5. Perl has three native data types: scalar, list, and hash.

6. A list is a simple collection of elements in a particular order. By contrast, a hash is made up of pairs of elements that are related to each other. Aside from the relationships between the key/value pairs, the order of the listing is not important in a hash. Indeed, a hash will store the elements in whatever order is most efficient from a memory usage point of view, so the order in which elements are stored may have nothing to do with the order in which they were input.

7. A function is an element of programming that works some sort of an operation on the data that is input to it. Functions, along with operators (and the line between the two can get pretty fuzzy), comprise the ability to "command" the computer.

8. A compiled language is one in which the programming instructions are converted to the processor's native binary language before the program is run. For example, C is a compiled language. Before a C program can be run, it needs to be processed by a *compiler*. By contrast, an interpreted language is one that is run directly from the program instructions, with each instruction converted to the processor's native binary language at the time of execution. Perl is an interpreted language.

9. A command line flag is an option that is given when invoking a program using a command line interface. Command line flags usually alter or augment the default behavior of the program with which they are invoked. The Perl interpreter can be used with many command line flags. Three examples are -d, which invokes the Perl debugger, -e, which executes code given on the command line, and -I, which modifies the list of directories which are searched for modules.

10. perlmod

11. perldoc differs from man in that it is able to provide more control over accessing specific information. Various flags exist that provide the ability to access information on specific functions, or specific modules, and to search the Perl file of Frequently Asked Questions (FAQ) by keyword.

12. If you can't find what you're looking for in Perl's built-in documentation, odds are you can find the answer to your question either in the camel book (*Programming Perl*) or on the www.perl.com Web site. Other places to try are the comp.lang.perl.* Usenet newsgroups and the various Perl mailing lists.

Saturday Morning Review Answers

1. Word processors create document files. In addition to the textual content, document files contain information about formatting, fonts, colors, layout, pagination, and other aspects of creating a document that will look good on paper. By contrast, text files contain only text. That is (in most cases) they contain only characters that are defined in the ASCII character set.

2. Programs are created in the form of text files. Program compilers and interpreters can be very picky about the characters and symbols that appear in programs, and the formatting information found in word processor documents will confuse the Perl interpreter. Therefore, you should use only text editors to create your program files.

3. Pico is a *text mode* editor, which means that it can be run in a purely command-line driven environment. NEdit, by contrast, is a *graphical* editor, which means that it needs a graphical environment in which to run.

4. When saving files in WordPad, you should save your files as *text document*. WordPad may try to get you to save your files in one of the MSWord document formats. Be on the lookout for this behavior, and don't let it save in that format.

5. Programming style is the combination of logical organization and attention to aesthetic detail that makes for clear, organized, readable code. Good programming style is important because it makes the logic of the program obvious. This makes for easier debugging, and easier editing of the code later. It also tends to promote clear logical thought, which makes for better problem solving.

6. Lines are indented to show that they are subordinate to an enclosing construct. Indentation makes it easy to see the boundaries of such a construct.

7. A comment is a programmer's message to the reader of a program. In Perl, comments are introduced by a hashmark character (#). Comments are ignored by the program interpreter, but form a vital mode of communication between programmer and reader. Comments are important as an element of good programming style, since they can be used to describe and clarify the accompanying code.

8. The string #!/usr/bin/perl is, in fact, not a comment. This is the way that Perl programs on Unix and Unix-derived systems are able to invoke the Perl interpreter from within themselves. The #! sign (called a *shebang* in Unix parlance) lets the operating system know that this program needs to be interpreted by the program that comes next on that line.

9. Lone rightward facing curly braces indicate the end of a block of code. These braces are placed at the same level of indentation as the statement that initiated the block of code, and therefore one can find the beginning or end of any block by simple vertical alignment.

10. A scalar variable is a name that represents a single piece of data. Scalar variables are identified by the dollar sign character ($) that precedes their names.

11. My name is jake

12. \n is an *escape sequence* representing a *newline* character.

13. A list variable is a name that represents a set of more than one data element. Individual elements are identified by position. Lists are identified by the at sign symbol (@) preceding the variable name.

14. $list[1]

15. A hash variable is a type of list in which the elements are organized in related pairs. Hash variables are identified by the percent symbol (%) that precedes their names.

16. An expression can always be evaluated to a single unified value.

17. A statement is a single unit of command within a program.

18. An operator is a means of combining or modifying terms within an expression.

19. eq is an operator that tests two texts strings to see if they are equal. It returns true if the strings are equal, and false if they are not.

Saturday Afternoon Review Answers

1. Command line arguments are available to Perl programs via the special variable @ARGV. $ARGV[0] represents the first argument, $ARGV[1], the second, and so on.

2. STDIN represents the standard input, which is usually the terminal keyboard. It is most commonly used with the readline operator to take input from the keyboard as in

   ```
   $input = <STDIN>;
   ```

3. The diamond operator is used as a sort of combination of the readline operator and @ARGV. The diamond operator reads a line of input from any file (or files) named on the command line.

4. Flow control is the means by which programs are able to make decisions about how to execute themselves. Flow control can be conditional, meaning that certain sections of code can be marked off to be executed only if certain conditions are met, or iterative, meaning that certain sections of code can be marked off to be executed repeatedly as long as certain conditions hold true.

5. if and unless

6. while, until, and foreach

7. A native function is one that is considered to be part of the core of the Perl language. That is, any installation of "Perl" would be able to use these functions, since they are built into the Perl interpreter and do not need to be further defined.

8. Nested functions always execute from the inside out.

9. The chomp function serves to remove the trailing newline character from a line of input. Whenever input is entered at they keyboard, its last character is always a newline because the user has to push the Enter key to send the input. Frequently, this newline character causes things such as string equality tests to fail. Therefore, it is almost always the case that input taken from the keyboard should be chomped.

10. A filehandle is a means of referring to a file. Using the open function, you can create filehandles for reading, writing, or appending. Filehandles are used to take input from or direct output to the files they represent.

11. Using the pipe character (|) you can link a filehandle to a process by means of the open function. The filehandle will then be used to take input from, or direct output to the process, depending on which side of the process name you put the pipe. Note that open cannot be used to access a process for both input and output at the same time.

12. Aside from the obvious fact that a directory handle refers to a directory while a filehandle refers to a file, directory handles are manipulated with an entirely different set of functions. opendir as opposed to open, readdir as opposed to the readline operator, and so on.

13. Careless use of the unlink function, especially from a program running with administrative privileges, can inadvertently delete crucial system files, effectively crippling your operating system.

14. A pipe is a feature of the Unix operating system that allows the output from one program to be used as the input in another.

15. The system function passes the output of the shell command directly to the program's standard output (unless otherwise specified), whereas the backquote operator captures the output of the shell command as a string.

16. You can avoid zombie processes by making sure that every child process that you create with fork has an exit condition. As long as all the children can exit, you won't create zombies.

Saturday Evening Review Answers

1. A regular expression is a general description of a piece of text. More than one piece of text can match a given regular expression. Regular expressions make use of metacharacters to describe types of characters that are to be included in or excluded from any matching text.

2. Character classes are created by enclosing a group of characters in square brackets.

3. /(F|f).*ck/

4. ds

5. The easiest way to assign the contents of a list to separate scalars is to simply assign the scalars to the list. Thus, given

```
@list = (1, 2, 3, 4);
```

one could assign the scalars thus:

```
($one, $two, $three, $four) = @list;
```

6. Transliteration is an operation performed on literal strings, whereas substitution is performed on regular expressions.

7. The fieldholder with the leftward pointing angle brackets denotes a field in which the content is left-justified, while the fieldholder with the rightward point brackets denotes a right-justified field.

8. If a line in a filled field has two tildes at the end, that indicates that the field will expand to accommodate data that is longer than the explicit fieldholder.

9. The $~ variable is used to denote the current output format. The default value of this variable is STDOUT, but if you change the value, you can get your program to print to standard output using a format that is nominally created for a different output stream.

10. The only real difference between a subroutine and a function is that the word "function" is used primarily to refer to those that are Perl native. User-created functions are almost always referred to as subroutines. Other than that, there is no real difference.

11. Subroutines allow code to be written once, but used in multiple places. This saves the programmer the work of rewriting code that he has already written. It also makes programs smaller and easier to read and follow. Finally, it forces the programmer to think in terms of modular methods of problem solving.

12. The @_ variable is used to pass arguments to functions. This variable can be thought of a localized version of the @ARGV variable. The function's return value is passed back to the main program in the related $_ variable.

Sunday Morning Review Answers

1. A module is a special type of package that allows the export of symbols. That is, whereas a package is a simple namespace management tool and may only be germane to a single program, a module is intended to be reused among many programs that may share a common focus.

2. The CPAN interface automatically makes connections to CPAN repository archives. In addition, CPAN will automatically download and install any modules upon which your desired module may depend. The CPAN interface is simple to use, and provides a great deal of automation for tasks that would ordinarily have to be performed by hand.

3. The special variable @INC represents the list of directories in which the Perl interpreter looks for package and module files. @INC can be manipulated on the command line with the -I flag, or from within a program by normal list processing functions.

4. require simply loads the module code and makes subroutines available for use, whereas use imports the module's symbol table into the main program.

5. A method is a technique of object-oriented programming. It is roughly analogous to a function, except that a method is called upon an object, which is a data structure that acts as a unit.

6. DBD modules contain the low-level drivers that enable DBI method calls to interact with the various database servers.

7. The program fails to create a statement handle, and fails to prepare the SQL statement before execution. The correct code should look like this:

```
#!/usr/bin/perl
use DBI;
$dbh = DBI ->
connect("DBI:mysql:database=perl:host=
"localhost", "perl", "e492a") || die
"couldn't connect to database";
$sth->$dbh->prepare("SELECT * FROM table);
$sth->execute;
```

8. fetchrow_array()

9. Notwithstanding the answer to Friday evening's Question 8, Perl is, in fact, both an interpreted AND a compiled language. Perl programs are "compiled on the fly" each time they are run.

10. The BEGIN command tags a block of code to be evaluated at compile time, before the program is actually run. Thus statements enclosed inside a BEGIN block will already be evaluated, and their values available at run time.

11. Scope refers to that part of a program in which a variable is visible. Variables declared with no modifiers are generally visible to the entire package or program in which they reside, whereas variables declared with the my function are generally only visible inside the innermost enclosing block in which they are declared.

12. The Perl Standard Library is that collection of modules and pragmas included with the standard Perl distribution. In other words, you need not do anything to install these modules and pragmas, since you should already have them.

13. You can see a list of installed modules by giving the command

    ```
    perldoc perllocal
    ```

14. A pragma is an instruction to the compiler.

15. The IO::Socket module provides object methods for making network connections and controlling their input and output.

16. A reference is an indirect way of passing data. References provide a pointer to a variable or subroutine's location in memory. References can be created explicitly, using the backslash operator, or implicitly, using anonymous variables or subroutines.

17. A symbolic reference is created when a reference is used without having ever been created. The interpreter acts as if the reference had been created and performs whatever operation is specified on the implied referent. Symbolic references can be useful, but they can also present a certain danger to the programmer, and should thus be handled with care. When in doubt, the strict pragma can be used to prevent the interpretation of symbolic references.

Sunday Afternoon Review Answers

1. HTML is HyperText Markup Language. It presents documents on the Web by means of various formatting tags and form elements.

2. The <FORM> tag indicates that whatever falls between it and the closing </FORM> tag is to be treated as an HTML form. That is, form elements indicated within these tags will be rendered on the client's browser, and the user can input data via these form elements.

3. CGI stands for Common Gateway Interface. The CGI is a way of passing Web form data to programs residing on the Web server. Thus, the data from a Web form can be passed to a Perl script, which may, for example, fetch data from a database sever, and reassemble it into an HTML document. In this way, a simple Web-based search engine could be created.

4. Because CGI causes programs to be executed on the server, there is always a danger that the action of these programs can be hijacked and made to perform actions that the programmer did not intend. Programmers and Web administrators need to take care that CGI programs are as secure as they can be, and that other system security measures are in place.

5. GET and POST are the two methods of passing data from an HTML form to a CGI program. GET sends the information from the form as part of the return document's URL, whereas POST sends data as an input string, and can be read from STDIN. In general, POST is more secure than GET, since it does not advertise itself in the URL, however anyone with even a modest knowledge of WWW software can figure out how to access the information passed in a POST operation as well, so POST should not be considered secure either. POST also has the advantage (or disadvantage depending on the situation) of not sending horrifically long encoded URLs.

6. The read function reads a certain number of bytes (characters) from the given filehandle. An optional offset can be given to define the particular starting point of the substring in which you're interested. It is used to read data from STDIN when processing POST operations.

7. The CGI module contains functions and object methods that greatly simplify the process of creating HTML documents on the fly.

8. The start_html method creates the initial headers that signal the beginning of an HTML document. Arguments to this method represent parameters that will be included in the HTML headers.

9. The CGI module's function-oriented mode allows the programmer to avoid the overhead of importing all of its object methods into a program where they are not needed. Since CGI overhead can become a real performance issue when there are a large number of clients accessing a Web site, this can be a major way of streamlining CGI program overhead.

10. A cookie is a piece of information passed back and forth between a Web server and a Web browser. Cookies are used to manage Web sessions, and keep track of the state of the browser.

11. SSI stands for server-side include. SSIs are a way of creating server-parsed documents on the fly.

12. mod_perl is a module that can be compiled into the Apache Web server. mod_perl essentially embeds a Perl interpreter within Apache itself, thus saving the processor overhead of having to start a new instance of the Perl interpreter every time a CGI script is run. This can greatly reduce the load on the Web server's processor, and make for faster and more efficient processing of Perl scripts.

What's on the CD-ROM

The CD-ROM that accompanies this book contains the following:

- Perl interpreter binaries for Red Hat Linux and Debian GNU/Linux
- Source Code Perl Distribution
- Freeware version of Adobe Acrobat Reader 5.0
- A self-assessment test to help you measure how much you have learned

System Requirements

The following are the system requirements for running the CD-ROM:

- A PC with a 486/DX or faster CPU
- Linux or Unix operating system (software for other platforms is available on the Internet)
- At least 32 MB of RAM
- A minimum of 350 MB of disk space
- A CD-ROM drive

Although the software provided with this book is intended primarily for Linux and Unix systems, Perl interpreters are available for almost every computing platform. Generally, the code examples in the book should work on any platform. The main exceptions to this are programs that use the operating system. You will need to supply proper syntax for executable programs, file names, and directory paths.

Index

G

Continued

Hungry Minds, Inc.
End-User License Agreement

READ THIS. You should carefully read these terms and conditions before opening the software packet(s) included with this book ("Book"). This is a license agreement ("Agreement") between you and Hungry Minds, Inc. ("HMI"). By opening the accompanying software packet(s), you acknowledge that you have read and accept the following terms and conditions. If you do not agree and do not want to be bound by such terms and conditions, promptly return the Book and the unopened software packet(s) to the place you obtained them for a full refund.

1. **License Grant.** HMI grants to you (either an individual or entity) a nonexclusive license to use one copy of the enclosed software program(s) (collectively, the "Software") solely for your own personal or business purposes on a single computer (whether a standard computer or a workstation component of a multi-user network). The Software is in use on a computer when it is loaded into temporary memory (RAM) or installed into permanent memory (hard disk, CD-ROM, or other storage device). HMI reserves all rights not expressly granted herein.

2. **Ownership.** HMI is the owner of all right, title, and interest, including copyright, in and to the compilation of the Software recorded on the disk(s) or CD-ROM ("Software Media"). Copyright to the individual programs recorded on the Software Media is owned by the author or other authorized copyright owner of each program. Ownership of the Software and all proprietary rights relating thereto remain with HMI and its licensers.

3. **Restrictions On Use and Transfer.**

   (a) You may only (i) make one copy of the Software for backup or archival purposes, or (ii) transfer the Software to a single hard disk, provided that you keep the original for backup or archival purposes. You may not (i) rent or lease the Software, (ii) copy or reproduce the Software through a LAN or other network system or through any computer subscriber system or bulletin-board system, or (iii) modify, adapt, or create derivative works based on the Software.

   (b) You may not reverse engineer, decompile, or disassemble the Software. You may transfer the Software and user documentation on a permanent basis, provided that the transferee agrees to accept the terms and conditions of this Agreement and you retain no copies. If the Software is an update or has been updated, any transfer must include the most recent update and all prior versions.

4. **Restrictions on Use of Individual Programs.** You must follow the individual requirements and restrictions detailed for each individual program in Appendix B of this Book. These limitations are also contained in the individual license agreements recorded on the Software Media. These limitations may include a requirement that after using the program for a specified period of time, the user must pay a registration fee or discontinue use. By opening the Software packet(s), you will be agreeing to abide by the licenses and restrictions for these individual programs that are detailed in Appendix B and on the Software Media. None of the material on this Software Media or listed in this Book may ever be redistributed, in original or modified form, for commercial purposes.

8. **General.** This Agreement constitutes the entire understanding of the parties and revokes and supersedes all prior agreements, oral or written, between them and may not be modified or amended except in a writing signed by both parties hereto that specifically refers to this Agreement. This Agreement shall take precedence over any other documents that may be in conflict herewith. If any one or more provisions contained in this Agreement are held by any court or tribunal to be invalid, illegal, or otherwise unenforceable, each and every other provision shall remain in full force and effect.

Get Up to Speed
in a Weekend!

Flash™ 5 Weekend Crash Course™
by Shamms Mortier
408 pages
ISBN 0-7645-3546-3

Red Hat® Linux® 7 Weekend Crash Course™
by Naba Barkakati
432 pages
Red Hat Linux 7 on 3 CDs
ISBN 0-7645-4741-0

Visual Basic® 6 Weekend Crash Course™
by Richard Mansfield
408 pages
ISBN 0-7645-4679-1

Dreamweaver® 4 Weekend Crash Course™
by Wendy Peck
408 pages
ISBN 0-7645-3575-7

Also available:

Access® 2000 Programming Weekend Crash Course™
by Cary N. Prague, Jennifer Reardon, Lawrence S. Kasevich, Diana Reid, and
Phuc Phan *600 pages* ISBN 0-7645-4688-0

Active Server Pages 3 Weekend Crash Course™
by Eric Smith *450 pages* ISBN 0-7645-4756-9

C++ Weekend Crash Course™
by Stephen R. Davis *552 pages* ISBN 0-7645-4689-9

C# Weekend Crash Course™ (Available July 2001)
by Stephen R. Davis *432 pages* ISBN 0-7645-4789-5

HTML 4.01 Weekend Crash Course™
by Greg Perry *480 pages* ISBN 0-7645-4746-1

Java™ 2 Weekend Crash Course™
by Julio Sanchez and Maria Canton *432 pages* ISBN 0-7645-4768-2

JavaScript Weekend Crash Course™
by Steven Disbrow *408 pages* ISBN 0-7645-4804-2

JSP Weekend Crash Course™
by Andrew Utter And Geremy Kawaller *408 pages* ISBN 0-7645-4796-8

Linux® Weekend Crash Course™
by Terry Collins and Naba Barkakati *450 pages* ISBN 0-7645-3593-5

**Each book comes with a CD-ROM and
features 30 fast, focused lessons that will
have you up and running in only 15 hours.**

Available wherever
books are sold,
or go to:
www.hungryminds.com

Hungry Minds™